THE

Red Letter

QUESTIONS

*Meditations on the
Questions Jesus Asked*

DON HARRIS

Bridge-Logos
Orlando, Florida 32822 USA

Bridge-Logos

Orlando, FL 32822 USA

The Red Letter Questions
by Don Harris

Copyright ©2007 by Bridge-Logos

Printed in the United States of America.

Library of Congress Catalog Card Number: 2007933093
International Standard Book Number 978-0-88270-332-9

Scripture quotations in this book are from the *King James Version* of the Bible.

G1.316.N.m707.35250

To Guy

It is because of his confidence, encouragement and vision
that this book is in your hands. He will be missed.

*"Know ye not that there is a prince
and a great man fallen this day?"*

Guy Joseph Morrell

President & CEO
Bridge-Logos Publishers
October 29, 1945 – May 11, 2007

Contents

Foreword vii

Preface ix

Part 1

Jesus' Questions Work to Perfect Us

If You Would Be Perfect 1

Part 2

Jesus' Questions Challenge Us Personally

What Are You Thinking? 29

Dedication 67

Preparing You for Understanding 109

Revelation—How to Hear 131

Hindrances to Hearing 139

Faith 171

Ministry 195

Part 3
Jesus' Questions Challenge Our Theology

Our Concept of the Messiah 239

The Bible 257

Symbols, Rituals, and Sacraments 295

Part 4
Conclusions

Who Is a Faithful and Wise Steward? 303

Finding Real Faith. 311

Index. 321

The Questions Jesus Asked 323

Foreword

A man with "all the answers," Don Harris set upon his career as a pastor. While directing a Christian children's home and school, he was as typical as any preacher, teacher or radio/TV evangelist you could meet anywhere—typical, that is, *until* the Lord Jesus presented him with some questions.

For several years, during his early morning devotional time, Don was carried back to the ancient discourses on the sandy shores of Galilee and the grassy hillside sermons to take a closer look at the questions of Jesus. He noticed that the Messiah frequently attempted to teach by asking questions, but Don's "answers" just didn't fit!

The Scriptures that had been so familiar to him became like another language. The messages were sometimes the *opposite* of what he had always believed. As the questions opened anew, he watched the irrational ideas that had plagued him dissolve into pure reason—and the contradictory doctrines that he had dared not even investigate, vanish!

The Red-Letter Questions describes the progression of insights and revelation given to Don during the journey that changed his life forever. These are the heartfelt thoughts of a man who, through traditional misinterpretation of Scripture, inadvertently disobeyed the God he claimed to love and serve.

The traditions of men and false assumptions had become part of Don's everyday life (just as they may be in ours). Discovering the truth behind these poignant red-letter questions set him free, and it will set you free as well.

The Red-Letter Questions is a fresh look at the recorded questions asked by the Messiah during His ministry on the earth. Let the questions transport you to the feet of the Messiah. Open your ears and your heart to hear His questions anew and find your own answers—answers that will cleanse and change you forever.

Lloyd Hildebrand
Publisher

Preface

The scene was the same every day. Early in the morning my wife, Pam, came into the room and found me in my chair, where she finds me every morning, as I was scratching through my Bible. "Whatcha looking for?" she asked.

My answer was always the same, "Lookin' for questions."

For most of my life I looked in my Bible for *answers*, but for nearly four years my early morning hours were devoted to my new assignment—looking for questions. When I first began my pursuit of *The Red-Letter Questions* in the Bible, my interest was quite detached from book development. It was pure intrigue. My fascination with Bible *questions* sprang from my disenchantment with Bible *answers*.

Since the age of fourteen, I had studied the Bible in a search for answers. At first, I needed only simple answers to resolve the simple questions of a youth who was just beginning life. As my life became more complicated, the questions became more complex. I needed more from my faith. So, naturally, I sought more from the Bible. Over time, I learned the languages, procured the translations, and reconstructed the history and the customs of civilizations past. I learned to dissect and analyze—*precept upon precept—line upon line—here a little, there a little*—until I was able to prove, codify, and solidify my theology into a flawless, inarguable reality.

Wasn't this the way I was supposed to do it? *Precept upon precept, line upon line, here a little, there a little?* Wasn't the Bible supposed to be my only source?

Didn't Job say, *"I have esteemed the words of his mouth more than my necessary food?"*[1] Job even wished for a Bible like ours when he said, *"I want the almighty to answer me. If He had only written a book, I would take it to myself and learn it and consider it as a crown to me."* [2]

Through this technique I learned how to find the most obscure answers to any of the doctrinal trivia that may arise out of my fundamental dogma. I could point to Scripture after Scripture explaining in clear terms exactly what I believed (and why you should, too!).

I had fallen prey to a twisted kind of biblical *Gnosticism.*[3] I had been convinced that the more I *knew,* the closer to God I would become. Somehow, I had it in my mind to get the answers I needed from the Bible. I was told that prayer should fill the disparity in my spiritual communications, but it was not a desire *to speak to Him* that made me feel so helpless— what I needed was to have *Him speak to me.*

I had, up to this point, gone to the Bible for the "conversation" I longed for. How many times I would open my Bible while considering a difficulty and say, "Well, let's see what God says about it." As I considered my lifelong pattern, I realized that my Bible had ever increasingly become my "god." *But I had my answers!*

---

1   Job 23:12
2   Job 31:35-36
3   Gnostics believed that spiritual development was linked to *Gnosis* (knowing).

Remember, a person who has all the answers has no questions. That made me, by definition, a "know-it-all." I was to learn the reality of this fantasy the hard way, over and over again, during the next twenty years.

In my mid-20s I commenced my first public ministry. It eventually included a church congregation, a children's home, a Christian school, and my first radio broadcast. All was well. In each of my decisions I justified my stubborn (and sometimes sinful) position by Scripture and solid apologetics. My positions were inarguable, my theology was flawless, and my heart was blackened by self-deceit.

After several years, my "Utopia" began to disintegrate. I watched helplessly as each part of my life, home, and ministry was all lost, one by one, over the course of seven short days. I felt a mistaken kinship to Job, as my life, work, and family systematically vanished, but that was because I still thought that I was right.

Not learning much from my mistakes, I began again. In the years that followed I watched helplessly as two more of my attempts at ministry failed.

Although I felt that I had the "answers," I realized that my faith was having no real effect on my life (i.e., I had no power over sin—many times not even recognizing it—nor had I any assurance of Jehovah's hand in my life). Again, all I had set my hand to do crumbled, and I found myself helpless to change anything.

These were the years when the renowned preachers were falling one by one. I saw local and national ministries accused of scandalous misdeeds. I became more weary and disappointed and spent several years avoiding anything spiritual. I was angry. I was afraid. I saw *myself* in them.

Could You Repeat the Question, Please?

My struggle to understand continued. What happened to these men? What happened to me? It became obvious to me that I had learned the *words* and missed the *message*. Although I knew all about the Bible, I did not know its Author. I had answers, but what was the question again?

Job wanted answers. I wanted answers. Is it such a ridiculous thought to seek answers by seeking questions, I wondered?

Then, one day, it all turned around. While halfheartedly listening to the Bible on tape, I heard the Almighty speak in thunder to Job, "*WHO IS THIS THAT DARKENS COUNSEL BY WORDS WITHOUT KNOWLEDGE? STAND UP LIKE A MAN AND I WILL QUESTION YOU AND YOU WILL ANSWER ME FOR A CHANGE.*"[4]

Could it be that simple? Could my problem have been that I had been looking for *my answers* when my real task should have been to find and answer *His questions*?

Mark records the familiar story about the Pharisees demanding answers from Jesus. Jesus responded with this proviso, "*I will also ask of you a question. Answer me and I will answer you.*"[5]

This became a theme, a key to my Bible study and indeed my entire spiritual life. Could it be that I had spent the sum of my life gathering answers to questions of no value? Could

---

4 Job 38:2-3
5 Mark 11:29

it be that all of us are striving to answer questions formulated in our foolish minds when we should be answering the wise and prudent questions formulated in the mind of our God and Savior? Could it be that we are not even prepared to ask questions until we have fully answered Him on the basic issues about which *He* questions *us*?

Mine is not a story of a man who thought he was "saved" but wasn't, nor is it a story of a man who finally found the "holy grail." Rather, mine is a record of a progression of faith that is not only *available* to everyone, I am sure it is His divine plan for us all. I felt then, and still feel confident in His salvation, but I had no *relationship*—just words with no *conversation*. I had an affiliation but no *interaction*.

I am a different man today because I stopped *asking* and started *answering*. The answers that I had wrested and wrung out of the Scriptures to fill the voids and inconsistencies of my own doctrines have since evaporated into the expanse of HIS understanding. *My vain interrogations* have since become ridiculous in comparison to *His questions.*

At first, I was vexed about the new journey that lay ahead of me. With all of my previous foundations in rubble, I contemplated the changes that were taking place in my thinking. It frightened me. I would pray, "Are all my concerns to be forgotten?" No answer. "When will I get to ask *You* questions again?" No answer. I winced. Again, I found myself questioning Him! This would be a hard habit to break. I learned to relax.

One day, when I least expected it, my assignment became clear, the price became evident, and the reward came into focus. What would I be trading to seek this new understanding? I would only be trading my own wicked ways, my unrighteous thoughts for His! Good trade!

Then the Scriptures spoke within me, "*Let the wicked man forsake his way and the unrighteous his thoughts let him return to the Lord, that He may have mercy on him ...for he will abundantly pardon ... for my thoughts are not your thoughts nor are your ways my ways, says the Lord, for as the heavens are **higher** than the earth, so are my ways **higher** than your ways and my thoughts than your thoughts.*" [6]

It was then that I *heard* within myself—as if He whispered to me personally, "*So are My questions **higher** than your questions.*"

I finally conceded, "*Okay, Lord, You ask and I'll answer.*"

His Questions Must Take Precedence Over Ours

If you can, imagine having a one-hour appointment with the Creator of Heaven and Earth in which He has agreed to answer all of your questions—*if* you so desire. Can you also imagine walking into such a meeting, laying all your own questions aside, and asking, "*Lord, what questions do you have for me?*"

When it occurs to you that His questions have more power to educate, illuminate, and inform than any of the meager answers you have ever garnered from your religious experiences, you will gladly desire *questions* from your Lord rather than *answers*.

---

6   Isaiah 55:7-9 (author's emphasis)

You will find that the mere contemplation of His questions can transform you. When this approach is applied to your study, you may find that it is necessary to experience a myriad of changes before you are even *able* to answer at all. Honesty may demand returning with a different answer at a later time.

Some of His questions will not even make sense until you are in the right place at the right time—with the right perspective.

His questions will require searching within and researching without. They will demand your time in meditation and your consideration throughout your day. They will appear and reappear in your everyday life. They will occupy the background of your thinking in nearly every situation. They will culminate in such peace and power and understanding that you will be changed forever.

It could take a lifetime to answer just *one* of His questions, but answering just one of His questions will change you *forever*! There are no limits to His ways of teaching. His ways, as it is said, are "*… past finding out.*"

So perhaps, like me, you will begin searching for *questions* in your Bible instead of *answers*. As a result of doing so, I have never been the same. You will not be the same either!

PART 1

Jesus' Questions Work to Perfect Us

If You Would Be Perfect ...

Imagine that you are a first-century Israelite. You have heard of Jesus traveling throughout all of Judea healing and causing miracles that have freed people from physical illness and demonic forces. On this particular day, you have made your way to Him because you know that if you see Him, He will grant your greatest need.

The din of the swarm in the street of the city quickly reveals His location to you. You push and squirm toward Him. You are nearer to Him now. He is ahead in the crowd by only a few feet.

His words can be clearly heard and you are drawn in, as you listen to His stories intriguing the multitude. He speaks riddles that perplex the religious leadership. He astonishes all with a parable that you are sure conveys some deep eternal significance. You wonder what it could mean and you find yourself pondering the gracious words that come from Him.

Finally, as He shifts through the crowd, you realize that He will walk right past you if only you stand still and let the crowd pass. He gets nearer and nearer until He notices you. You look at Him and now you wonder if this great man will grant your request.

Thoughts of unworthiness flood your mind, as you try to maintain hope that He will even listen to you. Then, He looks at you. No, He is looking *through* you—and beyond. Surprisingly, instead of you asking of Him, He asks you the amazing question, "What do you want?"

What will we answer when the King of kings, the Word, the Creator, the Messiah, the Son of God, asks us the question: *"What wilt thou?"*[1] In other words, He inquired: "What do you want?" "What can I do for you?" How will we respond?

We must examine our desires honestly.

Your Desires

Your desire to read this book or to go to a particular church, to study and even to pray—all of your desires—must be examined for reason and motivation. Why is this essential as we start out on this journey through the red-letter questions? Because your state of mind, your desires, and your motivation *will influence the rest of your discoveries.*

Your quiet, daily consideration of these subjects is the only way to be sure of your purity of heart. As you push through the crowd, remember, it is the pure in heart who will *see* God.

The original story and recent adaptations of the genie in the lamp vividly portray the circumstances of limited opportunities and the consequences of asking for the wrong things. Is it possible that you could miss the opportunity to

---

1   Matthew 20:21; Mark 10:51; Luke 18:41

gain the most important request of your life when you are asked, "What do you want?"

Have You Settled for the Status Quo?

Thirty-eight years is a long time to be sick and immobile. It is very possible that the paralyzed man who was waiting to be put into the healing waters of the pool at Bethsaida got used to living with his infirmity.[2] It's entirely possible that his condition came upon him at birth, making him nearly forty years old. But if it came upon him in his youth, this man could have been in his sixties. Maybe he, too, had pretty much settled on remaining in his condition for life.

Perhaps it has settled upon you that your illness or injury or even your state of mind will never get better either. Perhaps you have resigned a little of your fighting spirit and a little of your life to your problems. In other words, through the years you have just learned to live with it.

As an eighteen-year old young man, I suffered the near amputation of my right hand. I have now been with this impaired hand longer than I ever had the fully functional one with which I was born. It seems impossible, but I have become so used to its deformity, pain, and lack of utility that I can hardly remember what it was like to be any other way.

Dr. McCarthy was skillful and persevering and, with all the medical science that was available in 1975, he made my hand usable again. Through the years of surgery and rehabilitation, I used to wonder if my hand had ever really stopped hurting, or if I had merely become accustomed to the pain.

---

2 John 5

Because the median nerve had been cut, only three of my fingers have tactile sensitivity enough to feel anything other than extreme pain, heat, or cold. Although every effort was made to restore the hand, it was left scarred and dysfunctional. Many doctors were surprised that I was able to keep it at all.

Many years later, I met an orthopedic surgeon who noticed and expressed interest in my injury. I watched him trace my already-scarred skin with his fingers. He was tracing the lines where new surgical openings would go. He began to talk of making further repairs. He tried to engage my enthusiasm by promising more freedom, less pain, removal of scar tissue, and restoration of sensitivity. All I could think about were the five surgeries that had preceded my present condition, the pain of rehabilitation, and the fact that I was getting along pretty well.

In essence what the doctor asked me was the very question the Messiah asked the man at Bethesda, *"Will you be made whole?"* or "Do you *want* to be made well?"

I answered, "Nah, I'll be all right."

Why would anyone turn down an opportunity to improve a lifelong, impaired condition? The insight that will inevitably come from this excursion into the red-letter questions will be curative and therapeutic, but as you know, therapy *can* be painful.

This is the juncture where I faltered with the surgeon's proposal. How about you? Are you ready? Is it your *will* to be made whole, or has complacency crept into your life? Have you lost the sweet taste of being clean and complete? Have you so soon forgotten the glory of purity before your God and the wonderful forgiveness that washed over you and filled you with His very presence? Will you be made whole?

Can I revive in you a desire to be as you were the day Christ first cleansed your soul? Do you remember the fervor with which you attacked sin and shortcoming in your life at the beginning of your relationship with Him? Can the lost and forgotten ideal, long faded by time and disappointment, be renewed into the fresh hope you had in the beginning?

If not, you are in danger of fatal acceptance, of lukewarm mediocrity. As the years slip by, the hope of being totally free from sin will ebb away until that hope is transformed into a dream. The dream will eventually turn into a fanciful wish. The wish will degrade into mere preference. Finally, preference will become nothing more than a whim of impossibility.

You may have folded and given up, thinking that the fight is hopeless, but it's not! Jesus knows that you have been in your state for quite a while. He wonders if you have settled in and grown comfortable in your lukewarm condition and He asks you (as only He can) the amazing question, "Will *you* be made whole?"

The condition to which you have become accustomed hampers your ability to find the truth. When you become discouraged with the progress of your pursuit of perfection, you may resort to pursuing only the familiar and the physical. Instead of perfection, you may seek memberships, fellowships, and mere identification with the people who profess perfection.

Rarely does anyone embark on a true spiritual journey toward perfection. Even more rarely does anyone set out upon that journey twice or three times, but you must continue to try. Perhaps the reason is that the spiritual is nearly always misunderstood—and perfection doubly so. More likely it is because the spiritual cannot be controlled; therefore, it is *avoided* instead.

This more *physical* approach will set you off on a more *common* journey. This is the road everybody else has taken. It leads to familiar and conventional places and teaches orthodox and customary ideas and concepts while surrounding you with common and regular people.

One day, you will awake with the very familiar feeling of being back—exactly where you started—essentially the same person—with Jesus Christ, congregations, the Bible, and religion just *added* to all the other interests in your life.

The realization of this can be devastating to the Christian who truly desires to please God. Angry Christians, indifferent Christians, bitter Christians have all come from just such a set of circumstances. Isn't it a shame that the very ones who originally set out to *please* God become disenchanted with the prospect of doing so?

Mary Magdalene became a sad Christian in her pursuit of Jesus. Her sadness became His concern.

Your Disappointment

It was the fourth day of the week. They had to hurry as they took Jesus' body from the tree. At sundown the first day of the Feast of Unleavened Bread would begin and, therefore, it would become a high Sabbath day.

Mary was compelled to prepare His body for burial before the sun set. Along with the other women, she waited for the men to make arrangements to get Him down from the rugged pole and place him somewhere, anywhere, because the Sabbath drew on and preparations would then be impossible.

The evening grew cooler as the sun sped toward its bed in the western sky. Jerusalem is now in long shadows, having observed the Passover, and it now awaits the first day of the Feast of Unleavened Bread. Mary noticed that the sun had fallen well behind the escarpment of Golgotha, as the dreaded evening raced toward her.

Finally several disciples appeared with news that Joseph of Arimathaea had offered his new garden tomb. Gathering their supplies, Mary and her companions made haste. High Sabbath was upon them.

At last they placed the body in the tomb, having only enough time to hastily wrap it in linen. Mary looked into the face of Jesus, as she placed the napkin over it. Remembering the sound of the priest's shofar, long since having passed into silence, Mary had the ironic thought of all the families of Zion sitting at their Passover tables praying for Messiah to come.

Guards appeared at the tomb. Men she does not know gathered around the stone to roll it over the door opening. "Get out" they shouted, "or stay in there forever!"

Forced to finish, they left and returned to their homes. As they walked the darkening streets toward their homes, the sound of a hammer driving a steel pin through lead in the rock grew faint and finally muted in one last sickening thud that sealed the tomb.

Then they wondered if they would ever be permitted to do the right thing for the Savior they loved so dearly.

Early on the first day of the week, Mary appeared at the tomb, again bringing her spices, hoping to somehow prepare the body of the Messiah. To her surprise she found the door open and the soldiers gone. Taking this miraculous opportunity, she entered, only to find that He was not there! "Someone has stolen Him away!" she thought. She couldn't take any more and began to weep.

Mary searched for Jesus. He was with her all along, but not in the *place* where she was looking, not in the *form* that she was seeking, and not for the *reason* that she had come. She was so intent on finding Him that she missed Him! *She was so determined to find Him according to her own understanding that she ultimately mistook Him for somebody else!*

Have you found yourself searching frantically for Jesus? Are you frustrating yourself at every turn? You may make the same mistake Mary did by accepting things as miraculous that are not miracles, thus missing the true miracles and deeming them as commonplace.

You may become discouraged, sad, indignant, or mad. You may even be reduced to tears, but if your search is pure and your heart is right, you will not be disappointed.

In your tired condition, and regardless of your weeping, you will feel all frustration melt away like a bad dream when He unexpectedly appears to you and asks, *"Why are you crying?"*[3]

---

3 John 20:13

Your Disappointment

While seeking to be made whole, we can become discouraged when that goal is not readily realized. Perhaps you are looking in the wrong *place*. Perhaps you are looking for the wrong *reason*. Perhaps He *is* there, but in a different dimension, or with a different agenda than your own.

When He asks why you are crying, you may have to admit that the reason is because things are not the way *you* want them to be.

Over a period of time this frustration can begin to wear on the average Christian. It may even happen that you decide to give up on being a Christian. This *has* happened to others. It *can* happen to you. You wouldn't be the first to quit. It may seem that you are investing more than you get in return. It may be that you consider the price too high.

In the days following the death of Christ, the disciples had such thoughts and (just as perhaps you have done) they returned to the life they had left behind.[4] They went back to their nets. Losing confidence in the promise to become "fishers of men," they settled for the familiar, and they became *fishers again*.

Has this happened to you? Have you sidestepped "being born again" and now find yourself merely "becoming again" whatever it was that you were—only now with Jesus in tow?

Are you more like you used to be or are you more like the model that the Lord has in mind for you to be now? If you are

---

4 John 21

in the former condition, there is hope. Have hope in the red-letter questions, the questions of Jesus.

Like the disciples, if you have gone back to your previous ways, Jesus inquires, "How's it going? How are you doing now that you are in control again? Are you making any headway? Are you advancing? Now that you are in control of your life, are you answering all of your prayers for yourself?"

The disciples, now determined to be fishers again, struggle with their old job. The familiar smells and taste of the sea remind them of the days before they followed the Savior. These memories were pleasant to tell around the campfire when they were with Jesus, but somehow the sea seems to stink in their nostrils today.

Peter grunts as he hoists the net full of nothing to the side of the ship. Then a groaning shout comes forth from them all, as they heave it onto the deck for what seemed to be the thousandth time. His sweat, mixed with the sea spray on his sunburned back, glistens in the evening sun that has come to signal the welcome end of a day's misery. Looking through his dripping ringlets, he stares with salt-reddened eyes at the empty net, then up at his companions, then out to the sea.

"There!" he says within a rattling cough, his dripping finger indicating the next target for the unproductive net. Picking the flotsam, jetsam, seaweeds, and other putrid fragments from its web, he sighs, and prepares it for one more draught.

As the disciples begin to change the rigging to aim the boat toward the place where he pointed, Peter sat down to get his breath. Despair had reached its crescendo. In a wave of overwhelming defeat Peter thinks that perhaps they should make for the shore instead.

He looks up toward the shore now lit like fire from the double sun of water and sky. In the same instant a small but clear voice from the beach is asking, *"Children, have you caught anything?"* 5

It was Jesus, and He knew fully well that they hadn't!

Christians should not be surprised to learn that life does not work as well as it used to *before* the Father called them to repentance.

Once you have drawn life from Jesus, things can never be the same. Just as these discouraged disciples were, you may find that you cannot focus as you once could upon the goal of advancement, because you know that advancement comes only from the Most High.

Money can't be your goal now that you've seen riches that far surpass gold. All that this heaven and Earth have to offer now pales in your mind since you have envisioned the New Heaven and the New Earth.

You find that the "here and now" is a poor trade for eternity. Your lack of focus, lack of vision, the pale incentives, and the lackluster gold and silver make for a poor laborer, a preoccupied workman, and an uninspired employee.

Disappointment with God is real.

You may have become discouraged and taken actions that removed your Lord as your *boss.* Whether you have pushed farther than you should have or misunderstood your

---

5 John 21:5

boundaries or purpose, you have put *yourself* back in control of your life.

Your Savior is Waiting on the Shore
Does your mind reel as a result of its efforts to make sense of all this? How do truth and faith come together to make *real* the life that He expects you to live and that ultimately pleases Him?

These are the thoughts I had. It is in these helpless moments that our Savior offers refuge.

Look out over the gunwales of your boat. Look across the vast expanse of water between you and the shore. Who stands at the shore by the fire?

Jesus stands there waiting with explanations of why your fishing expedition has not worked so well. He stands there with *your* supper on the fire. What is there to eat for supper? The same fish that have been impossible for you to catch alone are on His menu!

His delicious provision is always dependent on following His instructions. Listen as His voice echoes over the water, *"Children, have you caught anything?"*

Since your contact with Jesus, you are *different*. You have been *changed*. You are not the same as you once were. You have been shown things that have effected change in you forever. Your outlook, your attitude, your demeanor all are different now. You have been made *incompatible* with the world.

If you are among the many who have become discouraged with the life of faith (for whatever reason) and gone back to "reality," look around you. How are you doing?

Jesus is standing right where you left Him. H
echo over the vast expanse that you put betwee
your Savior, when He asks you, "So, how's it goi

Your Decisions

Most of the problems that come upon us are of our own
making. Somewhere, at some fork in the road, like these poor
fishermen, we made a wrong decision. An honest evaluation of
our lives and the record of our life histories show that we are
helpless and unable to make quality decisions. For the most
part, we all are powerless to mentally determine the proper
way we are to live.

In reality, we were not called to make good decisions.
We are not called to make decisions at all. We were called to
follow.

Jesus makes our inadequacy clear and asks the question,
*"If you then are not able to do the small things, why do you
take thought for the rest?"*[6]

Christians must confess to the inability to make decisions
that are beneficial to life and godliness. Life is indeed a really big
job—and it just keeps getting bigger! It is full of opportunities
for us to do what makes us die. Not because we make deadly
decisions, but because it is *decision-making itself* that steals
life away.

The anxiety of predictable consequences of the decisions
we make on a daily basis adds pressure, exacerbates our
disquiet, and renders the decisions even harder for us to make.

---

6   Luke 12:26

13

By virtue of the fact that decisions that are made under this incredible pressure will now also be made in worried haste, it is even more likely that these anxious decisions will be wrong.

Making decisions extracts your joy by forever dangling the nagging question in front of you, "What if?" at every doubtful juncture of life. "What if I had done it this way?" "What if I had done it that way?" "What if I had not made that choice?" "What if I had chosen right instead of left? Left instead of right?" These thoughts drain the joy from your daily life.

No one likes making decisions, and there is a good reason for that. You are not *called to make decisions*. You are *called to follow*.

You are not to discern the lesser of two evils, the best choice, or to deduce by logic every assessment you have to make. You are to follow. But, follow *what*; follow *whom*?

Safety, for sheep, is found in *following the Shepherd!* **Trade the *choice* for the *Voice*.**

Decision-making is a creaturely activity and a vain endeavor that we need to reject. We should determine to do *nothing* until He makes the *right* way known to us. We have but one task. We must follow *Him*—our Savior, our Master, and our Good Shepherd.

There is a better way of life for the Christian than to wring our hands over decisions that are difficult to make (those life-altering decisions). We need not search through our memories for Bible verses, consult with "experts," weigh the alternatives, and then deduce our direction. We must trust and follow naturally, easily, and effortlessly.

This can only be done if we trade the *choice* for the *Voice*.

There are so many things that we cannot fix in life. So many things are out of our control. Why do we attempt to take on even larger things—make bigger decisions—take greater risks?

Ambition must be rejected as the world's way to advance through life. Ambition, clearly observed, reveals itself as mere vanity.

We make feeble attempts to make life better. We can't prevent a common cold, yet we feign to hold cancer at bay with vitamin supplements or hold heart disease in check with medications. We can't balance our own checkbooks every week, yet we claim to know what stocks will rise in value next year.

Planning proves to be nothing more than gambling. The security we attempt to provide for ourselves is nothing more than guesswork. Avoidance of future trials and troubles is merely the empty wish of the fearful. It is vanity to place so much confidence in our own abilities when they obviously lack in so many areas.

We need to wait and listen for the voice behind us saying, "This is the way, walk ye in it."[7]

Jesus exposes our inadequacies when He asks the question, *"If you then are not able to do the least, why are you anxious for the rest?"*

Determine to trade *your choice* of direction for *His Voice* of guidance. Right choices require knowledge beyond your

---

7   Isaiah 30:21

scope of living, beyond your mental capacity to remember, and beyond your ability to interpret information.

Determine not to be discouraged. The Voice requires only that you have *ears to hear.* How many times did the Messiah exhort us to *hear?* How many times does He need to say this for us to understand? It is not *what* you know, it is *Who* you know!

Don't short-cut your opportunities to be taught by a perfect Master by instead relying upon those around you to teach truth. Why would you ask for guidance among your peers when the One who knows best is living within you now—waiting for you to ask *Him*?

Your Direction

Perhaps reluctance to ask the Lord to explain His words or give us guidance on a daily basis comes from the same ego attribute that prohibits us from asking directions (even when it is clear to everyone around us that we are lost). Perhaps it is not as innocent as that.

Mostly, we feel a demand placed upon *us* every time *we* place demands on Him. That demand makes us uncomfortable, so, like the people of Moses' day,[8] we choose rather to ask our peers to communicate truth to us.

It was only a few hours until the temple guards would gather their swords and sticks for their visit with Jesus in the night. They planned to carry Him to His destiny of torture.

---

8 Exodus 20:19

Meanwhile, in a borrowed upper room, Jesus is dining with His disciples. He looks into the eyes of His friends and wonders how they will fare on their own. He begins to give them instructions. He warns of the impending arrests and persecutions they will endure. He assures them that they will not be alone. He tells them that the Holy Spirit within Him is eternal, untouchable by wicked men, and will soon be *commissioned as their Guide.*

Sorrow fills His face as He attempts to tell them that soon He will be leaving them. They do not understand. He tries again. "But now I go away to Him who sent Me, and none of you asks Me, 'Where are You going?'" They sit in silence.

He says, "A little while, and you will not see Me; and again a little while, and you will see Me, because I go to the Father."

Then some of His disciples said among themselves, "What is this that He says to us? We do not know what He is saying."

Now Jesus knew what they desired to ask Him, and He said to them, *"Are you inquiring among yourselves about what I said?"*⁹

They wanted to ask Jesus what He meant by His words, but none dared to do so. Why? We do not know, but it is easy to speculate that they were *afraid.* It would not be hard to believe that Jesus asked this question, framed in such an enticing way, for the very purpose of *creating* curiosity. Yet every disciple feared to ask.

---

9 John 16:19 (NKJV)

Whatever the reason they would not ask, Jesus was eagerly awaiting the opportunity to answer their long-anticipated yet never-realized question. They simply did not ask. They feared.

Look at the story again. Jesus warned, "There's not much time now—a little while, and you will no longer see me." He paused. No response from His hearers.

In your mind's eye can't you see Him lean forward a little, waiting for the unavoidable query to come? However, it did *not* come. His disciples were curious, *but they did not ask.*

He saw the curiosity cover their faces, noticed their wrinkled brows, watched them tug on their ears and stroke their beards, *but no questions came.* No, they took an alternate route. They turned to *each other* for answers.

Unfortunately, the directions missed by the disciples, the directions they were afraid to ask Jesus to clarify, were the *most important directions they would ever receive.*

Direction by revelation from the Most High is, no doubt, one of the greatest experiences in the life of any Christian. It forms a bond, a communicative bond, between our God and us. After all, the main difference between Him and gods of wood and stone is that our God speaks!

He gives revelation to *direct* us.

When you are perplexed about something that He is trying to teach you, and you forsake His counsel and turn to the wisdom of man; when He finds your nose in books studying Greek, Hebrew, and Latin; when He discovers that the concept, idea, or mystery that *He has been trying to reveal to you* is being bandied about in discussion groups, don't be surprised if you hear His question in your head, "Do ye inquire among yourselves of what I said? ...Why not ask Me?"

Your Perfection

You must *not* receive your evaluation of your own level of perfection from your peers and not from *interpretations* of the Bible (yours or theirs!), but from its perfect Author, the Lord Jesus Christ. He gives revelation to *perfect* us.

His daily guidance helps us to obey His commands and, by answering life's questions, He gives us comfort and assurance day by day. He is waiting and willing to communicate with us on a *personal* level.

I fear that our concern with being perfected is not our main interest. Most Christians are being taught that perfection is an impossibility; therefore, they don't consider it at all.

Paul was under no such delusion. He said, "... and this also we wish, even your perfection"[10] and, "... let us go on unto perfection ..." [11]

Jesus commanded, "Therefore you shall be perfect, just as your Father in heaven is perfect."[12]

We must place perfection higher on our priority list. Our desire for perfection must be higher than our concern for comfort or social standing; it must be higher than the desire for and preservation of our very lives.

10   2 Corinthians 13:9
11   Hebrews 6:1
12   Matthew 5:48

After your decision to follow Christ, after you begin to answer His questions, you will begin the process of your perfection.

After your blind eyes have been opened and He asks you to evaluate your new life, you will start down the road of being made perfect.

Perfection Can Require a *Second* Touch

When Jesus came to Bethsaida, the people of the town brought a blind man to Him and asked Jesus to touch him. Jesus took the blind man by the hand and led him out of the town. (I wonder what they talked about while they walked.)

After Jesus spit on the eyes of the blind man and put His hands on him, He asked the unsighted what he could see: *"Now how is your vision?"*[13]

I take some license in saying that the Lord used these words in this question, but it is clear that He *did* ask about the vision of this man who had previously been blind. Jesus wanted to know how *well* he could see *after* His healing touch.

What if the blind man, happy to have any sight at all, had said, "Oh, everything is fine. I am just so thankful to be able to see anything"? What if he never mentioned his lingering inadequate eyesight?

This did not happen. The blind man said, "I see men as trees, walking." Afterward, Jesus put his hands on the poor man's eyes again. His eyes were restored and he "saw every man clearly."

---

13   Mark 8:22-25

Would you confess to Jesus that you are happy for His forgiveness and His gift of grace, but that you still have trouble forgiving others?

Would you confide in Him that you still find it hard to withdraw from the pleasures that the world offers?

Would you be honest enough to admit that you still_____ _____? (Insert your imperfection here.)

Unfortunately, we may not be like this blind man. We *could* be so happy to be forgiven and finally be at peace with God that we would not dare to be so candid with Him. It doesn't occur to us to tell Him that, although we are happy for His forgiveness, we still do not love our fellowman as we should. (One more time our pursuit of perfection moves lower on the priority list!)

My Second Touch (or, what *we* talked about on the way)

When I read the blind man's story and contemplated his second touch, I wondered if there may be a second touch for *me*. This particular question asked by Jesus made a profound impact on my life!

I well remember how the story laid bare my paradoxical struggle with pacifism. I had met many who had become pacifists through their faith in Christ, and I wondered why I still felt that I had the right and duty to defend myself and my property even at the cost of another human life.

Many years ago when I first read this question, I felt no qualms about arming myself (*and* my wife). I felt no compunction about killing an intruder or marauder, and thought myself fully capable of doing so. I counseled my wife to do the same. I sensed it was my *duty* to defend and protect my family.

I could not fit the words *"Do violence to no man"* [14] into my Christian understanding. Nor could I understand fully the words, "Beloved, do not avenge yourselves, but *rather* give place to wrath; for it is written, 'Vengeance *is* Mine, I will repay,' says the Lord." [15]

I did not know it then, but a *second* touch was in store for me. I had to admit that *"I see men, but they are as trees."*

Trees are alive, but they have no *life*. A tree can be left standing when it offers a benefit or it can be cut down if it's in the way. I gave mankind the same consideration.

This is no longer true for me. Men are not as mere trees. The Creator did not breathe life into trees, but He did so to my brother and my sister, my fellowmen.

Today, the men I see *are* as men to me. Now, I see *every man* clearly. (For this reason I believe that Jesus, as He led the blind man to the outskirts of the city, talked to him about loving his fellowman.)

In Summary

Christ Jesus' questions are all about perfecting you. Your *perfection* demands that you analyze your *desires*, your *discouragements*, your *disappointments*, your *decisions*, and your *direction*.

Honest evaluations, corrections, and the willingness to change will carry you though this exam with flying colors.

---

14   Luke 3:14
15   Rom. 12:19 (NKJV)

Just as Jesus told the rich young ruler, your own perfection is contingent on "... *if you will be perfect ...* "

It is no insult to Him if you confess that you do not love your fellowman as you should. Nor is it an affront to Christ or His redeeming power to say that you still see men as trees. For, in confessing, you show your *desire* to see clearly.

Jesus knows that a second touch is needed to perfect you. He is waiting for you to honestly confess this fact to Him. Go to Him. Perhaps you will not like what He tells you, but you must go to Him.

You are faced with the responsibility of reaching your own perfection and completion. Scripture is clear that it *is* your personal duty.

If this duty *disheartens you,* consider *why* it is a discouragement to you. Have you resigned the dream? Do you think it is impossibility? Seek guidance for the next step. It will come.

Scripture shows that *direction* comes through revelation.

Yours is not to make *decisions*, but to follow—*naturally*. What could be more glorious than to see all things clearly—to love truly, to care intuitively, to understand fully by simply following your Guide?

When you contemplate the change that has occurred in you since the point of your visitation, you must be honest. The second touch, *your perfection*, requires your honest confession—and the will of God demands it.

23

When your head raises for the first time to view the world with your new eyes, don't be *disappointed* if things are not as you expected. You don't see everything clearly yet because there is another touch in your future. (There may even be many!)

You must look at your life in Christ, evaluate your shortcomings, and sincerely and honestly respond to His question, "Now how is your vision? How is your new life?"

As you read this book, you will not be called upon to make a decision between one idea and another, this particular doctrine or that one; however, you *will* be called upon constantly to *listen for the voice of your Savior* who promised, "My sheep know my voice and a stranger they will not follow."[16]

Let the Good Shepherd do His job—*leading* sheep.

Even though His promise was to never leave us alone, some Christians still won't follow Him, because they simply do not believe He *will* or *can* answer us. By the time you finish this book, you will never again doubt His willingness or ability to speak to you.

As you *hear* the truth, you will no longer fear His demands; you will no longer doubt His *ability* or *desire* to speak to you. The conversation you long for will become apparent in the words, "He who has *ears* to hear, let *him* hear."

The excursion upon which you embark, as you read the questions of Jesus, will stir thoughts you have never had. The red-letter questions are like that. You will experience change,

---

16   John 10:4-5

cleansing, and renewal, but only if honesty prevails throughout the interview to come.

When the eyes that see your inmost thoughts look into *your* soul, when the mind that converses daily with the Almighty formulates a question for *you*, how can you answer and not be *changed forever*?

PART 2

Jesus' Questions Challenge Us Personally

What Are You Thinking?

The Great Teacher repeatedly asked His students, *"What do you think?"*

It seems that we have little time to think anymore. (You may have even wondered when you will have time to read this book—much less have time to *really* think about it!) During the course of reading the red-letter questions of Jesus, you will be repeatedly called upon to take the time to consider your thoughts. The questions of the Lord do that naturally.

As we strive toward perfection, He asks us to evaluate our thought processes. Convictions, philosophies, ideas, and patterns will emerge from the deepest recesses of a mind that is engaged in conversation with its Creator. What a waste of resources it would be to rush through the reading of His questions and back into life again and never analyze the conversations, the words, and our interaction with the Lord Jesus himself!

As I started to locate and read the questions of Jesus, I noticed a pattern beginning to develop within my thoughts. To my amazement His underlying *purpose* began to emerge. It became obvious that He was teaching me to *trust my relationship with Him*.

Relationships are personal; therefore, personal questions became essential. It is the personal questions that make us squirm, but we must trust our Teacher and answer honestly.

Three Warnings

Before the Master could begin to instruct me with His questions, the warnings came—three *main* warnings or hindrances to the Spirit-led life that can cause error and harm. They became apparent as I began to answer the personal questions of introspection that He asked in the Scriptures. *(I will explore each warning with you in the chapters that follow.)*

As you contemplate His questions, these three warnings will also become apparent to you, but you must not take umbrage or become defensive about them. (You will know offense has begun when you feel the presence of fear *or* anger. These emotions are an indication that you are beginning to take *personal* offense.)

Somehow, I understood that if I failed to control my thoughts during these vital times of revelation and attempted to justify any of my offending behavior or rebellious thoughts, my search for His will and my journey toward perfection would abruptly end. I knew that He would cease to teach me. Within my own spirit I was hearing, *"You will never move past your last opportunity to make a change."*

At first, I thought I understood perfectly what He expected of me, but I didn't.

I thought that the life of a "person of true faith" would be an enigmatic and esoteric one. In other words, a "spiritual man" would be a sort of *maharishi* or deep-thinking philosopher with a half-glazed look on his face, a wise proverb on his tongue, and his hands together in front. (His fingertips would touch each other ever so lightly.)

After that idea evaporated, I was somewhat disappointed to learn that my thinking was entirely backwards! (This became evident over and over again!) I learned that to live a life of true and biblical faith is actually a very simple, daily practice.

I am sure that my concept, taken to the extreme, is the origin of a works-oriented redemption—mistaking *physical accomplishment* for *spiritual achievement.* (I *was* pleased to discover that He did not require that I become like a monk perched at the top of a pole, or some guru living on top of a mountain.)

Like the rich young ruler who had plenty of works to his merit, I heard, "Keep the commandments!" My thought continued, *"That part is easy, what lack I yet?"* I thought I understood, but I didn't. (Anyone thinking that living by faith is easy is in for an awakening!)

He wanted me, an *ordinary* man, to exercise discipline and heed the warnings that He has so clearly provided in the Scriptures. I felt that there *had* to be more to it than just these three warnings! (They seemed too easy—too good to be true!) You see, I thought I understood, but I didn't.

I am sure I am not alone in this. Perhaps you, too, have considered your life of faith to be solely a *spiritual* one, or maybe you have assumed that there *has* to be more to it. It may be that you have drawn a broad black line between your spiritual life and your secular life and never thought of them as being compatible, much less co-existing!

Maybe you have felt that what the Father requires of you is much more than a mere human can accomplish, and, therefore, you "spiritualize" His commands, making them more palatable to your material world. (Maybe you, too, *think* you understand, but don't!)

When I began to obey His commands, I discovered that those three warnings, those three commands I had at first perceived to be simple tasks, would demand nearly all my efforts; yet they were easily within my reach.

My confusion lifting now, I was sure that the key was to first *obey* Him! Whatever He says! (And I was right!)

Faith is a matter of the heart. "But the heart is desperately wicked," says the Prophet, and "Who can know it?"[1]

This is where life under the renewed Covenant really shines. We *can* know our heart—with a little help! We get that help at the feet of our Master when we honestly answer His questions.

Perhaps you are fearful of what may come next, as you journey deeper into His questions. (If you are not, you may not understand where we are going.) As you respond to His questions in order to pursue a life of faith, you will be required to face who you *really* are.

In the world in which we live, people seem to think that *saying it* makes it so. To the contrary, in the world of the Spirit there are no illusions, no smoke and mirrors, no fantasies; all of the vocal bravado means nothing.

---

1 Jeremiah 17:9

He who, "… *hears* these sayings of mine, *and does them*, I will liken him unto a wise man, which built his house upon a rock,"[2] the Master says.

Fear

In the Gospel of Matthew, we are given a story about Jesus getting on board a ship.[3] His disciples followed Him and "… a great storm arose on the sea," so that the boat was covered with the waves. Jesus went to sleep.

Then His disciples came to Him, woke Him, and cried, "Lord, save us! We are perishing!"

Jesus responded, *"Why are you fearful, O you of little faith?"*

Then He arose and rebuked the winds and the sea, and there was a great calm. So the men marveled, saying, "Who can this be, that even the winds and the sea obey Him?"

Panting and holding on to the swaying boat, their stomachs yet churning and their hearts still racing, as the waves took their last waning laps against the sides of their heaving vessel, Jesus asked His disciples, "Why are you so fearful?"

Consider for a moment that this question was not asked because Jesus needed to know the answer. Rather, the Teacher asked because He wanted His disciples to examine the *reason* for their own fear.

It would be pure foolishness for a fisherman not to be afraid of severe weather! But Jesus did not ask them *what*

---

2   Matthew 7:24
3   Matthew 8:23-27

made them afraid. Similarly, He doesn't ask us *what* we fear, but *why* do we fear?

When the Son of God asks us to consider our fear, what we are to do at that point is to consider *why* we are afraid! It is a natural human reaction to focus on *what* makes us afraid, but Jesus wants us to consider *why* we are afraid. Do you see the difference?

In an honest Christian this question should sober him or her and initiate self-examination. This self-examining process is an essential part of our Christian faith and is critical to what follows in our progression toward perfection.

Self-examination is like a meeting of the minds—just you and your Creator looking at "why?" It cannot be bypassed, done in haste or hurry, nor can it be accomplished in formulaic steps or procedures.

The process of self-examination is lacking in nearly every life, and certainly is non-existent in most conventional congregational worship. Our churches are noisy, our homes are noisy, our lives are noisy, and there is essentially no time at all set aside just to consider, in quietness, our own lives—before our God.

We must all take the time—quality, quiet time—to consider our own fears and reasons *why* we are afraid.

If you may feel that your fears are out of your control, you should remember that *the fear you feel is always in inverse proportion to the faith you have in Jesus Christ*—and your faith *is* in your control!

Many times within the course of my study, the questions of Jesus called me to quietness and reflection. It was only then that understanding would come forth.

His questions will call you to quietness and reflection, too. After your reading, don't hesitate to sit silently for a while. Take the time to think about nothing in particular; instead, consider the formulation of your own thoughts and fears. You will find that at the heart of your fear will be your lack of faith in Jehovah.

In the religious world fear takes many different forms, but lack of faith is the basis for all of them. Why *are* you so fearful? Do you feel that you should not tamper with your already-established religious faith?

Can you track down and name the fear you feel? Is it simply a fear of change? Or perhaps you have a fear of opening yourself to deception?

You will undoubtedly hear and see new ideas form as you answer the questions of Jesus. Sometimes these thoughts will contradict what you understand today as conventional Christianity. You will want to investigate them, even if they take you in directions opposed to convention.

Within your heart, you might feel a fear come about when you are told something different from what you, your parents, your grandparents, your denomination, your family, and your friends believe. You may find new concepts, beyond your present understanding, which you will want to study and know for yourself. Do you consider everything outside your present mindset to be "evil"?

Jesus responded to such fears, and asked, *"Why do you think* [of] *evil in your hearts?"*[4]

Good and Bad

"Evil" is actually a simpler word than we make it out to be in our modern vernacular. The Scriptures use the word "evil" as meaning the opposite of the word "good." Today, we can simply substitute the word "bad" or "unpleasantness."

In this example Jesus had approached a man that had been suffering from the palsy and said, "Son, be of good cheer; your sins are forgiven."

Then He asked some of the scribes who were watching Him why they thought evil (bad thoughts about Him) in their hearts. Jesus was not speaking about "sinful" thoughts. He asked about their *suspicious* thoughts. Sometimes, when we are unsure, or afraid, we approach "new" ideas with suspicion.

Jesus operated *outside* the conventional religion of the day. He still does. Do you see how the Father Jehovah had done a wonderful thing through His Son for this man by forgiving his sins? Yet, the religious leaders found themselves on the outside looking in and they felt left out. They responded by finding fault.[5]

This is a curiosity worthy of investigation. Many times, when we find ourselves on the outside looking in, we will find fault, as well. When something new presents itself to be included in life's "script," our first reaction is to initiate rejection and our first thought is suspicion. Why do we do that?

---

4   Matthew 9:4 (NKJV)
5   "And at once some of the scribes said within themselves, 'This Man blasphemes!'"

There is bad (evil) within the heart of man, so we naturally draw upon this to form our thinking. Jesus knew this and attempted to direct the Pharisees' attention to the source. He said, "An evil man out of the evil treasure of his heart brings forth that which is evil. For out of the abundance of a man's heart his mouth speaks."[6]

Suspicion *is* evil, and it is the suspicion in our own hearts that formulates in our minds and eventually, it comes out of our mouths. Why are we so suspicious? Why did the Pharisees say, "He is a blasphemer!"? It was because they were afraid.

We are afraid! We are afraid of losing our friends. We are afraid of being deceived. We are afraid of going against tradition and convention. Our fear of these things can be explained in no other way but as a bondage to the "role" we have decided to play.

When we consider the "script" by which we live to be a "closed canon" (nothing may be added to it or taken from it)—when we protect the role we play in that script, we are, by definition, hypocrites.[7]

Take another look at what John's record demonstrates. Jesus was assisting the Pharisees in discovering a fact about their own spiritual nature. He wanted to help them know what they could never understand on their own.

Jesus was helping them to see their bondage to family and tradition—their bondage to the "script." The discovery of this bondage would reveal something about themselves that could prove to be very frightening.

---

6   Matthew 12:34
7   root: *hypocrita* (Greek, meaning *actor*)

For the first time these Pharisees were being told that they were *not* who they *thought* they were. They were not a part of the family that they had claimed, nor were they even a free people, but were actually "slaves and servants to the kingdom of the damned."[8] (That's a lot to swallow in one afternoon!)

Could it be that you do not realize that *you* may not be who you think you are?

We all must come to this realization. Religion has served us a plate of answers—a "script," if you will. Many times these answers come before the questions are even asked. As we are served these answers, we begin to formulate in our minds who we *think* we should be. We decide what "part" we should play.

We decide, usually with good intentions, who we *need* to be in order for the "answers" to fit. A role begins to develop for us to occupy. The answers become a list, then a liturgy; the liturgy becomes doctrine; the doctrine develops into dogma; and the acting stage is set—set for hypocrisy. (We'll discuss more about hypocrisy later.)

Our evil thoughts, if unchecked, can develop into the dreaded and destructive posture of *defending* our position. When we resort to defending ourselves, we have stopped the learning process.

The Pharisees were not open to discover what was false about what they believed. Are *you*? What can be learned by someone who has no doubts? How much truth do you *really* know?

---

8 John 8:28-59

To help a group of Pharisees discover their lack of openness regarding what they really believed, Jesus once asked, *"If I say the truth, why do you not believe me?"*[9]

The life of a dedicated Christian eventually becomes a quest to find truth. But how will you know it when you see it? Is it possible to find something you have never before encountered?

I'm convinced that there are people who do not recognize the truth that sets us free. Matthew teaches that it is given for some to know the mysteries of the kingdom and for others it is not given.[10]

A psychologically unhealthy person ignores reality by the utilization of "escapism." That phenomenon takes place through his or her immersion into music, movies, songs, dance, drugs, television, sex, and hobbies. (The list is nearly endless.) The Christian's resistance to the discovery of reality often takes the form of immersion into the "church life."

When we are surrounded by those who believe the same things we believe, it can strengthen *any* idea—and it need not be a *true* idea.

It is ironic, but the protection against deceit that is practiced by most Christians (the involvement and saturation in their local congregational activities) can actually be an incubator of pretense and self-deception. The Pharisees felt they were right *because everyone they knew felt the same way.*

As His questions become more personal, they become more difficult. The answers cannot be quick or reckless, trite

9   John 8
10 Matthew 13:11

or clichéd. We must engage in intellectual honesty and personal integrity in our responses.

A wonderful question to ask *yourself* is, "If what I believe is *not true, do I want to know it?*"

Don't answer too quickly. The fast answer is not always the honest one. Many wish to answer, "Yes," and then quickly add the proviso, "But what I believe *is* true!"

That's not the question! The question is this, "If what you believe is not true, do you want to know it?"

Believe it or not, I have heard people answer this question, "No," even after giving it thought. That may be appalling to you, but if you decline to hear a theory, a premise, or an idea that goes against your present understanding, *perhaps your answer is "No," as well.*

If you would rather belong to a crowd than be correct in your belief, there is little hope for you to find the true, abundant life of faith that Jesus offers and expects you to live.

Maybe you are among those who ignore the natural, plain, and obvious evidences of truth in your life, or perhaps you are someone who refuses to obey the truth after seeing it clearly in the Scriptures.

Jesus wants to know why, and asks, *"If I say the truth, why do you not believe me?"*

He leaves us no alternative with this question. We have to admit its premise. That is, that He has *told us the truth* and we do not believe Him. We may *not* argue that He is mistaken or that we *do* indeed believe.

Upon this admission, we are left to answer *why*, then, do we *not* believe? The sad answer can only be that we do *not recognize* truth when we see it, or the truth is *uncomfortable* to our way of life; therefore, we are *compelled* to reject it, or both!

If something is true and it goes against your thinking, you must be honest enough to accept that truth into your way of thinking or be doomed to live in the quagmire of status-quo religion. You will be destined to have only books, liturgies, men, and traditions to answer your questions about life. If discomfort of truth causes you to hold to your own way, your progression toward perfection again has halted.

There comes a time in life when we must admit that the level for which we have strived certainly has not reached the perfection that is asked of us by Jesus. This becomes apparent in the dichotomy between our passions and His. When He was here on the Earth, He was often perplexed by what enthused people and how different their affections were from that of the Eternal.

The frustration this caused for Jesus is obvious in questions such as this one, *"... to what shall I liken the men of this generation?"*

After asking this question, He immediately offered this graphic description, "They are like children sitting in the marketplaces, calling to their companions, and saying: 'We played the flute for you, And you did not dance; We mourned for you, and you did not weep.'"[11]

Jesus used the example of spoiled little children to illustrate a point about the mindset of the people in His generation.

11   Luke 7 and Matthew 11

They wanted what they did not have, and what they were given, they did not want.

They had been given John the Baptist (in the estimation of Jesus he was the greatest prophet ever born), yet they dismissed him as a lunatic. They had been given the very Son of God and rejected Him because He was not what they had expected. By their rejection of the Messiah they made a huge statement, "He's not holy. He's not mighty. He's not sympathetic to our religion. He doesn't fulfill the prophecies; therefore, He is not the Messiah." Isn't it curious that the messianic role of Jesus was rejected on *religious* grounds?

Note the pattern of their deductions. They looked at the Son of God and decided that He was "evil" (bad.) They evaluated the Messiah by using their own understanding of what was good and bad, what was conventional and familiar.

We all do the very same thing. We cannot help it. We have a rule by which we measure the things that come into and go out of our lives.

Can we trust our own sensibilities? Isn't our sense of right or wrong (our sense of good and evil, our sense of what is just and unjust) warped and twisted, because of our sinful condition? Sure it is, but we must admit that.

The comparison given through Jesus' question can bring our passions into sharp focus. Have *we* refused to dance to His music? Have *we* any remorse concerning that over which He mourns? How would Jesus liken the men of *our* generation?

For centuries Almighty God has given many prophecies about His sheep, His people, the pride of their sin, and their subsequent separation from Him. He has voiced displeasure with sin, and on several occasions, He named the things that grieve Him most.

Listed in Scripture are seven things that He hates[12]—things that are an abomination to Him. Yet most people cannot list them.

How many of the seven can you name? Do you know what grieves the God you profess to love and serve? Can you list the things that he calls "bad?" How can you claim to be under the direction of a Lord from whom you receive instruction if *your* list of "bad" things is *different* from His?

His nature needs to become a part of ours. So that what He deems "good," we will deem "good," and what He sees as "evil," we will also see as "evil." Or, as Jesus put it, we are to *dance to His music.*

It looks as though we have not changed much from the people of Jesus' generation. We need to close these huge gaps between our desires and His, between our evaluation criteria and His, between our preferences and His.

The gaps are probably much larger than you might imagine, but not so large that they cannot be spanned. We must make changes in our thinking. There are many pauses that must be inserted into our speech, and many, many of *His* concerns added to our lists of "good things" (as well as dropped from our own lists of "bad things").

Have we become spoiled children who only want what we do not have and only have what we do not want? Have we become so bored with the things that excite our Father

---

12   Proverbs 6:16-19

Jehovah that we refuse to dance, sitting with crossed legs and arms until we hear *our* favorite tune? Does the news from across town that breaks His heart fall on our own ears as unimportant and mundane?

We should seek fresh revelation from the Father about *His* concerns and *His* loves, for only His music is worthy of our dancing, and it is solely to His sorrowful lamentation that we should mourn. Self-concern can preoccupy the heart of the most dedicated Christian.

To what shall I liken the people of this generation? They were like children—sitting in the marketplace—not even recognizing the music He played. Bored children—sitting and doing nothing of any eternal value. This distressed the heart of Jesus then, and it is still a distress within His heart today.

We baffle Him because we would rather have the things we want than the things He wants to give us. When we finally admit to ourselves that we really don't know "good" from "bad," we should then beware of comfort and contentment. This admission alone will help us avoid being content with error and comfortable with sin.

A true servant lays no claim to "a mind of his own"; rather, he serves only his Master's wishes. The gospels are replete with parables that portray those who claim a servant's position (an unselfish condition), when in reality they are not in servitude at all.

The pretexts, self-deceit, and purposeful misleading all end with the same result, but there will come a day when all pretext and hypocrisy will be exposed for what it is, and we will be exposed for who we *really* are.

Are these warnings for you?

When reading a parable about a wicked person who receives punishment, many times we naturally assume that person is somebody else—someone *unlike* ourselves. We most often assume the best about ourselves and the worst about others.

There is a question you must ask yourself as you examine these parables. Who are the warnings for?

In nearly every message today, we are given assurances (and sometimes even guarantees) of salvation and rewards. We are assured that we need not worry about anything because Jesus has made all provisions *for* us.

Above the din of our modern-day pulpits, this question of Jesus still beckons a response, *"What is this, then, that is written?"* [13]

When I found this question, I considered again the parable about a foolish man who had built his house upon the sand. Who is this foolish man? Did this man, who built his house on the sand, do it purposely? Did he ignore his own good common sense, ignore the instructions of his peers, and build his house on the sand, all the while knowing that when the storm came, his house would fall?

Who were the "many" that Jesus was talking about when He said, *"Many will say to Me in that day, 'Lord, Lord, have we not prophesied in Your name, cast out demons in Your name, and done many wonders in Your name?' And then I will declare to them, 'I never knew you; depart from Me, you who practice lawlessness'"*? [14]

---

13   Luke 20:17
14   Matthew 7:22-23

Who were the five foolish virgins[15] who took their lamps without oil to the wedding feast? These members of the bridal party were not reveling and having a wild time while *ignoring* the bridegroom. They were *waiting for the bridegroom*. Who are these foolish virgins who found themselves outside, in the dark, scrambling about and trying to make provision in the last day? If they are not well-meaning Christians, *what is this, then, that is written?*

What about the man who put his hand to the plow and looked back? He earned a place of unworthiness in the Kingdom of God by his actions. This was not a man who *refused* to plow. This man had *decided* to plow. He started to plow. He set out to accomplish plowing, but he turned back. Jesus said to him, "No one, having put his hand to the plow, and looking back, is fit for the kingdom of God." If this warning is not ours, *what is this, then, that is written?*

While teaching the Pharisees one day, Jesus told them a story about an owner of a vineyard. This lord set up his winery, making every provision for it. He hired a staff, put them in charge, and then left the country.

Upon sending emissaries, the lord found that the workers had grown wicked and selfish. So, he sent his son, thinking that his workers would surely reverence him. The story ended when the workers killed the son and tossed his beaten body out to the birds.

When the story concluded, Jesus stared at the Pharisees and asked, *"What do you think will happen now?"*[16]

---

15   Matthew 25
16   Matthew 21:40

Just as He expected, they answered with a reply that was commensurate with the offense. "He will miserably destroy those wicked men!" But they had not yet considered *who* was represented by the murderers they condemned in the story. They could not believe that the warnings were for *them*.

Are the warnings only for the lost? The lost in the world do not even *know* God. The lost in the world care nothing about the Lord Jesus Christ (they certainly don't call Him "Lord"!) Who is it that has built their doctrines on such shaky foundations? Who has hands upon the plow? Who is waiting for the Bridegroom today?

If *we* have nothing to worry about, then why were *we* given these warnings? If these Scriptures are not a warning for *us*, *what is this, then, that is written?*

It must be evident to you, my friend, that my warnings from the Father were not for me alone. Why else would He broadcast such warnings in the Scriptures? We must assume the warnings are for *us all!*

Inconsistencies

The inconsistencies in our thinking, doctrines, and our faith become apparent. We suffer from inconsistencies in our Christian lives because of basic misunderstandings or incorrect assumptions, illogical deductions, and incorrect definitions of good and evil.

When we hear the Messiah teach us and we evaluate His words as being impertinent, useless, bad, or unworthy of attention, we put ourselves in a precarious place *outside* of the care and understanding of Christ. When His warnings seem to be for somebody else, perhaps we need to correct our view of what is good and bad, real or imaginary, dogma or doctrine. We will need *discernment* to uncover these inconsistencies and repair them.

The world tears at our discernment. Hollywood, Madison Avenue, and mammon at large constantly wear away our correct understanding of good and evil.

The life to which Jesus has called us is simple and ignoble. Our rewards are on the other side of this life--not here. In respect to the Scriptures, we must be very careful to determine that we see mammon *exactly* the way our Father sees it—as being *bad*. At the same time we should resist our natural human tendency to embrace *pleasant* things as "good things."

On the last Sabbath day of Jesus' life, we find Him in the Temple antagonizing the religious leadership. Upon leaving, one of His disciples voiced a casual observation about the Temple of Herod. "What beautiful stones are these!" Jesus astonished them by responding with an agitated question. *"Do you not see all these things?"*[17]

He continued, "Assuredly, I say to you, not *one* stone shall be left here upon another, that shall not be thrown down."[18] His question goes to the very heart of the *evaluation* of what we *see*.

The disciples were obviously fascinated with the beauty of the Temple. They thought that it must impress the Master. Surely He thought it was as holy, great, grand, and glorious as they did. They were sure that this beautiful religious temple

---

17 Matthew 24 & Mark 13
18 Matthew 24

must be a "good" thing, but they were staring mammon in the face and did not know it.

"Don't you see what I see? Don't you realize what you are seeing?" He was amazed by the fact that they could not see what He saw clearly.

If I may lay aside intellect for a moment and capture your imagination, we can "put some pants" [19] on this story.

Today, if we were to walk with Jesus down the streets of our modern world, we likely wouldn't act any differently than the disciples did. We would probably seek to engage His enthusiasm about the "miracles" of modern man. Setting aside the fact that He is well aware of all the things that man has accomplished over the centuries, we would probably attempt to show Him around as if He were a visiting stranger.

We might take Him to Cape Kennedy and show Him the space center, while touting the accomplishments of our past and the promises of future endeavors.

We may boast to Him of mankind's great strides in modern building construction and the technological leaps we've made in electronics and satellite telecommunications. Perhaps we would point out our modern hospitals and brag about our medical and pharmaceutical progress.

The idea would be to impress our Lord Jesus with ourselves and our accomplishments while gorging Him with the "best of the best" in every area of modern civilization. (Can you imagine, for example, what He would think of the Internet?)

---

19   "Put pants on it" is a term I use to apply to what is usually considered a "spiritual" concept in order to make the hearer see it for what it really is—to "humanize" it or to visualize it as an actual occurrence.

Continue with me for a little longer as we ignore the foolishness of the thought of walking around with the Son of God, trying to impress Him with who we are, rather than sitting at His feet and learning about Him! (What a ridiculous endeavor it is to try to impress the Almighty with man, when man is so unimpressed with the Almighty!)

We simply don't see things the way Jehovah sees them. When His Son, Jesus, looked at the stones composing Herod's temple, He knew that they had merely been purchased by Herod, an Idumean who cared *nothing* about the things of God, His temple or His people.

Today, people point to many great "stones" that have been set in their churches and they flaunt man's accomplishments. But consider how Jesus would see these things. For example, what were the "whitewashed tombs" He spoke of "… which indeed appear beautiful outwardly, but inside are full of dead *men's* bones and all uncleanness."?[20]

We need to realize that Jesus sees things completely differently than we do. We might be inclined to show Him our accomplishments, but neglect to show Him our many failures.

We would likely show off our amber waves of grain, but hide from Him our homeless and hungry who have little of it.

We may proudly show Him our beautiful buildings, but not the alleys behind them that are populated with the ones who are unwelcome inside the buildings.

---

20   Matthew 23:27 (NKJV)

We would take Him down our streets, but distract His attention from the gutters.

If He were with us today, we would most likely try to impress Him with our most recent medical breakthroughs, but not our psychological failures. We might be proud of our rising standard of living, but not mention the rise in our disintegrating families.

Would He consider it an evidence of the Church's influence to see that the divorce rate hasn't increased in recent years, when He knows that it is really because marriage has become passé in many cultures?

We would, no doubt, show Him our worldwide satellite television broadcasting networks, but surely would be ashamed for Him to view its contents. We certainly would not brag to Him that the United States is now the largest purveyor of pornography to the world today via the miraculous Internet!

No, we definitely do not view things the way our Savior does. It would be difficult for anyone with understanding to overlook what is so obviously wrong with our world in order to admire any "right-ness" in it.

I remember a sports car in the 1970s that everyone wanted to own. Everyone, that is, *except* auto mechanics—for they knew what was *under* its shiny "skin." When you know that the inner workings of something are severely flawed, it is difficult to get excited about its appearance.

This is what was in the mind of our Messiah when He looked at those temple stones. He wanted the disciples to understand that they needed to change *their ideas about good and evil,* just as He wants us to evaluate our own understanding of good and evil.

At this point, anxiety may have found a place in you. You may be wondering just what is it that you think is *good* but is actually *bad* in His sight. You might be concerned about what you think is *right* but He considers *wrong.* Let me assure you, if you have no fear at this point, you are either right in every area of your life, or you are not paying attention!

I was also very uncomfortable with this awareness, but it is the very state of mind that Jesus was trying to bring about when He asked questions of His disciples, the Pharisees, and other religious leaders of His day. We must face the inevitable prospect that we may be wrong.

Oh, to have a mind that is not hemmed in by prejudice, stifled by tradition, or fenced in by preconception! Such a mind would be able to have all knowledge within its grasp! To develop these qualities we must start with the possibility that *we may be wrong.*

Of course, we are all subject to error. If we have agreed that we could be wrong, we must ask, wrong about what?

When awareness comes and your eyes are open to this danger, you will feel fear. (This is just good sense. Remember, it is *ignorance* that is bliss.) We will only overcome pure fear with pure faith; and faith begins with bravery in the face of fear. We must be brave if we are to understand.

Brave or fearless?
Bravery is something we don't hear much about today. Oh, sometimes there are movies or novels that portray men and women as brave—people who go against all odds, risking life

and fortune, but these people who are portrayed as "fearless" are poor examples of bravery.

Fearlessness *can* be merely a product of ignorance. As a matter of fact, there is no true bravery in ignorance. Rather, bravery *requires* fear in order for it to be pure bravery.

In the Garden of Gethsemane on that fateful night of treachery, Jesus was well aware that He had been betrayed, and He awaited the hour when His archenemy would have free reign.

As He prayed, He was distracted as He saw within His mind a party that was organizing to capture Him. He knew they were preparing for the Crucifixion and, although He was well aware of all that would soon befall Him, He had the courage to stay in the Garden, to wait for them, and to face them.

When Jesus heard the distant sounds of their approaching, His heart undoubtedly leapt at the realization that the end was upon Him. His brave heart must have skipped a beat at the sound of a twig snapping from a tree branch. The armed party of religious thugs were making their way through the Garden toward Him.

As the very Son of God, He was sure that He could call on legions of angels to rescue Him, but He determinedly shook off all thoughts of escape. Instead, He considered the beneficial effect that His death would have for you and me!

Whispers were followed by silence, as He heard the noise of their walking stop just short of the moonlit circle of His disciples. He stood erect, looked them in the eye, and resolutely walked straight toward them. Bravely, Jesus asked (as if He did not know), *"Who are you looking for?"*[21]

The Messiah is our perfect example of real bravery. He knew exactly what was happening, but He did not turn and run. He did not stand in the face of His enemies, unafraid. In spite of His fear, He stood there *bravely*.

Our Savior magnifies the idea of bravery to astounding measures when He looks at His disciples and asks, *"...do you think that I cannot now pray to My Father, and He will provide Me with more than twelve legions of angels?"*[22]

He declares that escape is within His prerogative; yet, though it will cost His life, He continues to press toward right. This is indeed true bravery.

The quest for truth will require us to examine our newfound truths and assess the possibility of escape back into the "Sunday-go-to-meetin'" lifestyle from which we came (because that escape *will* be available!)

As we face the questions of Jesus and re-evaluate our hearts, we will receive the needed re-programming of our minds! It will require bravery to make it through all His questions.

The fear we feel, as we continue to closely examine our answers to the questions of Jesus, will require the *necessary* ingredient of bravery. We cannot consider what others may do to us, think of us, where we will fit in with them, or what doctrines and ideas we are going to have to accept or discard because of the insights that have been given to us.

---

21 John 18:4
22 Matthew 26:53 (NKJV)

Think of the finish line: When everything we believe has been examined and thoroughly tested, only *true revelation* is left. When we have answered His questions and considered life from the perspective of His rationale, we *will* emerge confident and faithful.

Like our Savior, we have to determinedly walk *toward* our own execution. We need to walk past the escape opportunities. We must take up our crosses, *die to self*, eliminate our own thinking and preconceived ideas, *deny* our egos, and *lose* our lifestyles!

Only now will we fully engage the promise, "If anyone desires to come after Me, let him deny himself, and take up his cross, and follow Me. For whoever desires to save his life will lose it, but whoever loses his life for My sake will find it."[23]

Warning One: Beware of the Flesh

Simplicity first ...

The subject of comfort and complacency goes to the heart of every human endeavor. Biologists have named it the "survival instinct." In every animal on Earth it goes against nature to "subtract" from ourselves.

Perhaps this is why Jesus mentions denial of self so often. He even asked a question to illustrate that "adding" to ourselves is merely an illusion.

"Which of you by worrying can add one cubit to his stature?"[24] "Therefore do not worry, saying, 'What shall we

---

23   Matthew 16:24-25 (NKJV)
24   Matthew 6:27 (NKJV); Luke 12:24-38 (NKJV)

eat?' or 'What shall we drink?' or 'What shall we wear?' For after all these things the Gentiles seek. For your heavenly Father knows that you need all these things. But seek first the kingdom of God and His righteousness, and all these things shall be added to you. Therefore do not worry about tomorrow, for tomorrow will worry about its own things. Sufficient for the day *is* its own trouble."

His question is sure to make us feel somewhat ridiculous about ambitiously worrying over our state in life. It guides our thinking toward the realization that there is very little we can accomplish by worrying about the necessities of life.

Perfection demands that these superficial concerns be absent from our thinking. This is a subject that is often sidestepped. We have even coined phrases like "Nobody is perfect" to make us feel better about not pursuing perfection.

However, according to the Scriptures, we are *called* to perfection. He wants us, and He *expects* us to be perfected. In our hearts we know that He has not asked us to do something that is impossible. Rather, in His call to perfection there is a promise. If we will even *attempt* to advance to this level, we will surely find *every provision* made for our daily sustenance.

The daily pursuit of comforts and security will severely hamper our progress toward perfection. We should learn to allow ourselves to be "uncomfortable." Trusting Him in everyday life instead of trusting in the arm of flesh or our own abilities is *difficult*, but it is not impossible.

The things of the world wait eagerly to rush in and fill the void in the discontented life. Do not fear lack! Fear makes us ripe and ready to receive the worst of all worldly powers—mammon, the destroyer of faith and virtue. Mammon will not require virtue or faith to manifest itself, just your allegiance and attention.

As we seek the Kingdom of God (pursue perfection), we know within ourselves that Jehovah's provision comes to us as we are obedient and submissive to Him. He is our Lord and Provider, and we rightfully link right-living to His supply, because we have His promises.

Ambition within us must be curbed. The desire to increase our stature by *taking thought* (by taking our life into our own hands) is most treacherous to faith. When the hand that steers our life is revealed to be our own, we need to relax and submit to His control. Let go of the controls and make an opportunity for Him to guide you onto another course.

Keep in mind that the saying, "The Lord helps those who help themselves," *is not Scripture;* nor can this idea be supported by Scripture. Little by little, as you let go of *your way* and fasten to *His way*, you will move toward perfection.

Servitude

The idea of letting the Father provide your needs must be in the back of your mind at all times. The best strategy to accomplish this is a proper *outlook*. We are to be *servants*. A servant is *provided* food and provision by his or her Master—and a servant never even considers ambitious thoughts in order to climb above the station to which he or she has been assigned.

Our Lord and Master, Jesus, illustrated this concept when He asked a very pertinent question, *"And which of you, having a servant plowing or tending sheep, will say to him when he has come in from the field, 'Come at once and sit down to eat'? But will he not rather say to him, 'Prepare something for my supper, and gird yourself and serve me till I have eaten and drunk, and afterward you will eat and drink'? Does he thank that servant because he did the things that were commanded him? I think not.* So likewise you, when you have done all those things which you are commanded, say, 'We are unprofitable servants. We have done what was our duty to do.'"[25]

Jesus asked His disciples if this particular servant received appreciation from his lord because he did the things that were commanded of him. You can almost hear the sarcasm in His voice when He answered His own question, "I don't think so!"

His question puts our understanding of who we are into the proper perspective. As servants, we need not worry about our next meal. Our primary duty is to recognize Jesus as Lord. In order to accomplish this recognition, we must understand that we are but *His servants.* We must put our provision (food, drink, shelter, and clothes) in second place to our *duty* to our Lord.

How do you view your life, as a child of God, as a servant of God, as a friend of God? How we view the roles of our lives affects the daily activities and philosophy by which we make small decisions. Our lives, time, money, and pastimes all emerge from our self-image and our perceived station in life.

When we do not consider our time as our own, we *spend* it differently. The way a person spends his time at the *work place* is different from the way he or she spends the time he or she

25 Luke 17:7-10 (NKJV)

considers to be his or her own. Can a mere cashier *spend* the money in the till?

Intentions / Actions = Faith / Works

If we are to learn the truth, we may have approached this subject backwards. Instead of examining our *intentions* (faith), perhaps we should do as Jesus did and examine our *actions* (works). Our lifestyle, checkbook, acquaintances, pastimes, luxuries, and what we have stored up for ourselves for the future say much more about us than any mere words we profess could ever do. The way a person lives his or her life tells exactly how he or she views his or her *station* in life.

Like it or not, a great indicator of our true way of life, philosophy, and dedication is our pocketbooks. A person who is bankrupt in one area of life is likely to be bankrupt in others. When we deal with our money correctly, it is likely that we deal with life correctly. Jesus knew this. That is why His questions about our stewardship in the Kingdom were couched in questions of *personal* finances.

The importance we place on ourselves and our own needs on an everyday basis is a straightforward indicator of our priorities. Occupying the position of a servant can easily eliminate ninety percent of our failures in this area. As servants, we have less to concern ourselves about; we have fewer pressures, and we face fewer opportunities to displease our Master. We have only to do what we are told.

Instead of striving to be in charge, let's take the position of *"least."* Let's adopt a servant's attitude and become *good* servants. Only then will we have opportunity every day to show faith in our Almighty God.

Mammon can only affect those who give themselves to it. Jesus said, "He who *is* faithful in *what is least,* is faithful also in much; and he who is unjust in *what is* least is unjust also in much."

Then He asked the question, *"Therefore if you have not been faithful in the unrighteous mammon, who will commit to your trust the true riches?"*[26]

It is the unrighteous mammon of life and how we handle it on a daily basis that indicates both to ourselves and to our Lord exactly how we will handle true riches. When we look at our personal economy, how we spend our time, money, and how we use our talents, we may be amazed to discover how much of our life is dedicated to the mere gathering and re-distribution of wretched mammon.

What about the basic necessities?

Does Jesus begrudge a person basic necessities? We see again that our Savior sees life differently than we do. We must admit that we could get along with *a lot less* than we presently have. Traps of peer pressure, style, the commonly held ideal of three square meals a day, fear of hunger (or, worse yet, fear of our children being hungry), all add to the pressure surrounding the gathering of provisions.

Seeking basic necessities can severely hinder our goal toward perfection. Jesus asks two questions that indicate that these may be problems for us, *"Is not life more than food?"* and, *"Why do you take thought for clothing?"*[27]

---

26 Luke 16:11 (NKJV)
27 Matthew 6:25

A spiritual person is not required to merely *lack* food and clothing. Jesus warns of the anxiety that accompanies mind and heart when we depend upon our own wits and abilities. These things may keep us from reliance upon our heavenly Father.

We insult our Lord when we don't consider His promises as being trustworthy. His frustration is evident when He exclaims, "Look at the birds of the air, for they neither sow nor reap nor gather into barns; yet your heavenly Father feeds them! *Are you not of more value than they? ...* Consider the lilies of the field, how they grow: they neither toil nor spin; and yet I say to you that even Solomon in all his glory was not arrayed like one of these. *Now if God so clothes the grass of the field, which today is, and tomorrow is thrown into the oven, will He not much more clothe you, O you of little faith?*"[28]

If your food consumption fell to the level of eating only to satisfy hunger, not only would you cut your food bill in half, or even less, but your health would flourish! If your notion of what to wear was determined by the criteria of it being sturdy, durable, and warm, instead of by what is stylish, chic, and fashionable, your budget could easily allow for your needs. (And you would be a better individual for having eliminated an element of respect with regard to a person's outward appearance.)

If you can see the difference between banqueting and food, style and clothing, you are beginning to see things the way your Master does.

Pride will be discovered over and over again as the foe of the spiritual person. The contentment, complacency, and

---

28 Matthew 6:26-30 (NKJV)

comfort that the Savior warns us about are all found in our lifelong adversary, pride.

From the beginning, original sin was enveloped in the pride of physical hunger, beauty beheld by sight, and ambition:

> *"So when the woman saw that
> the tree was **good for food**,
> that it was **pleasant to the eyes**,
> and a tree **desirable to make one wise**,
> she took of its fruit and ate."*[29]

These same three categories of temptation were presented to Jesus—*bread* for His belly, the *beauty* of the cities, and instant *fame* that would undoubtedly come from being saved from a fall from the pinnacle of the Temple.[30] He overcame them all. He overcame, so *we* could overcome every sin as well!

The Apostle John lists these categories of temptation in the same order. "For all that *is* in the world—the lust of the *flesh*, the lust of the *eyes*, and the *pride* of life—is not of the Father but is of the world."[31]

These three (and thank our Father there are *only* three) are at the root of every temptation. If we deny ourselves nothing, if our lust for beauty is daily satiated by owning, eating, wearing, and displaying the best of the best, if we make our own provision well into the future, instead of daily relying upon the heavenly Father, we will become dry kindling for the inevitable "fiery trial"!

---

29 Genesis 3:6 (NKJV, author's emphasis)
30 Matthew 4
31 1 John 2:16 (NKJV, author's emphasis)

Ego, pride, and self-preservation will daily bind us to the three temptations cast upon mankind. Jesus is warning us to avoid these traps, but how? Controlling these three basic temptations on a *daily* basis, as the Lord has instructed, will equip us to overcome the larger temptations of life.

Perhaps this is why the Apostle Paul taught, "... godliness with contentment is great gain. For we brought nothing into *this* world, *and it is* certain we can carry nothing out. And *having food and clothing, with these we shall be content.* But those who desire to be rich fall into temptation and a snare, and *into* many foolish and harmful *lusts* which drown men in destruction and perdition. For the love of money is a root of all *kinds of* evil, for which some have strayed from the faith in their greediness, and pierced themselves through with many sorrows. But you, O man of God, flee these things and pursue righteousness, godliness, faith, love, patience, gentleness."[32]

Wow! Maybe Paul heard the Master teach, "Seek ye first the kingdom of God and all these things will be added to you."

The first of the three warnings that came as I searched the red-letter questions was, "Beware of the flesh."

I took to myself His radical ideals of simplicity in dress, provision made only to the level of my daily necessity, and dependence upon Him for advancement in my life (forsaking ambition). When I did this, however, I became conspicuously different to those around me.

Sometimes, I am ridiculed and accused of "tempting God" or being just plain lazy. I found, though, that the peer pressure I may suffer from my peculiarity was not only good practice

---

32   I Timothy 6:6-11 (NKJV)

(suffering persecution in many cases), but it proved to be the very thing I needed to accomplish my perfection!

A great stride toward perfection is likely to be found within your nearest trial. (You may even feel that trial coming on you now.) How will you fare?

Servant or Sovereign?

The key is to be a *servant,* not a sovereign. The American mindset is that we are all *sovereigns;* we make our own rules; we are free people. Mind you, this kind of thinking is in direct opposition to the station we are called to in Christ. The *Kingdom* mindset is that we are to be *servants.* We are to be servants who serve a good and kind Master.

Life as a servant can *seem* heavy because of the way we evaluate the load of our lives. The load can seem heavier when we *despise* the cargo. However, evaluation of the load is the duty of the Master, not the duty of a servant.

Bear in mind that because a mule cares nothing about money, he carries a load of bricks with the same power and outlook as he would carry a load of gold. A true servant is not concerned about the load he or she carries, but only that his master is pleased by his or her doing so. When we are servants, whether the load be slag or silver, diamonds or dirt, what can it matter?

Sovereigns, on the other hand, have the *privilege* and the *power* to argue, avenge, and complain. They can pursue ambitions, acquire wealth, and drape themselves in velvet if they so desire. Servants do not. Servants do not insist on having their own way. Servants learn to *suffer,* to *let,* and to *allow.*

Servants do not sue each other. The way of a sovereign, however, is to insist, "I will not be cheated! I will not suffer for anyone's wrongdoing!" Paul was discouraged with the people at Corinth because they were suing each other at law.

*"Dare any of you, having a matter against another, go to law? ... I say this to your shame ... But brother goes to law against brother ... it is an **utter failure** for you that you go to law against one another.* **Why do you not rather accept wrong? Why do you not rather let yourselves be cheated?**"[33]

A servant *allows* himself or herself to be cheated. An American who has the mindset of a sovereign is *never* to lose *anything ever*! Look again, "... it is an utter **failure** for you."

We sue, we insure, we secure, and defend that which we consider to be our own. What does an indentured servant have to insure? What does he have to protect and defend? What would a true, lifelong servant who is consecrated to his or her Master do in the case of harm or loss? He or she would simply go to his or her master.

Matthew tells a story of a man who came to Jesus looking for something he was sure He could give him. He said, "Good Teacher, what good thing shall I do that I may have eternal life?" So Jesus said to him, *"Why do you call me good?* No one is good but One, that is, God. But, if you want to enter into life, keep the commandments." The young man said to Him, "All these things I have kept from my youth. What do I still lack?'"

It is very interesting to note how Jesus answered his question, "If you want to be *perfect*, go, dispense with your

---

life and come, follow Me. But the man went away sorrowful, for he had *great possessions.*[34] He did not trade his eternal life for his possessions, but he did forfeit his *perfection*.

Then Jesus said, "Assuredly, I say to you that it is hard for a [man who provides for himself] to enter the kingdom of heaven."

Once again we can see the misdirection of modern interpretations. The subject was not the depletion of goods, keeping the Law, or doing good deeds. The subject was *perfection*. Are we seeing here that "entering the Kingdom" is only done by those who pursue perfection?

When this truth came to me in my search for the questions of Jesus, it was obvious that my warning to "Beware of the flesh" could be heeded simply by abiding in my proper role as a *servant* to the Most High. The plan of Jehovah for His people to achieve perfection was *and still is* servitude.

---

34 Mark 10, Matthew 19

Dedication

A re you a dependable person?

There is a story in the gospels of a man who came to his friend at midnight and made a request of him. "Friend, lend me three loaves; for a friend of mine has come to me on his journey, and I have nothing to set before him."

Can you, in your wildest imagination, conceive of the Lord Jesus equating His Father as someone who would say, "Do not trouble me; the door is now shut ... I cannot rise and give to you"?[1] Yet, this is the common interpretation.

I am always surprised when someone who is teaching on prayer uses this parable. From this story they attempt to teach that if we just don't give up, eventually the Lord will answer our requests. Just keep on praying! That is not what is taught here at all.

This parable shows the disparity between *our* commitment to the Lord and *His* commitment to us. He assures us that *He* will answer speedily. As a matter of fact, He continues, "... *everyone* who asks receives, and *he who seeks*, finds; and *to him who knocks* it will be opened."

---

1   Luke 11:5-8

67

He need not assure us of *His* friendship, for that stands sure. However, He questions *our* friendship. He asks, "Do I have a friend upon whom I can depend in the long night—who has only the interests of his Master at heart—who would rise at midnight to give bread to a stranger?" He asks, *"Do I have such a friend in you?"*

There is a beautiful hymn that is entitled, "Satisfied With Jesus." Its chorus declares over and over, as if we need to verify *Him* as being worthy of *our* friendship:

"I'm satisfied, I'm satisfied, I'm satisfied with Jesus ..."

Then, the ending takes the hearer by surprise with a probing question:

"But the question comes to me, when I think of Calvary, is my Master satisfied with me?"

Have we seen this parable backwards all these years? Of course we are satisfied with Him! *He* is the faithful one in this partnership! Now, we can see who the characters in the parable represent. It is *Jesus* who stands at the door and knocks! *We* are the sorry friend in bed who "cannot rise and give" to his friend at the door.

Dedication to be a servant to our Master requires sacrifice. When called upon, we rise when we feel like it and we rise when we don't. This is *servitude*.

It is when we do that which we *do not want to do* that our level of dedication will be evidenced. Where sacrifice is absent, so is dedication.

We must be certain that we live our lives as dedicated servants, not simply doing what we are pleased to do. A servant does only as he is commanded! His life is not his own. He has been bought with a price and paid for by his Master.

Yet another question of Jesus that has been transposed in our thinking is found in, *"What will a man give in exchange for his soul?"*[2]

Look again! He didn't ask what a man would *take* in exchange for his soul; rather, He asks, "What will he *give?*"

There is a price upon eternal life. If we don't pay it, we don't get it. There is an exchange that must take place. I know this idea flies in the face of much modern theology, but the Scriptures are plain about it.

The words on the Bible's pages will not allow the modern idea of salvation that merely *adds* Jesus to our present life. We are told we must "accept Jesus," but He is not focused on whether *you* accept Him! The question is does *He* accept *you*?

The Scriptures teach that we are to bring a sacrifice to Him in order to be redeemed. Many have learned that the sacrifice made for us is the blood of Jesus,[3] but we cannot offer what is not ours to give. David said this best when, in his darkest hour

---

2 Matthew 16:26 (NKJV)
3 The blood of Jesus certainly cleanses us, as 1 John 1:7 says, "...and the blood of Jesus Christ His Son cleanses us from all sin" (NKJV). And the blood certainly makes salvation possible, as it says in Ephesians 2:13, we "are made nigh by the blood of Christ." And we are granted access by the blood, as is made clear in Hebrews 10:19. We are now able...to enter into the holiest by the blood of Jesus."

of sin, he would not offer to the Father *that which costs him nothing*.[4]

Many of us have acquired a western, Gentile state of mind that hinders our understanding of the Bible's references regarding the practices of ancient Israel. To many, the Old Testament is just that, old.

We should realize that the Covenant under which we have been redeemed is the *same Covenant that God made with Abraham*, and it has been extended to us who are "afar off."

What is the price that we must pay for our souls?

I would like to take you to the streets of Jerusalem, circa 28 A.D. A man preaching in the streets is being challenged by the religious leaders to take sides in the ongoing debate about the tribute being given to Caesar. The leaders asked Him if it was lawful to pay taxes to Caesar.

The Preacher asked them to produce a piece of money; then He outsmarted them with a question, *"Whose image and inscription does it have?"*[5]

Many, who read the Preacher's final words in this passage, "Render therefore to Caesar the things that are Caesar's, and to God the things that are God's," are too quick to apply their meaning only to taxes, money, and such matters.

The other, more neglected message is the very subject with which we are presently dealing. What sacrifice can we give in order to inherit eternal life?

---

4   2 Samuel 24:24
5   Luke 20:22-25

The government under which money is issued has always determined its value. Caesar put his image and name on each coin to identify to which kingdom the coin belonged and to assure its value. This gave both the seller and the buyer confidence in the value of the instrument that was being used.

The Kingdom of God has a currency as well, and it is a coin of great value. The value of this coin is determined by the King, and it is never subjected to private evaluation by anyone. Though we have arbitrarily valued and devalued it from time to time, its true worth has remained constant.

It still brings joy and pleasure to God when this "coin" is given in offering. Anyone wishing to offer it as tribute must first discover it and possess it before giving it as a gift. What is this coin?

When Jesus was handed the penny and asked, "Whose image and superscription hath it?" the ownership of the coin became obvious. Caesar's profile and his name were boldly inscribed around its perimeter to make its owner and evaluator unequivocal. It was unmistakably the property of Caesar.

We may find some similar clues in the Scriptures to help us identify the "currency" of the Kingdom by searching for the "image" of the King. In Genesis 1:26-27, we can see the image of God impressed upon the form of man. The creation story tells us that we have His image. "In the image of God created He him."

What about the King's superscription? The priests of Jehovah were commissioned to "... put My name upon the people" through the Aaronic blessing.[6] Also, the promise of

Revelation 3:12 states, "Him that overcomes ... I will write upon him the name of my God ..."

From beginning to end, the Bible declares *us* to be the property of God. We have been minted by *His hands*, "coined" in *His mind*, valued by *His love*, and guaranteed by *His grace*. We are His most valued possession! We have His image and His inscription!

He further states this concept in the parable of the ten coins. From His own heart of compassion, Jesus told of a woman who had ten pieces of silver, "*... if she loses one piece, does she not light a candle, and sweep the house, and seek diligently till she find it?* And when she has found it, she calls her friends and her neighbors together, saying, Rejoice with me; for I have found the piece which I had lost."

Then to make the parable unmistakable, He adds, "Likewise, I say unto you, there is joy in the presence of the angels of God over one sinner that repents."[7]

We overcome the world by *serving Him*. Relinquishment of selfish control inscribes His name upon us, making Him alone the One who is privileged to determine our value.

Tribute to Him can be no less than to "... render unto God the things that are God's." We are God's own creation, and He demands no less than our service as the only reasonable tribute. "I beseech you therefore, brethren, by the mercies of God, that ye present your bodies a living sacrifice, holy, acceptable unto God, which is your reasonable service."[8]

---

7   Luke 15
8   Romans 12:1

Look in the mirror and consider what you owe to God. Look at your life and service, and ask, "Whose image is this and whose name is written here?"

So, what *was* the price that was paid for us? Remember that I said the blood of the Messiah was *not* the sacrifice that the Father requires? Please, don't misunderstand what I am saying about this. Salvation is *impossible* without the shedding of His blood, but *His blood is not your sacrifice.*

The blood of the Messiah was offered to make your sacrifice *possible.* With His blood He sanctified the Temple, the altar, and *you!* He prepared the sanctuary for you to make the exchange!

What is our sacrifice? What is it that we must *give* in exchange for our soul?

Paul answered this question for us, "I beg you to present *yourself* as a sacrifice—it is your reasonable *service.*"

What will a person *give* in exchange for his or her soul? We can only offer what is ours to give. The price has never changed from the day the Messiah taught these concepts by the Sea of Galilee until now.

Unlike most of His sayings, this passage is recorded in *every* Gospel account.[9] "For whosoever will save his life shall lose it; but whosoever shall lose his life for my sake and the gospel's, the same shall save it. He that loves his life shall lose it; and he that hates his life in this world shall keep it unto life eternal." He must have said this often. It is unavoidable in any gospel account. It is unavoidable in every Christian's life.

---

9   Matthew 16:25, Mark 8:35, Luke 17:33, John 12:25

We are called to sacrifice *ourselves* on the altar that was cleansed by the blood of Jesus, our Messiah.

Surely, Jesus had the necessity of your sacrifice in His mind when He asked, *"Will you lay down your life for My sake?"*[10]

Perhaps you remember the massacre that occurred in a Colorado high school that later became known as the "Columbine Tragedy." It is told that one of the murderous boys, upon choosing his next victim, Cassie Burnall (well known in her school to have a Christian testimony), demanded that she deny Christ in order to save herself. She did not deny Him and lost her life as a result.

Can you imagine yourself proving your allegiance to Christ, as godless communist hoards overrun the city in which you live, while demanding that you deny Christ or die?

We may gain some transitory satisfaction in thinking that we would never deny our Savior, even if threatened with death. However, when the dramas we create in our minds are discarded, and the "cameras" we envision are no longer recording our heroism, the real-world mammon and hard-core temptations fall upon us to take their full effect.

What we do when we find ourselves under the scrutiny of our peers and what we do when those peers are nowhere to be found can be quite different!

We fail tests everyday. No, not by blatant and public denials of Christ, but through private denials, the choices made in offices and homes, and by the directions taken in conversations and lifestyles.

---

10   John 13:38 (NKJV)

You see, many may say they are willing to die for Christ, but few are willing to *live* for Him. His question is, *"Will you lay down your life for My sake?"*

We "lay down" our lives by laying them *aside*. We "save" our lives by living them without denial—living in comfort and self-satisfaction. Many people live in a dichotomous state of limbo, not wishing to blatantly deny Christ, but never depriving themselves of anything they want.

Is there a place in our idea of faith where we can neither deny Christ nor ourselves? Is there a way to lay down our life *and* keep it? Can we gain the whole world and *not* lose our own soul?

These questions must be answered honestly within yourself—not once, but once a day or perhaps even many times a day! This is what Paul meant by a *living* sacrifice. Self-denial *is* the price of eternal life.

If you feel power now to commit to a lifestyle of denying self, you are hearing the voice of the Shepherd. If you are steadfast with regard to the task of exchanging your life for His, He wants to take you further.

He asks, *"Are there not twelve hours in the day?"*

John tells the story where this question appears. Jesus had just been informed that His good friend, Lazarus, was dead. He decided to go to him. The disciples warned that if He went to Bethany, the Jews would stone Him!

Some reading this account mistakenly assume that in receiving the warning from His disciples, Jesus suggests they go in the dark of the night. But read again what Jesus said after asking about the number of hours in the day, "If anyone walks in the day, he does not stumble, because he sees the light of this world. But if one walks in the night, he stumbles, because the light is not in him."[11]

The Messiah is not suggesting that they hide by cover of darkness; but is rather recalling to them His earlier words, "I must work the works of Him who sent Me *while* it is day; *the night* is coming when no one can work."[12]

Likewise, we must dedicate only to the eternally important. Messiah wants us to know that there is only so much time to work (especially those of us who now live in this last century, upon whom the ends of the world are come). We should be keenly aware of our *time* constraints.

If you feel the nudge of the Holy Spirit, if you hear the voice of your Shepherd calling you higher, when, dear sheep, will you accomplish this task? There are only twelve hours in a day. The night comes ...

Paul's words are ever so pertinent on this subject: "Therefore let us not sleep, as others do, but let us watch and be sober. For those who sleep, sleep at night, and those who get drunk are drunk at night. But let us who are of the day be sober, putting on the breastplate of faith and love, and as a helmet the hope of salvation."[13]

When there is work to do, little is more aggravating than a sleeper. Jesus, in His most weighty hour, found His disciples asleep. I cannot help but feel that His frustration continues

---

11   John 11
12   John 9:4 (NKJV)
13   I Thessalonians 5:6-8 (NKJV)

today when He reveals His will to a person who constantly puts off the work he has been given to do.

Jesus inquires, *"Why do you sleep?"*[14] Arise! Get on with it! Why are you waiting?

The time for which the prophets waited is now upon us! What has captivated our attention? What has so consumed our lives that we have little more than church attendance to our merit?

Jesus is, most likely, still asking, *"Could you not watch with me one hour?"*

Our Savior is meticulously engaged in the time in which we live. He looks around and rather than finding us watching, He finds many of us sleeping—unconscious and unconcerned with the things of eternal significance.

We, the workers He has called into the vineyard, stand watching the clock, waiting to punch out. Do we have not an hour to share with our Savior?

Perhaps simplicity of lifestyle has even more to offer than just peace of mind?

People who ignore the promptings of the Holy Spirit are likely to be more concerned with present temporal issues. They can give little attention to the perfecting of themselves. Can it be that they really *love* the Lord they claim to serve?

One day, Jesus found impetuous Peter on the shores of the lake. He was disappointed in himself for having denied

---

14 Luke 22:46 (NKJV)

His Lord and discouraged about ever being used for ministry again. On this day the Savior he had once followed caught him reviving his former fishing business.

Jesus begins His "question therapy" on this disciple.

***

Peter watches his friend closely as Jesus took a place across the smoldering fire, now stinking with fish bones thoughtlessly thrown there. He looks first at the fish in the net and then back at Peter. *"Simon, son of Jonas,"* says Jesus. Peter looks up, glancing around to avoid the eyes he knew so well. He repeats, *"Simon!"* Jesus finally gets the attention Peter has been so purposefully misguiding. Peter sees Jesus' finger carelessly flip here and there, pointing around at the nets and fish and finally at the fish bones lying in a pile between them. Then He smiles and in a half chuckle He asks, *"Do you love me more than these?"*[15]

Peter says, "Yes, Lord."

Jesus wonders if the disciple is merely attempting to make amends or if he really understands the question. Maybe Peter is sorry that he quit and returned to fishing? Is it just the pungent burning fish bones that make My offer appealing? Does he just want a second chance to prove himself as faithful now that the furor has died down and the danger of death has disappeared?

The Savior tries again. But He doesn't ask, "Do you love me more than fishing, do you want your job back, do you

---

15   John 21:15 (NKJV)

want me to forgive you for what you did." Instead, Jesus asks, *"Do you love me?"*

Any of us who have had and raised children can hear instantly the underlying motivation in the words, "I'm sorry." Is there a parent anywhere who has not asked his child, "Are you really sorry, or are you just sorry that you got caught?"

What a horrible accusation to make. Yet, we all know that there *is* a difference.

There is a sorrow, Paul says, that leads nowhere; and there is a sorrow that leads to repentance. *Listen to his words in this letter to the Corinthians.* You can hear him apologize for being hard on his hearers. No doubt he considers their temporary discomfort worthwhile *if* it leads to repentance.

"… I made you sorry with my letter … though only for a while. Now I rejoice, not that you were made sorry, but that your sorrow led to **repentance**. For you were made sorry in a godly manner … For godly sorrow produces repentance *leading* to salvation … for you sorrowed in a godly [way] …"[16]

The sorrow Peter felt that day on the shore produced in him the determination and will that were necessary for him to continue, to become even better than he was before! That determination took him all the way to Pentecost, where he received the power to finish the work that had been begun in him! Eye to eye with the Savior, so that there is no mistake this time, he answers, "Yes, Lord!"

---

16 2 Corinthians 7:8

But Jesus is not finished with Peter. He continues the therapy. He said to him the *third* time, *"Simon, son of Jonah, do you love Me?"*

There is a place of clearing—when sorrow appears, repentance is real, and forgiveness is granted. It is with this principle in mind that I present the idea that perhaps Jesus was taking Peter to just such a place.

Peter's heart was, no doubt, heavy with the guilt of having denied the Lord publicly three times during the night of Christ's torture. Now, even in his Lord's presence, the weight of shame was coloring his every thought, slanting every word of conversation, and nagging every promise of loyalty he espoused.

Even as the Lord asked Peter *for the third time* if he loved Him, Peter felt as though the Lord had no reason to believe such a coward as he. But the Lord kept asking, *"Do you love Me?"*

It was not by chance that Jesus asked Peter the same question three times; for it was three times that Peter had denied knowing Him. There was a clearing, forgiveness, and cleansing that took place in the third affirmation of Peter's love for Christ.

Finally, Peter came to the conclusion that his love for the Savior *could* stand this test, "I do love Him" he thought, "and if anyone would know that to be a fact it would be Jesus, from Whom nothing may be hidden."

He laid aside the fishbone he absentmindedly played with, stood to his feet, stepped a little closer to Him, looked into his friend's face and said, "Lord, You know all things; and You know that I love You."

He finally sensed the balanced account and the forgiveness of his teacher. I am sure a smile crossed Peter's face as he realized what was happening. The Savior, now satisfied with Peter's declaration, reaffirmed the commission to feed His sheep.

A new stage in Peter's life and faith then took place. His past forgiven, his impending conversion, and the infilling of the Holy Spirit changed this fisherman once again into a fisher of men!

If these questions have been difficult, if my statements have been hard, I am sorry. However, I do not apologize if they spark the diligence, the clearing, the indignation, the holy fear, the vehement desire, or the zeal that they produced in Peter.

Move on the prompting to make changes in your life! Affirm allegiance to the Savior by an honest declaration of love for Him. He may ask again and again if you love Him, but this should only make you love Him more.

We should not be grieved when we are questioned by the Lord about the genuineness of our love for Him. It may be that we are on the threshold of a new summit, about to graduate to a new level of faith, or finally ready to receive our commission in total.

As we survey our new opportunities and evaluate the price tag on true dedicated living, and although He may smell fish bones in our fire, would to God that we will have what it takes to answer, "Yes!" when He asks the third time, "Lovest thou Me?"

Relationship

As my journey through the questions of Jesus continued, I noticed that the revelations He gave me were placing demands on my *relationship* with Him. If I was to depend solely upon Him, whether to guide me in doctrine or in everyday life, I am forced to trust the relationship we share.

It is because I doubted my own relationship with my Lord that I turned to others whose relationships with God I *did* trust; but that was the method that *created* my problems. Haven't we all experienced this doubt? Haven't we all, because we did not trust our relationship, placed confidence in other people for guidance and truth? Why else would we not go to Him?

Jesus wonders how mankind, having the Spirit of His Father residing within, hearing the testimony of the Scriptures that bear witness to the experiences of those in history enjoying His unfaltering supervision, can consistently decide NOT to come to Him.

He asks, *"Why judge ye not of yourselves what is right?"*

Why do we need to verify our revelation with others, or worse yet, why do we only receive the revelations *of* others as doctrine. Take some time to think about this. Why do *you* not judge within *yourself* what is right?

Is personal revelation trustworthy, or should we only accept the ideas of other people as a correct understanding of Scripture? Many who aspire to reign over us as intermediaries quote 2 Peter 1:20 as a warning, "Knowing this first, that no prophecy of the Scripture is of any private interpretation." From this, it is argued that we are not to *privately* interpret the Scriptures in any way we wish, but we are to consult with those who "know."

So far, in our investigation into the questions of Jesus, you have undoubtedly witnessed your understanding of the Scriptures opening in ways that have been backwards to conventional Christian thinking. In this you are hearing the Teacher. You are hearing the voice of guidance. Could this be the reasoning behind Peter's exhortation?

Peter exclaimed, "And we heard this *voice which came from heaven* when we were with Him on the holy mountain. And so we have the prophetic word confirmed, which you do well to heed...."

It is unfortunate that this passage (and the previous one) have been used to prove the exact opposite of their intended message. The subject being discussed here is *the voice from heaven*—the voice that was *heard* by Peter. If his idea, interpretation, or revelation, which "came from heaven," go against convention, so be it!

As for "... no prophecy of the scripture is of any private interpretation ...," the meaning is self-evident. We *do well to heed* the Scriptures according to our own *revelation*, because they are not subject to any private, singular, or conventional *interpretation*.

I've been told that if I go in a direction that is different than conventional understanding, I risk adopting heresy; but I want you to know that not one person in all history has *ever* been led astray by the Spirit of the Almighty! We are to obey His voice.

Realize that it is not the *voice* that we have difficulty trusting, it is our *relationship* with our Guide that we mistrust. The Lord Jesus made this truth evident by stating, "My *sheep* know My voice."

If our relationship is sure, then the voice is trustworthy. If we doubt the voice, our *relationship* is dubious as well.

All that many of us are sure of is that we know how we feel about Him, but we must know how He feels about us in order to really trust His guidance. However wonderful it is for you to believe in Him, it makes all the difference in the world to know that He believes in you and knows who you are.

Remember the story of the demoniac of Gadera? Jesus asked the demon, *"What is your name?"*

The demon answered, "My name is Legion, for we are many."

Why did He want to know the demon's name? In the heavenly realm names have meaning. The name of the demon would *reveal who he was*. It would describe the disposition, nature, or personality of the demon. His name actually *described* him to the Master.

Jesus also said that a man who breaks any of His commandments (even what that man determines to be the least commandment) and teaches others to do the same shall be called "least" in the Kingdom of Heaven. What a horrible name to be called for all eternity!

The Scriptures indicate that we will have a new name one day. Is it possible that this will be a name that describes us perfectly? Why are we to strive for perfection? The heavenly name He has chosen for you describes the perfection for which we strive today.

Let's spend the rest of our lives aspiring to *that* name. It is the name with which we were named "before the foundation of the world." This is the name that is inscribed on the white stone mentioned in the Book of the Revelation. On that "day of Jesus Christ," when we see it, we will know it, and we will understand that all along He knew our potential and capabilities.

When we commune with Him, He reveals bits and pieces of that perfection to us. As we obey, more is given. "Being confident of this very thing, that He which has begun a good work in you will perform it until the day of Jesus Christ."[17]

Yes, my friend, the Messiah has high hopes for us because He places great value upon each person—much more than He even esteemed *himself*. He showed this when He gave himself as a lamb!

The lamb is the epitome of servitude. It has no other purpose than to give; no other reason but to serve. The lamb always provides food and clothing; it offers resistance neither to the one who shears it nor to the one who slaughters it. No wonder that this innocent animal became the symbol of redemption.

As we evaluate our relationship with Him, we can make no mistake about the love our Creator has for us *if* we understand the value He places on sheep. In this picture He places your life in great esteem and deems His own as expendable.

---

17 Philippians 1:6

Jesus prophesied His own death. The Savior's words made His intent clear: to give Himself "the lesser" for us to receive "the greater." We can clearly see His appraisal of Himself as our servant and find a new message in Jesus' question, *"How much then is a man better than a sheep?"*[18]

Let us join Jesus as He walks in the courts of the Temple. We see the sacrifices being offered to the travelers from distant cities coming to the Feast. He takes this opportunity to teach us how much we mean to the Father by making a comparison. He holds out His hand, points toward a handmade cage containing five sparrows, and asks about the disparity between these merchants' evaluation of life and the Father's.

At that very moment, you hear one of the tradesmen call out, "Five for only two coppers!" Looking into your eyes, He asks, *"Are not five sparrows sold for two copper coins? And not one of them is forgotten before God."*[19]

Why would the Father care so much for these birds? In order to understand, we must see life as He does. He had watched these tiny birds from their beginnings; He knew their parents and watched the death of their grandparents. He had fed them every mouthful of food, just as He had all the fowls of the Earth. He had watched Mama Sparrow lay and hatch her eggs and He had become acquainted with all her young.

One day this sparrow was going about, trusting in Jehovah to find food, and she was taken in a snare and placed in a cage with four others. She was carried to a noisy street in Jerusalem to be sold, along with four other captives, for two copper coins.

---

18   Matthew 12:12
19   Luke 12:6 (NKJV)

Jesus, pointing at the flailing, flopping birds that were trying to escape the cage, asked His question to illustrate the point that we do not evaluate life *or* death the way He does.

We show our own evaluation of life when we are taken by surprise at the words, "Do not fear therefore; you are of more value than many sparrows." When we discover such a high evaluation of ourselves by the Savior, how can we mistrust His guidance?

Jesus is puzzled by our mistrust of Jehovah as a good Father to us. Why do we not judge in ourselves what is right? Why are we afraid to communicate with Him? "… you will not come to me, that you might have life."[20] After all, Jesus asks, *"If a son shall ask bread … will a father give him a stone?"*[21]

The crowd's guts growled as they milled around wondering if Jesus would again perform the rumored miracle that had brought them there. They waited and waited.

Finally, He spoke, "You came here for bread, didn't you? I am the only bread worthy of seeking. I am the bread of life. Therefore eat my flesh and drink my blood if you are so hungry!"[22]

"Wow! What did He say? He must be a nut! I'm going home," some of them said. Some waited and then left. Still others (but only twelve) stayed and followed.

The disciples looked around and saw only footprints in the sand where perhaps thousands had stood before. Jesus

20 John 5:40
21 Matthew 7:9
22 John 6:54

looked at His closest companions and asked, *"Will you also go away?"*[23]

I was not pleased with the disciples' response, but for some reason, the Lord Jesus seemed to like it. Their attitude seemed to be, there is no place else to go. Later, in contemplating this question, I realized that they did not say this because there was indeed no place to go. They were convinced that Jesus was the Messiah and confirmed their faith by answering, "What are we going to do—find someone who preaches a kinder and gentler gospel? You have the words of eternal life."

Sometimes, even when you *feel* like you have no choice but to stay faithful, it is because of a resolve that was cultivated from a seed planted in you before the foundation of the world. It is His choosing that makes us faithful. It is our calling that makes us endure. It is because He called us that we know we can do this—we can achieve His high calling.

Jesus looked at His disciples and with deep gratification said, "I knew you would stay. *Have not I chosen you twelve?"*[24]

Near the end of His time on Earth, Jesus was heard praying for us in the Garden "... that they all may be one, as You, Father, are in Me, and I in You; that they also may be one in Us ... I in them, and You in Me; that they may be made *perfect* ... that they may behold My glory which You have given Me; for *You loved Me before the foundation of the world.*"[25]

It seems that wherever the love of God toward us is mentioned, eternity is mentioned also. The origin of that love

23 John 6:67
24 John 6:70
25 John 17

comes out of an era known in the Scriptures as "before the foundation of the world."

Whenever the subjects of predestination, foreordination, and election come up, theology seems to turn away or just mumbles some indiscernible jargon in an attempt to define and explain their meanings. (Okay, can't we admit we don't fully understand everything and move on?)

The references to election are a beautiful picture of love and acceptance that is essential for proper comprehension of our *relationship* to Him! He chose us before the foundation of the world![26] We can rely upon His choice. Therefore, we can rely on His voice.

We can and we will make it! We will not disappoint Him. We can trust Him to finish His work. We can trust Him to keep us from harm. We can trust Him to guide us in our everyday lives. He will keep us from going astray. He will teach us the doctrine of His Father.

Persecution

If we hold to the ideas presented in the Sunday schools and in many common "Christian" writings, even many sermons that are preached from the pulpits of America—we may form an erroneous concept about the mission of the Messiah. Ours is not much different than the mistake His disciples made centuries ago.

The problems of hunger, disease, and political oppression are as present today as they were in the time when Jesus and

26   Matthew 25:34, Ephesians 1:4

His disciples lived. It is no wonder that everyone believed that when the Son of God would come to the Earth all things would be set right—all oppressors would be vanquished and all divisions of inequality would be leveled.

It is no secret that we live in a tumultuous world. Problems abound among nations and powers. They are all vying for the envious positions of control and rule. However, we do not find programs of equality, justice, and conquests of tyranny on the agenda of the Messiah.

Contrary to peace, He warns that we should rather *expect* conflict. As a matter of fact, His denial of mankind's dream of peace appearing is evident in His question, *"Do you suppose that I came to give peace on earth?* I tell you, not at all, but rather division."[27]

The revelation and salvation He brings is to save us while we are in the *midst* of the world. He said in the Gospel of John, "I do not pray that You should take them out of the world, but that You should keep them from the evil one … Sanctify them [set them apart from the world] by Your truth. Your *word* is truth."[28]

It is the Word of God, the voice of the Shepherd, the revelatory, guiding words to our Spirit that is the *word* of which He speaks here. This *word* will separate us from the world and maybe from friends and family, as well.

There is a cup that is poured out to all believers that will be hard to swallow; it is the cup of persecution. Along with this cup, a baptism by fire awaits some who follow Him closely.

---

27 Luke 12:51 (NKJV)
28 John 17

In order to avoid the baptism of martyrdom, Peter followed Jesus to His persecution "afar off." We learn by experience that following "afar off" will exempt us from persecution, but at what price?

A woman who has the future of her two sons on her mind stands before Jesus. When He asks her what she wants of Him, she answers, "That you would grant that my two sons would reign with You. One can sit on Your right hand and the other on Your left."

As usual, Jesus provokes thought with a question, "You do not know what you ask. *Are you able to drink the cup that I drink, and be baptized with the baptism that I am baptized with?*"[29]

The hierarchy of the spiritual world is populated with those who have suffered. We *want* to be worthy. We *want* to be perfect, but are we able to drink from the cup of persecution?

The apostle warned Timothy, "... all who desire to live godly in Christ Jesus will suffer persecution."[30]

The rule of reciprocity, applied to this Scripture, condemns many. This equation can be written in several ways, none of which places the lukewarm believer in a good light. Those who *do not* live godly or *desire* to live godly *shall not* suffer persecution.

Though a person who is familiar with the Bible should not be, many are surprised when the origin of persecution comes from *within—within* churches, *within* circles of friends, and

---

29   Mark 10:38 (NKJV)
30   2 Timothy 3:12 (NKJV)

within families. We are not only hurt, but we are taken unaware when the words of Jesus become true for us that "... a man's enemies will be those of his *own* household."

All of those who live godly in Christ *shall* suffer persecution. If we are not suffering from our friends, and family, we must ask ourselves why? Could it be that we do not *desire* to live godly? Have we followed, but "afar off" in order to avoid such hateful treatment?

Jesus desired for the "churchmen" of His day to see that that they were indeed afraid of the truth He bore in His public testimony. Just as He had asked the disciples why they were afraid, He asked the mob that was coming to fetch Him why they would arm themselves against such a meek and passive man.

It is sometimes purported that the men who came that night were Roman soldiers, but they weren't. They were men who had been assigned to the Temple as guards. They were a "Tuesday night visitation committee" of sorts.

Think about it. Would Peter, the fisherman, have even *considered* swordplay with a trained Roman soldier? No, these were, in our vernacular, deacons and elders of the First Whatever Church of Jerusalem.

These men who came to the Garden for our Savior were scared, but why? Jesus even said, "I was daily with you in the temple teaching, and you did not seize Me."[31] It was as if He was asking, "What are you guys afraid of?"

---

31   14:48 (NKJV)

How did He know they were afraid? It was obvious because they armed themselves with swords, sticks, and clubs to attack Him.

Understanding our adversaries will help. If we learn *why* our enemies hate us, we have learned little. If we learn that our enemies are pitiful and helpless, trembling and unsure, we will have great openings of power and grace to endure.

Our enemies are afraid of us. They don't even know exactly why. They don't know what we know and it worries them! Don't be surprised if the attacks from these *insiders* are cruel and humiliating. They do not know who they are fighting. This is the power behind the words, "Forgive them, Father, they know not what they do!"

The Messiah asked Saul, *"Why do you persecute me?"*[32] Saul had *no idea* why or of whom he was truly afraid. So it is with our detractors.

If we can, we should make our foes comfortable. Let them know there is no need to overreact. Our example is found in the question Jesus asked those men on that night, *"Have you come out, as against a robber, with swords and clubs to take me?"*

Neither a martyr's baptism nor beatings alone necessarily constitute persecution. Sometimes persecution comes with merely a comment or a look. Sometimes it is experienced as a bypass in the conversation or a reluctance to ask your opinion about weighty matters.

---

32 Acts 9:4, 22:7, 26:14

Persecution is evident in statements like, "Well, that's just Bob—we all know *his* opinion." "Sorry, but we have decided to let John teach this class next year. He has a lot to share. I hope you will support him." "You are just a novice. When you have been at this as long as I have you will have a more precise theology."

Persecution, couched in humor, wrapped in kindness, or elevated to spiritual dimensions is still persecution.

There was a time when Jesus was teaching about the spiritual lineage of those who do the works of the Father. He said to those listening, "Those who ... do the works of Abraham are Abraham's children. You are not of Abraham. If you were of Abraham, you would believe in Me."

Then, in a rage they answered, "We be not born of fornication!" Why did they say that? Was it to prove they were the children of Abraham? No, they were calling public attention to the fact that the parents of Jesus were not married when Mary was found with child. They called our Messiah a bastard—publicly!

The people of Judea used a play on words to torment the worshipers of the god of Ekron, a city in the land of the Philistines, their lifelong enemy.[33] The name of this god was Baal Zebub. The Jews slurred the name to "Beelzebub" meaning, "Lord of the flies."

Since flies were associated with dung, a chuckle and a smile would come across the face of anyone who used this name when describing the dung-god of their rival country. This was

---

33 2 Kings 3

a word most foul, and for them to use it in reference to the Messiah was purposely hurtful.

They called Him a dung-god. A name, properly interpreted, that cannot even be printed in this book. To the listening crowd, Jesus asked, *"If they have called the master of the house Beelzebub, how much more will they call those of his household?"*[34]

Jesus warns that persecution WILL come. Don't be surprised when it does. Rather cherish it. Note that both of these cited instances were epithets that were hurled at Jesus by the religious leaders who were claiming His Father as their Father.

Whence will our persecution come? I resolved to endure persecution and not retaliate. If we determine to continue in faith, regardless of what our friends say to us and about us, we have won half the battle.

The other half of winning the battle is to *rejoice* in this persecution.

The early followers of the Messiah found themselves standing before the same council that had crucified Him. They were told to cease preaching and teaching in His name. We have an idea of the attitude of these followers about their persecution in the following Scripture:

"And through the hands of the apostles many signs and wonders were done among the people. And they were all with one accord in Solomon's Porch ... Then the high priest rose up, and all those who were with him (which is the sect of the

---

34 Matthew 10:25 (NKJV)

Sadducees), and they were filled with indignation, and laid their hands on the apostles and put them in the common prison. ... And when they had brought them, they set them before the council. And the high priest asked them, saying, 'Did we not strictly command you not to teach in this name? And look, you have filled Jerusalem with your doctrine, and intend to bring this Man's blood on us!' But Peter and the other apostles answered and said: 'We ought to obey God rather than men.' ... and when they had called for the apostles and beaten them, they commanded that they should not speak in the name of Jesus, and let them go. So they departed from the presence of the council, rejoicing that they were counted worthy to suffer shame for His name. "[35]

Have you read in this story that Peter and the other apostles prayed to be released from prison? Where do you see them complaining? Perhaps they learned from the Messiah that release from trouble may not be the best route?

Since the warning to "beware of the flesh" opened my eyes to the value of suffering, I do not spend so much of my time trying to avoid it. Rather, I inspect it and search for my perfection in it. I look at persecution now as a barometer of my level of dedication. Its presence exhilarates me—and its absence frightens me! I see suffering and persecution as custom-made tools to bring about perfection in my life.

Paul said that he would be glad for tests and trials and persecution in order that the strength of Christ would be made perfect in him.[36] The writer of Hebrews[37] states that the perfection of our Messiah came through suffering. We should expect nothing less.

---

35 Acts 5 (NKJV)
36 2 Corinthians 12
37 Hebrews 5:8-9

Should we pray to be saved from trouble? Is it your desire to serve your God in perfection? Our most troublesome hour is our gateway. Persecution is our opportunity. Death is our door.

Persecution, our own cup of trembling and oppression, is life to us and should be cherished with joy. If it is wrung out to us by our Father, let us drink it to the dregs!

Listen to the words of Jesus, as He contemplated His own martyr's death: *"Now My soul is troubled, and what shall I say? 'Father, save Me from this hour?' But for this purpose I came to this hour. Father, glorify Your name."*[38]

Warning Two: Beware of Hypocrisy

No one will readily admit to being a hypocrite. Most people have good intentions. My own intentions to do good through ministry were real. I wanted to be used of God to help others, but like so many others, I didn't understand that what mattered most was to do His will, to obey Him—on an everyday basis. For this reason, the Messiah sometimes uses a back-door approach to show us that many, even good-intentioned folks, are fully engaged in hypocrisy.

Hypocrisy has become a liturgical word that is used nearly always in religious parlance. Today it seems to be only a negative term, but it was not so at its beginning. It comes from the root for the word "actor," a person who is acting out a role, pretending to be something or someone they are not.

38   John 12:27-28 (NKJV)

97

There was time when school teachers, doctors, people who worked in government, even lawyers, held their occupations because they felt a *divine* calling to do so. They did not pursue their vocations merely for monetary reasons alone.

During those days, professionals like these were not motivated by mere money, just a desire to do what was right and to fulfill a commission by God to serve their fellowmen who were in need. This problem of professionalism is not an indictment against all professionals or ministers, but today many ministries have become less of a ministry and more like a business. Professionalism is one of the worst things that could happen to the gospel ministry.

Long ago, in a little town, Jairus' dear daughter lay dead. Sympathize with this heartbroken father as we enter his house to view the body of his child. At first glance, Jesus' comments seem insensitive, uncaring, and perhaps even a little foolish. He walks into the room where the precious girl is lying and asks, *"Why do you make this commotion and weep?"*[39]

In order for us to understand the reason He asks those attending the funeral of a little child why they are weeping, we have to understand some of the background of this story. We need to know who it was that Jesus addressed when He walked into the room.

Those who were crying and mourning were not *truly* grieved persons. They were paid professionals. They were *hired* mourners.

It is said it was so shameful to have a funeral at which no one wept, that folks were compensated to take time from work

---

39 Luke 8:53, Mark 5:39

to come and mourn at funerals. The cost was just considered to be part of the funeral expenses. As the idea became more commonplace, the poor and indigent would show up at the house of the sick and dying and loudly mourn, hoping to receive a coin or a gift.

These in attendance over this dead child were false mourners, and they were proven to be so by their own actions. They showed themselves just as willing to lament as they were to laugh. They could switch from sobbing to snickering with no effort at all.

Without knowledge of this custom, we may wonder at the abrupt change in the demeanor of these "mourners" when Jesus told them to stop their weeping and declared that this beloved daughter was not dead. The Scriptures record it this way, "… they began to laugh at Him, 'knowing that she was dead.'"

They switched to laughter easily because they were only *pretending* to grieve. True sorrow makes no room for humor. Rather, it despises it. But these pretenders were willing to laugh *instantly*. Why? They were *paid professionals*.

These mercenary mourners were at the girl's bedside for purely selfish reasons. There was no genuine concern for the girl, the real mourners, or the family of the dead. Think of how the truly mournful family must have felt to hear the falsetto wailing of the crowd one minute and hear them explode into laughter the very next moment.

Without understanding this custom of hiring mourners, we may have wondered about the insensitivity of this crowd in the presence of the grieving family. But think about our customs today. Isn't similar behavior exemplified by those who make their ministry into a profession?

Every day pastors preach flowery words at funerals of the dead to gratify the friends and families without giving them a reason to continue living. Month after month, thousands of dollars are spent on weddings that are conducted by ministers who pretend to add God's blessing to the union, but many times they are not even acquainted with the couple. Every year millions of dollars are spent padding pews and paving parking lots while the people who sit and park in them search for Truth to no avail.

When truth is bypassed for gain, effect, or goods, it is nothing short of hypocrisy. When we allow the end to justify any means, whatever our profession, we are nothing short of actors who are playing a part for gain. When we want the benefits of virtue, without cost to ourselves, we are no better than hypocritical thieves playing the part of honest persons.

Hypocrisy can rear its visage in almost every area of life. We are called to help our fellowman, but, like it or not, many times even this can be an act of hypocrisy. Take, for example, the Bible story about the poor man who had a splinter in his eye. His neighbor was compelled to help him by removing the splinter.

Jesus reveals this man's hypocrisy when He asks, *"Why do you call attention to the splinter in your brother's eye?"*[40]

Here again we see Jesus asking a question so that we can gain understanding—not so that He can gather information. Notice His interrogative, "Why?"

---

40 Matthew 7, Luke 6

Jesus didn't ask him why he did not help his brother by removing the splinter. He asked this man *why* he was calling attention to (KJV: *beholding*) the splinter in his brother's eye.

His question could have been answered, "Well, because I feel sorry for my brother and I want to help him," or "I want to minister to my brother," or several other honorable responses, but they would only be honorable *if they were true!*

Many times the speck that is made so important by the minister could be carried in our brother's eye without immediate consequence and be totally unnoticed by anyone. Nevertheless, Jesus asks *why* we call attention to it. He does not ask why we are *trying to remove* the splinter from our brother's eye. That answer would be obvious.

The Master went on to show that there is nothing *inherently* wrong with the ministry of splinter removal. It is a good and honorable thing to do, but *first* He said, (and I'd like to draw your attention again to these words) remove the beam—remove the board, remove the two-by-four, get rid of the plank—the log—in your own eye! He explained that only then can we see clearly enough to remove a splinter from our brother's eye.

The red-letter questions did it again for me! Through His question, I experienced self-analysis and introspection into the reasons *why* I desired to minister. Why *do* we *do* those things we call "ministry"?

We often demand from others what we so desperately need for ourselves. I realized that many times the reason we do what we do is solely to divert attention away from those areas in our lives where *we* need help. *Ministry* becomes a very sinister enterprise if it serves to divert attention and facilitate our pretense.

Hypocrisy *is* a very evil activity, and it will altogether stop the revelation of God. Do you see the Savior's warning to me, "Beware of hypocrisy?"

If what we do is done because we want to accomplish something *other than the obvious ministry* to our fellowman, we are likely to be involved in hypocrisy. Our main duty is to remove the beam from our own eye. It is only in this condition that we can see clearly enough to remove the speck from our brother's eye.

What happens if we try to remove a brother's speck when we have a beam in our own eye? We can do damage because *we cannot see clearly.* Our own vision is impaired and injury is the result. (Perhaps this is why the numbers of "casualties" in congregations are so alarming.)

If you have ever been made to feel shame about shortcomings in your life, you may have experienced the pain that comes when someone brings attention to a speck in your eye. It is no comfort, but your injury was most likely done as an act of hypocrisy.

There is nothing wrong with splinter removal, mind you, as long as it is not done for the ulterior motive of diverting the discovery of our own sin. We must admit, however, that if splinter removal is to be done free of hypocrisy and free from sin (and I believe it is), we are left wondering just *who will* perform this splinter removal?

In reality, Jesus himself, our Pastor and Shepherd, *is* the sinless One who can remove specks, splinters, beams, and boards. Only He can see clearly enough to do so.

Jesus asked several questions to reveal hypocrisy. When the Pharisees accusingly demanded to know why He did not wash His hands before eating, Jesus didn't say (and He well could have), "Your rules and traditions demand that I wash my hands—I don't care about your traditions."

When asked about His hand-washing practices, Jesus retorted with a question for the purpose of exposing their hypocrisy, *"Which of you shall have an ass or an ox fall into a pit and will not straightway pull him out on the Sabbath day? Don't you violate your own laws?"*[41]

I can't help but believe this was the first time the Pharisees ever considered that they *did indeed* violate their own laws. Jesus knew that these wicked religious leaders had convinced themselves of truth, justified their sin, and enjoyed living in the religion they had created for themselves. Therefore, when they were confronted with the accusation of violating their own laws, it probably came as a surprise to them.

Jesus was concerned that their law was supreme over the good of their fellowman. Why had they even raised the subject of hand washing? Jesus had just healed a man on the Sabbath day. His example made it clear that deliverance of their fellowman was not as important to them as their hand-washing law.

The deliverance of our fellowman must be the crux of ministry. If ministry, doctrine, or business becomes more

---

41   Luke 14:5, Matthew 12:11 (With author's addition)

important to us than the truth, it is hypocrisy. Hypocrisy can taint everything we do—even those works that are birthed from our best intentions.

The Pharisees were the religious "ministers" of the day. Their works were formed around how they would *appear* to those watching them.

Jesus told them what He thought of them, "[You] *Serpents, brood of vipers! How can you escape the condemnation of hell?* "[42]

He was well aware of their hypocrisy and asked, *"How can you believe, who receive honor from one another, and do not seek the honor that comes from God only?"*[43]

I hear the sound of hopelessness and despair in these questions. It is as if it would be *impossible* for them to escape damnation as long as they were concerned with their outward appearance. It is as if all means of help and hope are useless against their mindset, and damnation inevitably awaits them.

If we have a trace of this hellish philosophy, hypocrisy, in us, our eternity is threatened. Jesus called it the "leaven of the Pharisees." When He found Himself alone with the disciples, He charged them, "Take heed, beware of the leaven of the Sadducees and the Pharisees and the leaven of Herod."[44]

When I read this warning, I wondered just what was the *leaven of the Sadducees, Pharisees, and Herod?* I had never connected these three types of men together, as Jesus did, but I knew He did it for some reason.

---

42 Matthew 23:33 (NKJV)
43 John 5:44 (NKJV)
44 Mark 8:15

I wanted to find out what that reason was! So I read what I could find in the Scriptures about the Pharisees, the Sadducees, and Herod, attempting to find some link in their personalities, their manner of living, or something else.

What I found in common was that all three cared about what everybody else around them thought of them; *and* whatever people thought of them was what determined and ultimately influenced their judgment on all issues. It was their policy, philosophy (or as Jesus put it), their "doctrine."

The leaven of the Pharisees is apparent in the words, "… they feared the people."[45] These same words appear over and over in accounts regarding the religious leadership and their interactions with the community.

What about Herod? How did he resemble the Pharisees? Remember the story of the damsel who danced before him and afterward asked for the head of John the Baptist? The Scriptures record that Herod actually *liked* John and would go to hear his preaching.[46]

There was a time when he was inclined to have John killed for condemning him and his wife, but he "feared the people," so he didn't.

On his birthday Herod was tricked into an oath to grant the daughter of Herodias (his wife) a wish. She requested the execution of John. He did not want to do it, but "for the oath's sake," he did. He considered the people who heard him swear.

---

45 Mark 11:32, Mark 12:12, Luke 20:19, Luke 22:2, Acts 5:26
46 Mark 6:26, Matthew 14:6-11

The leaven of the Sadducees was the same leaven as the Pharisees *and* Herod. The Scriptures record the moment when the disciples understood Christ's warning, "Then they understood that He did not tell *them* to beware of the leaven of bread, but of the *doctrine* of the Pharisees and Sadducees."[47]

Paul bears out the assertion that leaven is a false philosophy of reputation protection when he says, "Do you not know that a little leaven leavens the whole lump? Therefore purge out the old leaven ... Therefore let us keep the feast, not with old leaven ... but with the unleavened *bread* of *sincerity and truth.*"

Sincerity and truth cannot coexist with hypocrisy.

I was warned of the "leavenous" doctrine of hypocrisy. If we regard what others think of us, our priorities will be compromised, our actions will become guarded, and our motives will be suspect.

If we fear being all by ourselves because of a differing doctrine; if we fear we will lose our friends when we obey the Scripture; if we fear losing fellowship at church because we no longer believe what they are teaching; if we fear the loss of family members due to breaking lifelong traditions—*that fear will keep us from apprehending what our Lord and Master has instructed and taught.*

The Lord Jesus waits to impart revelation. This revelation will change lives forever. It will change us for the better *if* hypocrisy is left behind, but if we try to mix our revelation with hypocrisy, it will all unravel and leave us in worse confusion than before.

---

47 Matthew 16:12

Many truths have been bypassed and/or rejected for the sake of social concerns. The Scriptures warn that a person doing this will be worse for having known the right way; it would be better for him or her not to have known the way of righteousness than to have known it and departed.[48]

It will not be easy to admit hypocrisy. As a pastor, a church leader, as a man upon whom many depended for guidance, it was especially hard for me to admit that my life was a sham. What made it so difficult was that my heart was right. It was my head that was so full of baseless doctrine, groundless theology, and conventional understanding of what a "man of God" should be that there was no room for sincerity.

According to those around me, I had to be a certain kind of man. I had to be a certain kind of preacher. I knew that the consequences of transparent living, sincere, heartfelt convictions, and living by a true faith would not be pleasant.

Thankfully, I was given an opportunity to walk away from it all. The personal changes cost me nothing but my own private repentance, because my life was all taken away before my changes were made. It was His mercy that allowed me to accomplish this.

I have no wonderful testimony of confessing my hypocrisy from a pulpit and being forgiven by good church members, or even of being run out of town on a rail in order to entice readers to obey, because the Lord knew that I did not have what it took to face those who were unsympathetic to my revelations. Had it come to that, I may not have obeyed.

---

48 2 Peter 2:22

Perhaps those reading this book *do* have what it takes. Maybe you won't have to lose it all—and maybe you will. No matter what the costs, though, be strong and obey. I wish for you glorious results. (I certainly have enjoyed some!)

Preparing You for Understanding

The questions of Jesus seemed to come to me in random order. At first I scoured the Scriptures looking for questions. Here and there I would find them, one at a time. "Wow!" I said to my wife, "There must be fifty of 'em." Later, I was to find that there are more than *150!*

When I compiled the questions into the original book, *The Questions of Jesus*,[1] I arranged them into chronological order. I wish now that I had preserved the original order, for the order the questions came to me played a great part in His teaching me.

I attempt to duplicate in this writing, the very stages of learning through which Jesus took me. I remember how it felt as I neared the end of my study. When I would encounter an idea or fact that was foreign to my belief, I thought that if I had come across that particular principle or doctrine at the *beginning of my studies,* I would not have been able to be obedient to the revelation. But His order *prepared* me to learn.

Salvation is of the Jews.

---

1 *The Question of Jesus*—© 2003–2007 Think Red Ink publications www. ThinkRedInk.com

Perhaps we are alike; nurtured in conventional western Christian churches, already secure in a basic appreciation of what Christianity is. If that is so, you, too, suffer with acceptance and appreciation of your *Hebrew* heritage.

I grew up thinking that the Jews were horrible hypocrites, that they were religious people who were only trying to make the "easy way" of faith more difficult by imposing their "Old Testament," works-oriented framework upon the glorious "New Testament" ideal.

Their ideas were to be shunned. What they despised, I was to hold as acceptable. Their approval was to be considered the *seal of heresy*. I was sort of an anti-Semite Christian.

Through the years, as I have shared the insights granted to me by the Spirit of the Messiah, I have found that, unfortunately, many people have a similar view.

"That stuff is for the Jews!" I would hear in answer to my views. It was as if "the Jews" were operating under a different plan—a different covenant. Can this be so?

Jesus, while actually addressing another issue, made a statement within a question that opened my mind to a new understanding. He asked the Pharisees, *"Have you not read, 'I am the God of Abraham, the God of Isaac, and the God of Jacob?'"*[2]

If Jesus, the Son of God, the Messiah, *our* Redeemer, has no problem associating with the "Father" of the Old Testament, His ways and philosophy, why do so many modern Christians

---

2   Mark 12:26

feel no remorse at their statement, "That stuff is for the Jews"?

When I considered my attitude about the God of Abraham, Isaac, and Jacob, I wondered if *He* was really *my* God. I hardly *knew* Abraham, Isaac, and Jacob—could I know that I *indeed* worshiped *their* God—Jesus' Father?

When Jesus spoke to the Samaritan woman at the well, He informed her, "You worship [who] you do not know. We know [who] we worship—for salvation is *of* the Jews."[3]

This woman was closer to Orthodox Judaism than *I* have ever been. Her culture, though removed from true Judaism, was still very similar. They called upon YHVH (Jehovah) by name, they looked for Elijah and Messiah, and (though distorted by wicked kings of the past) they kept all the Feasts of Israel, and still *He condemned her understanding of religious matters.*

This realization frightened me a little. Once again my search for His questions left me wondering if it is possible to be sincere in what I believe and still be wrong.

Jesus says that He will one day declare to a certain group of people claiming to have done a lifetime of works *in His name*,[4] that *He never knew them.* This statement alone proves to me that it is not only *possible* for sincere people to be utterly wrong, but, by the numbers He uses in His example, it is also highly *probable!*

After the story of the multitude of people who were named "Christian" being rejected, the Lord begins to teach about improper *foundations.*

3 John 4:22
4 Matthew 7

"For no other foundation can any man lay than that which is already laid by Jesus Christ himself."[5]

Basic to any foundation of worship is the entity that is being worshiped. If we do not know *Who* we worship, it reveals our sandy foundation. It was their *foundation* that damned these "sincere" workers.

Now, that realization frightened me a lot! Could it be that I, too, worshiped a God I did not know? Worse yet, was I worshiping a God who did not know me? I was compelled to examine my foundation.

A scriptural evaluation of the salvation of mankind will reveal that it is based upon the ancient covenant with Abraham. It neither is based in faithless works (compliance to the Law of Moses) nor can salvation be secured by an effortless (dead) faith.

Redemption is not based upon the words of the Apostle Paul, nor is it dependent upon the decree of the local (or universal) Church. All Scripture, from beginning to end, testifies that the covenant with Abraham was the "promise" under which we, who number as the sands of the seashore, shall be saved.

Abraham's covenant of faith spans the Bible. It is present in every word of the Law, every precious promise of redemption, and it is present in every sermon of Christ. If we do not know this man, Abraham, *and* the Father with Whom he entered into faithful contract, *and* the covenant of promise that made

---

5 1 Corinthians 3:11

room for us in His coming kingdom, we indeed "worship, we know not what."

An anti-Semitic "Christian" is, without a doubt, attempting to reside in the most insensible arrangement that anyone could ever occupy. If we despise Jewish influences in our Christian faith, we will have a difficult time resolving our ideas of Christianity with the Scriptures—for salvation is, indeed, *of the Jews.*

Jesus told a story that brought all these ideas into clear view for me.

A king hosted a wedding feast for his son. His dearest friends and closest comrades were bidden, the feast was ready and awaited them, but they began to make justifications for their absence and asked to be excused.

He sent for them again, but they answered once again that they would not come. (These, who were bidden first, clearly represent the Jewish nation of old.)

The wedding host was hurt and furious. He commanded that his servants go and get the lame, blind, and maimed to attend his wedding supper. They could barely fill the house as a result! (Obviously, these ailing people correspond to the despised Gentiles who later were invited to replace the ungrateful, doubting Jews.)

From here we Gentiles rejoice and give thanks for being given the opportunity of becoming recipients of the Father's grace and blessing, and so we should. However, we need to realize that we are *default winners* of this race. It is not an honor to be the last team player picked! We must remember that we are all halt, blind, and maimed in the eyes of our Host and are lesser than the guests He expected.

The story continues to unfold. Its message is not just for the unbelieving Jew, but heralds a warning to the boastful Gentile, as well. One of these guests failed to place any importance on the customs held dear by the King who invited him. (Perhaps he was a bit anti-Semitic, or maybe he just preferred his own familiar ways.) He seemed intent on doing things in his own style and insisted that he could maintain his own "identity" by wearing his own clothing instead of donning the wedding garment that was customarily expected by his Host. "After all," he may have insisted, "I am not a Jew; why would I want to look like a Jew?"

The attitude of the Host toward this insensitive Gentile wedding guest is evident in the Scripture: "But when the king came in to see the guests, he saw a man there who did not have on a wedding garment. So he said to him, *'Friend, how did you come in here without a wedding garment?'* And he was speechless. Then the king said to the servants, 'Bind him hand and foot, take him away, and cast *him* into outer darkness; there will be weeping and gnashing of teeth. For many are called, but few *are* chosen.'"[6]

"Ye worship ye know not what." Haunting, isn't it? When we insist upon the comfort of our own *identity*, we risk the displeasure of our Host. Loss of "self" and release of our own identity must occur for us, who were invited as a mere addendum, to sit in seats not intended for us.

We are obliged to adopt ways that please our Host, or we will be doomed to be cast out—speechless. Only when we take

---

6   Matthew 22:11-14 (NKJV)

on His ways and forget our own, will we win His heart and show our desire to become part of the family He called *first*. When we answer the *call* of invitation and present ourselves in obedience and submission, we can then await His approval—to be *chosen*.

Many are called—few are chosen.

One day while passing through Samaria and Galilee, Jesus walked along the hot, dusty road. Wafting across the landscape were voices, which were nearly imperceptible to the ears of the Messiah, but were heard faintly across the landscape, "Joshua! Teacher! Have mercy on us!"

The ten lepers, standing far away from the road, dared not approach the public byway with their blistered and decaying flesh for fear of being stoned. Although the sun- parched rocks and radiant desert sand distorted their distant, shimmering images in the heat, Jesus could see them out among the rocks, waving their hands in the air. He cupped one hand to the side of His mouth and shouted, "Go show yourselves to the priest and make the offering Moses commanded."

Can any western Gentile *really* understand what Jesus commanded them? Among this beleaguered band was a man who would be despised by any Jew—even if he had the flesh of a child. The Samaritans were hated by the Jews because their ancestors accepted Babylon's corrupting influence, allowing it to pollute their worship, many years before this man was even born.

You see, he was from the same nation as the woman at the well, the one who was told, "Ye know not what ye worship."
The Jewish Teacher called out instructions to this half-Jew, this Samaritan, this stranger to Israel, to perform an act that the

man likely did *not* even understand. His Jewish companions likely *did* understand, having been taught the Torah from their youth; but chances are that this Samaritan had no idea what the Law required of a leper.[7]

He obeyed anyway, "… and as he went he was cleansed." Perhaps he went along with his friends because he had nothing to lose, or maybe it was an act of his resolute faith. We do not know. What we *do* know is that, of the ten, this man, this one despicable man, returned to give thanks to his Healer.

His comrades went on, happy to be healed, but this one man returned, and in doing so, enjoyed the mercy and acceptance of the Messiah. *"Were there not any found [of my Jewish brethren any] who returned to give glory to God— except this foreigner?"*[8] And He said to him, "Arise, go your way. Your faith has made you well."

Thankfulness is far too rare. It should not be so among the redeemed, especially those having opportunity by grace *alone*.

The other nine lepers who had been cleansed may very well have been grateful, but they did not say so. The grateful heart of the stranger won the love of Messiah.

Could the man who was cast out of the wedding party be considered to be a *thankful* man? The guests who donned garments that were strange to them may have been a little uncomfortable, but they appreciated their Host, and enjoyed the feast to its conclusion.

The Jews were called, but they did not answer. The Gentiles were also called, and although they answered, they yet awaited

---

7   Leviticus 13
8   Luke 17

to be chosen. Many have answered reservedly, holding their works in check, refusing the Jewish garb, standing now by faith *alone*.

Paul understood both conditions well. He warned, "And if some of the branches were broken off, and you, being a wild olive tree, were grafted in among them, and with them became a partaker of the *root* and fatness of the olive tree, do not boast ... You will say then [boasting], 'Branches were broken off that I might be grafted in.' Well said. Because of *unbelief* they were broken off, and you stand by faith. Do not be haughty, but fear. For if God did not spare the natural branches, *he may not spare you either*."[9]

Remember that we, the wild branch of Gentile believers, have no roots that are *worthy* of preservation. Our *roots* are in Israel! If we ignore this fact, we will forever lack proper scriptural understanding. If we focus on the "New" Testament and forget "the rest of the story," we will greatly hamper our progression. We may even render it *impossible*.

We are admonished to study the Scriptures. Consider what is meant when the Bible uses the word "Scriptures"—certainly not a black, leatherbound book in the King James Version, a book that is divided into the Old and New Testaments. Remember, such a book did not exist in the day when this advice was given!

Jesus and His contemporaries studied the Torah and the prophets! When we neglect the Old Testament, we neglect the very document to which the Bible refers as "the Scriptures."

Reluctance to read and study the Old Testament will deprive us of the basis from which the Messiah taught in

---

9 Romans 11

nearly every sermon He preached. He expected us to have this framework firmly established *before* we attempt to interpret His messages. His entire ministry was conducted under the Law of Moses and the covenant of Abraham; and was subject to all the prophecies.

Jesus was an Old Testament student. He was an Old Testament preacher. He was an Old Testament prophet. Our redemption was promised in these writings. Our covenant of salvation began there. Our hope of resurrection is prophesied there.

Modern Christians are not doing anything new in their neglect of the Scriptures. Jesus frequently asked his followers, *"Have you not so much as read?"* and *"Did you never read in the Scriptures?"*

He was astounded that the Jewish people, whose entire existence was based in Scripture, had never read the Scriptures. Can He feel any differently about us?

Often, we nearly brag that our life in Christ is a matter of faith, but faith in what? Is our faith merely in what we have been told? Do we simply believe in a story we have heard? Is ours a faith that is based in obscure and pious sacraments? Can we have true faith if it is based only in a dogmatic understanding of religion? Perhaps we claim we have faith in God. Well, the Scriptures tell us that even the devils *believe* in God.

In what do you place your faith?

We are to place our faith in the testimony of Scripture— *all* Scripture. If we incorporate both the old and new (and it is possible to do that) there is a danger that with the success of this endeavor, we may be called heretics by our closest companions.

If that happens, we will be in good company! Paul lamented over what his brethren testified of him, "They cannot prove the things of which they now accuse me. But this I confess to you, that according to the Way which they call heresy, so I worship the God of my fathers, *believing all things which are written in the Law and in the Prophets.*"[10]

How can a Christian—the Apostle Paul—believe *both* the Law *and* the Prophets and write two thirds of the New Testament? How can someone believe both? It is not only *possible* to do so, but it remains as a challenge to you and me to do so as well.

When the Scriptures are taken as a whole, with dispensationalism and denominationalism left behind, they unfold the wonderful gospel story in all its fullness and power. They are not, nor have they ever been, a threat to pure faith in God or His Son, Jesus Christ. We may not discount even one word.

We must, as Paul did, "believe *all* things" which are written there. Otherwise, our faith is destined to become void, empty, and useless. If we dodge information because it threatens the status quo, we exemplify our lack of confidence that what we believe is true.

We doubt because we do not read the Scriptures, and we do not read them because we have doubts. How will we finally end this perverted circular reasoning to emerge into true faith?

---

10   Acts 24:14

Faithlessness and confusion such as this disturb the Lord Jesus. Once He cried out, *"O faithless and perverse generation, how long shall I be with you? How long shall I bear with you?"*[11]

Perverse? Why did Jesus use the word *perverse?* Faithlessness colors and perverts everything we do and say. When faith is nonexistent, thinking becomes worldly and goals become creaturely. As thinking degrades, perverted minds become absorbed in *self* and begin to fear uncontrollably.

When our mind is no longer an instrument, but rather our prison, we have then become *perverse.* We lose the joy of following and we start chasing. We stop living and begin surviving. We become defensive and overly concerned with superficial events while the spiritual holds little of our interest.

In order to continue on our journey of revelation and perfection, we must think the way our Master thinks. Without understanding and a familiarity with Scriptures, this will be an impossible goal.

Do you remember Jesus' boat trip with His disciples? Jesus intended to warn them about hypocrisy. As was His custom, He spoke in a metaphor by saying, "Beware of the *leaven* of the Sadducees and Pharisees and of Herod."

His disciples, misunderstanding him, were concerned only with their own skins. The spiritual had once again eluded them and they felt only condemnation in the words of the Messiah. They *thought* Jesus was talking about bread. Why would *they*

---

11   Matthew 17:17 (NKJV)

think of bread? It was because they had forgotten to bring bread for the trip.

How can such an insignificant act of minor neglect interfere with such an important revelation? What is it that we must learn from this story? We find the answer in the questions of Jesus.

He chided the disciples and reminded them of the loaves and fishes. He forced them to answer as He brought to their recollection just how many extra pieces they picked up from the ground after they had fed the thousands.

Then He asked, (as if He did not know), *"Just how is it that ye do not understand?"*[12] In other words, He was saying, "Think about it, boys, what is on your mind today, *yourselves* or the *Kingdom?*"

Their minds were clouded, preoccupied, and hence *perverted* by living without faith. He wanted them to recognize that it was their lack of faith that caused their lack of understanding.

They were afraid because they had no bread? *When the Bread of Heaven was a passenger in their boat?* They were mentally fastened on their own imperfections. Their lack of prudence mixed with their lack of faith and concluded in disastrous results. The mixture of oversight and doubt caused them to miss a dire warning and important revelation. How many messages have we missed because we were thinking about our own skins?

The Lord Jesus has been good to us in that He has placed the life of faith "low on the shelf." We can reach out to higher

---

and loftier ideas as we prove faithful in the baser and mundane. If we can believe that He can (and will) supply bread to sustain life, we can believe He will provide the "Bread of Life" as well!

Jesus speaks this same fact a bit more negatively, "... you do not receive our witness. *If I have told you earthly things and you do not believe, how will you believe if I tell you heavenly things?*"[13]

In asking this, the Savior indicts many of us, including me! I am not sure how this is done in our minds, but we have an uncanny ability to make the Son of God all powerful and all knowing in one area of theology and, at the same time, ill-informed and guessing in another.

Sometimes we are *not sure* of the facts. We know that God *is sure*, but when we *are* sure (or think we are), we wonder if there may be a translation error—a misapplication of the customs and manners of the day ... well, you get the point!

Why would we doubt the words of Jesus, or attempt to change their meaning? Our minds reject that which contradicts the facts we have established. If what Jesus says is *incongruent with our understanding*, we assume He cannot mean what He says.

My friend, we must allow Jesus to speak, for He says only what the Father tells Him to say.[14]

---

13   John 3
14   John 8:26 "... and I speak to the world those things which I have heard of him." (KJV).
John 12:50 "... whatsoever I speak therefore, even as the Father said unto me, so I speak." (KJV)
John 14:10 "... the words that I speak unto you I speak not of myself: but the Father that dwelleth in me ... (KJV)

Once Jesus said to a man who was lame, "Rise and walk!" Lack of understanding in the people who were there at the time may have made them say that He could not possibly have meant what He said. Only their lack of understanding would cause them to think, "When Jesus said, 'Rise up,' He meant to cheer up; and that perhaps 'Walk' simply meant to 'live a good life'!"

His piercing question must be answered, "*... which is easier, to say, 'Your sins are forgiven you,' or to say, 'Arise and walk'?*[15]

For Jesus, fixing a foot is just as easy as cleansing a soul! We *easily* trust Him for salvation, but have problems believing His promises of provision and guidance. We seem to feel that we can work out the common stuff on or own, but eternity—well, we'll just *have* to trust Him for that.

It is blasphemy to challenge His abilities or to subject Him to our very limited experiences and understanding. When we rank His message beneath scientific "fact" or laws of physics, yet believe He will save us, we engage in a paradox that will ultimately pervert our faith. When we make His words subject to our own theology, when we doubt His Spirit-led instructions, warnings, and admonitions for Christian living, yet do not doubt His ability to heal a lame man, we use a logic to guide our lives that is unknown in the universe.

As He revealed these things to me, I said to myself over and over, "Just shut up and learn." My problem was in attempting to make the Almighty jump through *my* theological hoops. Using the "here a little, there a little, precept upon precept" study method, I could make the Bible into a Baptist "statement

---

15 Matthew 9:5 (NKJV)

of faith," but in my heart I was sure that I could as easily build a theology for *any* faith or *any* denomination using exactly the same process.

The biggest change came when I learned that the Word of God is *not a book*, but a *living person*. The Word of God is not a liturgical diatribe to be dissected and manipulated. It is part of the eternal Godhead!

According to John 1, *the Word of God is Jesus Christ Himself.*

This truth was a major key to my understanding. I saw that there was a vast difference in the Scriptures, the words written in the Bible, and the *living* Word of God.

Jesus asked, *"Do you not understand this parable? How then will you understand all the parables?"*[16]

When I read this question, I immediately scanned the page backward to see exactly *which* parable He was talking about. I *had* to know! (Do *you* want to know?)

I have, on occasion, said to someone, "The Bible teaches there is a parable that is essential to understanding *all* parables." No response.

I would try again, "Jesus said that if you cannot understand *this* particular parable, you cannot understand any of them!" No response.

---

16 Mark 4:13 (NKJV)

I couldn't help but explode, "Don't you want to know what it is?" All I got was a shoulder shrug and a disinterested look.

Amazing! Are we the only ones who *want* understanding?

"... a sower went out to sow. And it happened, as he sowed, that some seed fell by the wayside; and the birds of the air came and devoured it. Some fell on stony ground, where it did not have much earth; and immediately it sprang up because it had no depth of earth. But when the sun was up it was scorched, and because it had no root it withered away. And some seed fell among thorns; and the thorns grew up and choked it, and it yielded no crop. But other seed fell on good ground and yielded a crop that sprang up, increased and produced: some thirtyfold, some sixty, and some a hundred. And He said to them, 'He who has ears to hear, let him hear!'"[17]

I must have read this five of six times before I really *heard* the Messiah's indispensable words. *"He who has ears to hear, let him hear!"*

The disciples were curious as to why He would not speak plainly to them. I was curious, too! After all, much of what we modern Christians mistakenly believe [and incessantly argue about] is because *He* did not plainly tell us about these doctrines.

Consider what the modern church would resemble today if Jesus had left a detailed book, a catechism, a liturgy, or a statement of doctrine for the Church? Something written down would eliminate many theological disputes. Better yet, a videotape!

17 Matthew 13:3-9

We wouldn't wonder if the bread at the Lord's Supper should be leavened or not. We would just look it up! We wouldn't wonder if the wine should be fermented. We would just look it up! We would never again worry about how a man is saved, baptized, joins the church, or whether he is qualified to be a Sunday school teacher, etc. We would know *everything* we needed to know in no uncertain terms!

So, why *didn't* He make these things clear and unmistakable? Actually the Lord answers this question. In His words, "To you it has been given to know the mystery of the Kingdom of God; but to those who are outside, all things come in parables, so that 'Seeing they may see and not perceive, And hearing they may hear and not understand; Lest they should turn, And *their* sins be forgiven them.'"

When the Spirit of God asked me how I expect to understand all parables when I did not understand this one, it became clear that His parables, His doctrine, the truths of Jehovah, cannot be found like treasure. They are not to be mined like silver. They cannot be earned as a reward; they cannot be possessed by education. We need to *hear* them as the Almighty sees fit to give us understanding.

It is not up to us! This ability to *hear* is not a product of hard work, but is bestowed upon whomsoever *He* wills! What assurance do we have that we will *ever* receive it? When dealing with a sovereign God, we can have no such assurances, but we do have *hope*. We must believe that He is *and* that He is a rewarder of those who diligently seek Him.

Are you ready to *hear* the word of God?

Reading the words of God requires no readiness—only ability and desire. Ability and desire have little to do with *hearing* the Word of God. We are receivers. We can make ourselves ready to hear, but whether He speaks is entirely up to Him. A radio that is on and tuned to the station will hear *when* the station transmits, but it has no control over the station's *transmitter*.

Is the Almighty speaking to you?

Many *assume* He speaks, but unless we have a working receiver that is tuned to His frequency, we really can't be sure. Spend some quiet time listening. A person's whole life could parade in front of him within ten minutes of silent meditation.

This communion with your Father could be a distressing situation, requiring repentance, or perhaps He will have a word of comfort! We will not know unless we take the time to listen. When we rise up, we will carry His voice in our consciences to guide us throughout the day.

Jesus has always pointed men toward their consciences. His recorded words are, *"What do you reason in your hearts?"*[18]

Contrary to what we are frequently told, we can trust our consciences. Troublesome judgment, justification of sin, erroneous beliefs and doctrines come not from *obeying* a pure conscience, but from *ignoring* it. It is only the conscience in a sinful or willful man that cannot be trusted. So why not *avoid* willful or sinful behavior and keep our consciences clear and reliable?

The Apostle Paul highly valued his conscience and trusted it as a dependable guide. He asserted before his judging council,

---

18   Mark 2:8 – 8:17, Matthew 16:8, Luke 5:22

"... Men and brethren, I have lived in all good conscience before God until this day."[19]

John, the Beloved, remarked, "For if our heart condemns us, God is greater than our heart, and knows all things."[20]

When we need to employ conscience and are called upon to reason within our own hearts, when we find ourselves in need of guidance, we must know *how* to do this.

If we have evil in the heart, the conscience is unusable as a guide. We *can* know there is evil in us. Jesus asks a question to put us on track, "*... How can you, being evil, speak good things? For out of the abundance of the heart the mouth speaks.*"

What comes from your mouth? Is it doubt and uncertainty or faith and power?

Temperament and language are our conscience's tattle-tales. An agitated and angry man has an irritated and restless conscience. Sleeplessness comes from a soul yearning to converse with God. Bitterness is in a man who feels he has been cheated by an untouchable enemy. Judgment becomes the default response in a life that is lived in selfishness. The list is endless because of our wickedness.

We must not merely learn to speak good things, but we must *become better*, through repentance. Only then can good things be heard from us.

---

19   Acts 23:1 (NKJV)
20   1 John 3:20 (NKJV)

Jesus knew the need for our repentance, and He asked, *"... How can you, being evil, speak good things? For out of the abundance of the heart the mouth speaks."*

Warning Three: Live the Life He Commands

What will it take for us to realize that we have created a god in our own image? We cannot choose Christian faith by simply choosing a denomination that suits us. Nor can we walk past the Scriptures, as if we were at a smorgasbord, picking and choosing what we like and ignoring what we don't.

If we find that our favorite holiday is an abomination in the eyes of the Almighty, will we balk? Will we justify our actions, or will we say, "Be it unto thy servant, Lord, even as You will"?

If we insist on our own way, if we deny our clear calling, if we choose rather to *belong* than *be right*, there is hardly any hope that we will find the true Messiah and live a life that pleases the Father. Our lives in such a case are filled with practices that disgust our Father in Heaven. Our minds are preoccupied with self and gratification of flesh. Our fears have become our faith, while true faith strikes fear in our hearts.

We call the King of the Jews "King" while denying our Jewish heritage.

We call ourselves "disciples," yet we exercise no disciplines.

We call Jesus "Lord," "Boss," and "Ruler" of our lives and cannot relinquish any of our own traditions at His beckoning for us to do so.

Jesus asks, *"Why do you call me Lord ... and not do what I say?"* [21]

His question is a good one, and it deserves an honest answer!

21   Luke 6:46

Revelation–How to Hear

I can only assume that your reason for reading this book, studying the Bible, attending a Sunday school or Bible class is that you seek a deeper understanding of the Scriptures and a closer walk with Jesus Christ.

In order for this to happen, you must receive revelation. Where do you think you will receive this needed revelation or, more importantly, *how* do you think you are going to receive it?

The understanding of the mechanics of revelation—how it actually happens—will help you to know what to expect when it comes. I'm sure that in the course of your studies or in listening to a sermon, revelation *has* come to you, but understanding the mechanics of *how* this happened will go a long way toward receiving more from God.

So, how do you *think* revelation will come to you?

Some people feel that if they use a different translation of the Bible, or if they understand the "original" language of the documents, they will understand further, and more will be revealed to them. In reality, however, revelation does not come through study.

Jesus taught, "… no one knows the Son except the Father. Nor does anyone know the Father except the Son, and *the one to whom the Son wills to reveal Him*."[1]

Remember when Jesus said that the Kingdom of God does not come with observation?[2] He was trying to reveal the fact that the Kingdom of God does not become visible by discovery or simply by looking for it. It comes only when the Father *wills* it to come in the hearts of His Believers.

The Apostle Paul taught that the Kingdom of God is "*not in food or drink*."[3] (This signifies that the Kingdom is not discovered by *doing* something.)

In the Lord's Prayer we hear Jesus teach us to pray, "Thy Kingdom come, Thy will be done." It is clear that we are to pray that His Kingdom *does* come.

Jesus also teaches that the Kingdom of God is within *you*. When we couple the thoughts that the Kingdom of God is within us and that it does not come simply by looking for it, we are left with this intriguing question: *how does the Kingdom of God come?*

Furthermore, *what is* and *where is* the Kingdom of God? How is the Father revealed? These questions are not unrelated thoughts; they are similar in their manner of revelation by the Spirit.

The Kingdom of God is *within us,* but it comes only to the heart and mind of the believer, *as* it is revealed. The Father is revealed to the believer at the *will* of the Son.

---

1   Matthew 11:27 (NKJV)
2   Luke 17:20
3   Romans 14:17

The Kingdom of God will only reveal itself to hearts and minds through the *Word of God*. Unless we understand what—or more perfectly, *who*—the Word of God is, revelation may very well be right in front of us and remain unrecognized.

When the seventy disciples were being commissioned to work miracles among the people, heal the sick, and raise the dead, Jesus taught them what to do if they were not received by those to whom they ministered. He told them that they were to shake the dust off their feet and, as they were leaving, to say, "The Kingdom of God has come nigh unto you."

Once, when teaching about the Kingdom of God, a Pharisee stated that to love Him [the one God] with all the heart, with all the understanding, with all the soul, and with all the strength, and to love one's neighbor as oneself is more than all the whole burnt offerings and sacrifices.[4]

Jesus' pleased response was, "You are not far from the Kingdom of God."

Obviously, this man did not realize that he was hearing the Word of God! He *heard within himself* the truth about the ministry of the Messiah, and that truth came out of his mouth. However, he did not recognize it as such.

This can happen to us, too! How sad it would be to seek the Kingdom of God while it is right in front of us (or within us) and not know it!

The Word of God spoken to the heart of the believer *is* this revelation process.

---

4 Mark 12:33

Revelation will not come from reading, although the Word of God can be heard while reading the Scriptures. It will not come through preaching, although the Word of God can be heard in preaching.

As Paul revealed, "... you received the word of God which you heard of us, you received it not as the word of men, but as it is in truth, the word of God ..."[5]

We need to slow down here. I loathe listing both Scripture and my opinion, one after the other, in rapid-fire succession, as is so common in our modern Bible-teaching practices; but I am hoping you will see the definition of "the Word of God" start to emerge.

The Word of God

I want you to see the kinship of the Kingdom within you and the revelation of the Father. I want you to see the prerequisite will of the Father in your revelation. In short, I want you to recognize the Word of God when you hear it.

You have heard it before; now, see it in Scripture. The experience of understanding, of finally "getting it," or the "Ah ha!" experience *is* the voice of the Shepherd to your spirit, the will of the Father to make it so, and the weeks of your preparation coming together in one instantaneous flash point of *hearing the Word of God.*

Remember, "He that has *ears to hear,* let him *hear.*"

---

5 1 Thessalonians 2:13

We are frail and faulty human beings, and have mistakenly attached our revelation of God and His Kingdom to the mouthpiece (or any physical conduit) from which that revelation came. If we attach the Word of God to a sermon, we will tend to seek sermons as the means for hearing the Word of God. If we attach the revelation of God to reading the Bible, we will feel that the Bible is the source of revelation.

This is how we become attached to evangelists and pastors, to denominations and philosophies. Although hearing sermons and reading the Bible can be a large part of revelation, they are *not* what we should seek. We need to seek the *Word of God* to our spirits. We should seek first the Kingdom of God.

If we continue to misunderstand what the Word of God is, we will constantly seek the Word of God from the wrong sources or through the wrong conduits. The understanding of Who the Word of God is changed forever my relationship with the Father, and my very life!

The Scriptures

The Scriptures are a trustworthy record of revelation and how it came to the hearts of the men and women of the past, and we can learn many things from *their* revelation. When another person's experience becomes our own, we have experienced something quite different from mere reading or learning. We have encountered the true *Word of God*.

To seek no further than another person's revelation will tempt us to act upon *another's* revelation as if it is our own. As surely as we do this, we will be disappointed.

Let's use an exaggerated example to illustrate the danger of acting on the revelation received by another person. The Lord's command to Moses as he stood at the Red Sea was, "Raise your staff over this sea and I will make a way for the children of Israel to cross over."

This instruction was revelation to *Moses* and when he obeyed, his action saved God's people from sure destruction. It was the *Word of God* to Moses, but if you or I (or anyone else) were to arbitrarily take those words of instruction to ourselves and attempt such a feat, we would be severely disillusioned!

So, what *do* we need? Do we need Moses' revelation, or do we need to hear the Word of God within ourselves as Moses did? To put it another way, if, as with Moses, we stand facing a barrier—a sea of seeming impossibility—and the Word of God speaks to us and tells us to hold our staff over our sea of trouble, thus making a way for crossing, *we can count on our obedience to that Word to somehow make a way of crossing!*

The Scripture shows us the patterns of Jehovah's movements and dealings among people. It lays out for us the format of how He does things, and we can learn from these records His predictable manner and the behavior He requires of us.

From the record of Moses, we may learn that we likely will not receive the Word from God to deliver us *before* we reach the sea. Equally important, we can learn that when the Father *does* speak to us, He is leading us *to say* or *to do* or *to move upon what He tells us.* From reading about Moses' experience we can learn that it may not happen instantly. The wind may have to blow all night, for example.

We can also learn that when we cross this sea, the very way He made for us may very well provide a way for our enemies to follow us.

There are many lessons we can learn from the Scriptures, but we cannot arbitrarily extract leadership or revelation from them and randomly apply it to ourselves. We must seek the Word of God to our own spirits.

The role of the Scriptures in revelation is that they give us the pattern of God's movements—what to expect and how these things will occur. The Scriptures describe what attitudes we are supposed to maintain, and they warn about the pitfalls that hinder revelation and communication.

When Jesus asked the question, *"What did Moses command you?"*,[6] He focused our attention upon the Scriptures so that we could learn from them that it is possible to learn from the revelations of others.

If we are not faithful in the revelation of other people, if we don't *know* the revelation given to other people, if we don't *read* the revelations of other people, there will be way too much for us to learn in our short, sinful lifetimes.

The Scriptures are a gift to *us*. The experiences of Moses, Elijah, Abraham, David, and the prophets are for *our* learning. They are not merely metaphors and they are certainly not revelation to our own spirits, but we can and should learn from them.

---

6   Mark 10:3 (NKJV)

"Now all these things happened to them as examples, and they were written for our admonition, upon whom the ends of the ages have come."[7]

---

7   1 Corinthians 10:11 (NKJV)

Hindrances to Hearing

As Jesus stood before the high council to be condemned, He spoke words to the high priest that gave offense to one of the servants. The servant slapped Jesus across the face! He struck Jesus because he did not like what Jesus had said.

After being slapped by the priest's staff member, Jesus simply asked a question, *"Why do you strike Me?"*[1]

We also can be guilty of striking the Messiah when what He tells us does not line up with our religion. Oh, we may not physically strike Him, nor may we accuse Him of not telling the truth when He speaks, but we twist His words and filter them through our own religious understanding so that they fit better with what we presently believe. These actions can be considered nothing short of assaulting the Savior and despising the Word of God.

John quoted Jesus, "He that rejects Me, and receives not My words, has One that judges him ..."[2]

We must believe that the Scriptures are true! If the Scriptures are not true and not trustworthy, and we cannot depend upon them, we are lost! In our present sinful condition, there is

---

1   18:23 (NKJV)
2   John 12:48 (NKJV)

little hope of receiving revelation if we constantly attack the Scriptures and try to make them say what they do not intend or imply.

The Scriptures can supply us with understanding so that we do not miss revelation when it comes.

Two Israelites walked toward the afternoon sun. The bright yellow ball was nearing the horizon but neither of them noticed it. They saw only their own sandals and the soiled, swinging borders of their garments as they walked with bowed heads and downcast eyes.

"How could this be?" they asked no one in particular.

They were so apparently gloomy that a stranger who met them as they traveled asked, *"What kind of conversation is this that you have with one another as you walk and are sad?"*[3]

The Lord Jesus had appeared to the two disciples on the road to Emmaus, but they did not know Him. They were forlorn and saddened by the fact that their Lord had been so ill-treated, despised, and persecuted, even to death.

From this condition, they extracted the thought that He must *not* have been the Messiah; He must *not* have been who they thought He was. They deduced this because what had happened to Him was not according to their assessment of what had been written in the Scriptures.

The Stranger asked them a question to realign their deductions, "O foolish ones, and slow of heart to believe in all that the prophets have spoken! *Ought not the Christ to have*

---

3   Luke 24:17 (NKJV)

suffered these things to enter into His glory? And beginning at Moses and all the Prophets, He expounded to them in all the Scriptures the things concerning Himself."[4]

His question directed them to the Scriptures, but they were forced to think about them *another way.* These men knew the Scriptures, but *from the Scriptures* they had drawn wrong conclusions; therefore, the revelation of truth was shut off to them.

Then Jesus pointed out, by way of His question, that Messiah *should* have suffered these things. Everything they experienced was exactly according to Scripture. It was only their *understanding* of what they had read, known, and understood that was faulty.

From His question *we* can learn that it is indeed possible to be in the presence of Christ Himself and not recognize Him *because* our understanding of His words is faulty. We must consult the Scriptures to establish if what we see in front of us does indeed align itself with the biblical record.

In addition to the Scriptures, another source for revelation of the Word is through the minds and mouths of other people. It is very common to hear the Word of God preached, written in books, or even broadcasted. It may touch us and move upon us in such a way that could change our lives for the better.

This may sound contrary to my earlier comments, but remember, the Lord Jehovah has spoken through individuals for centuries, even people of ill repute who were steeped in wickedness. Once, He even used a braying donkey!

---

4 Luke 24:25 (NKJV)

To arbitrarily discount the ministry of people is not wise; but to grant wholesale license to them is sheer madness. It will require the witness of our own spirit to avoid the pitfalls.

One of these pitfalls is affection for our helpers. If we wrongly attach the revelations of other people to our deliverance, we can mistakenly seek more of the words of others in order to hear the revelation of God. There is nothing basically wrong with seeking revelation from other people, as long as you understand that the Word of God is a *spiritual hearing* of *spiritual words* and not necessarily the perfectly laid-out and understood sermon. When we cannot discern the difference in poetry and theology, we are "ripe" for heresy.

Revelation has little to do with being moved *emotionally* or *intellectually* by the words of people. Some people seem to lean toward intellectual stimulation, while others are intrigued with the emotional aspects of preaching. Pick your poison!

We should be very careful to whom we listen and *why*. We should guard every thought that comes into our minds. We *can* be led astray by people who twist words and we *can* be led astray by Scriptures in their control, but *we can never be led astray by the Spirit of God.*

When the Scriptures seem to contradict themselves, we know that our understanding is faulty, but how can we understand when the words of people are faulty? Jesus taught us that there are individuals in this world, who, whether knowingly or not, can falsely "speak for God." Since a prophet is simply a man who speaks for Jehovah, such men are, by definition, false prophets.

Jesus shows us that the process of fruit inspection is to be used in order to know a false prophet when we hear one.

He did not tell us to listen to what the false prophet says, criticize what he says, or scrutinize what he says according to the Scriptures (although these are common understandings of how to know a false prophet); He said, "You will know them by their fruit."

To turn our minds in the right direction, Jesus asks a question, *"Do men gather grapes from thornbushes or figs from thistles?"*[5]

It is very interesting that thorns and thistles growing near vineyards, constantly being worked by harvesters, make it very possible to find an occasional grape stuck on a thorn! God's people, mingled among and found within the circles of false prophets, are like grapes stuck on thorns. Jesus wants us to know that those grapes, although they are found on the thorns of the thistle, did *not* grow there.

However, how did the grapes get stuck on the thorns and thistles in the vineyard? It happens through the process of proselytization[6] of God's people.

It is a common practice among false prophets to proselytize. Proselytization is the only way for a false prophet to gather "fruit" to himself, because he cannot produce it on his own. Jesus taught that an evil (bad) vine *cannot* produce good fruit, and a good vine *cannot* produce evil (bad) fruit. This fruit is nothing short of the true conversion of a lost soul.

The Pharisees were masters at the proselytization of God's people, but Jesus condemned it. He told them, "You compass

---

5 Matthew 7:16 (NKJV)
6 Proselytization is simply gathering people previously committed to Jehovah and merely convincing them of a new doctrine.

sea and land to make one proselyte, but in doing so you make him two-fold more the Child of Hell than yourselves."[7]

Grapes stuck on thorns are disconnected from the vine! They are punctured and dying! Although they may look good and fresh, it is only due to the short time they have been stuck there. If you watch them, you will see them shrivel and die.

While the grapes look good, they can fool you into thinking that this person is attached to the vine and is telling the truth. Be wary as you look at how many grapes are stuck to the thorns of false prophets. There are many *wonderful* people involved in false ministries today!

Keep in your mind this question of Jesus, *"Do men gather grapes from thorns or figs from thistles?"*

We must seek from God pure revelation to our own spirits. When we seek revelation from books, novels, or from preachers, sermons, and the like, we subject ourselves to the danger of being led astray. To have the power that comes from our revelation, so that we can know that we have heard the voice of God, it is *imperative* that we receive our *own* revelation from the Messiah—personally.

However, there are many things that can enter into the equation and render us unable to receive such revelation. One of these things is disobedience to the revelations of other people.

Stay with me! I don't want to lose you at this point. This statement may seem contradictory, but it is not!

---

7   Matthew 23:15

Words of Men

The Word of God *can* come from others, but it must ultimately be made your own. We must tread carefully here. The Bereans were doubtful of Paul's message. They examined what he had to say by the Scriptures.[8] When they realized that he had indeed spoken truth, they embraced *his* revelation, though it was foreign to their thinking and religious faith.

On the other hand, we are warned to, "Prove all things; hold fast that which is good."[9] Had the Bereans rejected Paul's revelation, they would have been fated to a life of confusion and the despair of a false foundation.

When a man who claims enlightenment speaks, it does not necessarily mean it is to be taken as the Word of God. However, no matter what he says, however strange it may be to our ears, if the Spirit witnesses to us that there is truth in his words, we are obligated to investigate both him and his message. But, even if his message is inarguable by the Scriptures, if we find no place in our own spirits to believe it, we are compelled to leave it alone.

The witness to our spirits alone does not condemn him as a false prophet, nor does it mean that we are in unbelief. It simply means that the revelation has not yet come. If it is true and has been made real, we are required to follow. If we don't follow, we cannot progress in our journey toward perfection.

As I was studying the questions of Jesus and learning how revelation comes, He warned me of certain actions on my part

---

8   Acts 17:11
9   1 Thessalonians 5:21

that would stop this revelation process. Revelation will cease when we are not faithful in that which belongs to another.

Jesus asked a deep question that needs more than just a single glance, *"And if you have not been faithful in what is another man's, who will give you what is your own?"*[10]

Many times when teaching about responsibility to those with whom we work or even to our own children, we might say to them something along these lines, "If you don't take care of what is yours, I am not going to put into your charge something that belongs to somebody else."

For instance, if our child does not take care of his bicycle, we are very reluctant to loan him our car. If an employee does not take care of his own tools, we certainly do not want to trust him with ours.

On the subject of revelation this Scripture means so much more than the mere maintenance of temporal and tangible items in our lives. Read His question again, carefully. You will find that it is saying the very *opposite* of the concept we use to train employees, children, etc.

Jesus did not say that we need to be faithful in that which is our *own*. He said we need to give attention to that which is *another man's*.

As far as revelation is concerned, if we have not been faithful in the revelation of another man, will we receive revelation of our own? If we have not been faithful in the revelation given to Moses, why would the Father give us our own revelation? If we have not been faithful in the Word of God that was given

---

10   Luke 16:12 (NKJV)

to the prophets, why would Jehovah confer upon us personal instruction?

Well, the simple and obvious answer is that He *would not!*

The Almighty God gave Moses revelation in the Ten Commandments. If we find ourselves in violation of the Ten Commandments, if Moses' revelation is not enough to move us toward righteousness, if the words of Moses cannot inspire obedience in us, then why would we expect to be given new or added revelation into the minor details of our lives?

We cannot expect Him to give us our own revelation because we have not been faithful in that which was already given to *another man.* The rich man in the parable of Lazarus begged that a new revelation be given to his brothers to avoid the place of destruction. He was answered, "... they have Moses and the prophets; let them hear them."[11]

We must find ourselves wholly obedient to the revelations of the men and women of Scripture. We should never find our lives in contradiction to what they taught, preached, or how they lived. Never should we find ourselves breaking a commandment of Jehovah, no matter how many times we have run it through our "filters" and changed it so that we can continue to live as we always have.

Stop the practice of filtering the scriptural commandments that were revealed to the godly men of the past! Before we can receive anything from God, we must first focus on being fully and wholly obedient to these revelations that were given to others.

---

11 Luke 16:29

Dual Citizenship

When I began to obey the revelations of other men, I became open to new revelation myself. This was only the beginning.

If you have followed this far and been obedient to what the Lord, through His Holy Spirit, has revealed to you, you now are open to receive new revelation, too! Consequently, the very hour He reveals something to you that requires action and you refuse—that is the very hour when that revelation will stop!

As we go through His questions together, we will find characteristics necessary to hear and obey the revelations. Even if we do not quite understand, we have "opened" ourselves. If we have repented, our lives are now a fresh, clean page upon which He can write the instructions for our remaining years.

He wants us to establish exactly who we are in this Kingdom of God. What is our citizenship? He teaches us that there is duplicity of identity, a dual citizenship, that could be very difficult to understand at first.

One day, Jesus and His disciples approached the Temple. As they walked into the court, at one side of where they were standing was a box with a hole bored in the top. It had likely been laying there since the days of Jehoiadah.[12]

As people walked through, they dropped a coin through the hole in the top of that box. One of the officers of the Temple noticed the disciples standing there and asked, "Does

---

12   2 Kings 12:9

your Master pay tribute? Is your Master going to pay the Temple tax?"

It is a curiosity to me that he even asked the question. Why was the Master's tax- paying practices in question?

Here we see the personality, or the lifestyle characteristic of Jesus Christ; it was so dissimilar from everyone around Him that He was *expected* to be different. He was expected to have different convictions. He was expected to do *something* different than everyone else. Why?

When your life starts to develop into the life that Jesus Christ has for you, you will find that *you* are different, as well. People will begin to inquire about your thoughts on particular Scriptures. They'll ask what *you* think about certain concepts, doctrines, and philosophies. Why?

People know that what you think is likely to be different from what everyone else thinks. They know that you are being led by a very different power and ideal, a different philosophy, a different *Spirit*.

Peter determined to ask Jesus about paying the tribute at his next opportunity. As he came into the house, Jesus anticipated the inquiry and asked him a question instead, *"What do you think, Simon? From whom do the kings of the earth take customs or taxes, from their sons or from strangers?"*[13]

Peter, not willing to put himself in the category of the children of the kingdom then occupying all Israel, said, "We are strangers."

---

13   Matthew 17:25

149

Jesus then asked, *"Are the children then free?* Nevertheless, lest we should offend, we will pay the tax."

The most familiar part of the story is what followed. Peter went fishing in order to receive the piece of money that was needed to pay the Temple tax.

Often overlooked was Jesus' very important question to Peter, which exposed the fact that our allegiances are necessarily divided while we are inside this kingdom of Earth. We have a *dual* citizenship—one is real, the other is unavoidable.

We are not children of this Earth! We are children of another kingdom and the way we see things is obviously going to be different. We *should* be doing things that don't make sense to other people.

We will be incessantly prodded and our patriotism will be questioned, but we must not forget the Kingdom from which we come and will someday occupy!

The natural tendencies to fight for rights and privileges in this kingdom will subside as we begin to see the Kingdom of God unfold before our eyes. Human patriotism tends to shed an unconditional love for those who are worthy only by virtue of the real estate they occupy.

To the contrary, prejudicial hatred for those who are on some other pile of dirt is often expected of a "good" patriot. Jesus taught us to go against this foolish, albeit natural "hatriotism," through one of His questions.

The loving Savior asked, *"What good is it to love those who love you?"*

It is a natural tendency for us to love those who love us, but it is not our *nature* to treat well those who despitefully use us and persecute us. A citizen of the Kingdom of God does not do good only to those who treat him well, but he or she does good to all.

When we understand who we are and the citizenship that we hold, we will understand that we *should* be marching to a different drumbeat. We are not of this world and thus should always have a very different state of mind than those who are!

It is most difficult learning to live in the Kingdom of God *only*, and letting the citizenship of earthly, political constructs fade into an immigrant status. We must move our focus from our temporary affections here on Earth.

When an ambassador travels to a foreign country, he is coached and taught the customs of that land in which he is to live so that he won't needlessly or unknowingly offend, and so that his own reputation as an ambassador will not be dishonored.

As citizens of the Kingdom of God, our own reputations in this country are always at risk. If we are to be ambassadors here, we must protect our reputations at all costs.

Do you hear the sound of negativity or finality in His voice when Jesus asked the question, *"How do you make salt salty again?"*[14]

The obvious answer is, "Well, you can't! It's not possible."

---

14   Matthew 5:13

151

We hear His agreement to our reply in His own answer, "It is thenceforth good for nothing than to be cast out and trodden under the foot of men."

Early in my life, I was taught that if we do not live in a certain way—a way that is pleasing to God—we will be cast out of the Kingdom and trodden under His feet. I have since learned that the Messiah was not speaking of the Kingdom of God rejecting us. He was talking about the men occupying the land of our *ambassadorship*.

Notice His words, "trodden under the foot *of men*." Jesus is giving us a warning, "They will tread upon you and will discount everything you say—unless your relationships and reputation are sterling!"

The Great Teacher puts a high value on reputation, and contained within that fact is the message that once it is gone, it's gone *forever*. We cannot get it back. This is why solid repentance and grave vigilance are necessary to develop and maintain the briny flavor the world so desperately desires in the people of Jehovah.

As we receive revelation from God and hear within us His words, there will be things that need to be changed in our lives. We must make those changes and make them *permanent*.

True permanent repentance is absolutely necessary so that we will make decisions according to the way that the Master has made so clear to us. There is no other way to maintain our cherished reputations. We must operate from *conviction*, not *convenience*.

Operating from convenience will allow us to do one thing one day and the opposite the next. We may have a "conviction" in the presence of a particular person or group and not have that same "conviction" when we are at home or alone.

If we are found operating from convenience, our reputation will be ruined and, as surely as salt cannot be made salty again, we will not be able to gain back that reputation.

Another problem area that affects reputation stems from an "American mindset" that declares to any antagonist the refusal to suffer. This attitude demands that we will not be wronged or cheated.

There will be plenty of persecution for that person whose faith is in God alone, the person who strives to enter the narrow gate. We will be stoned (figuratively, I hope), persecuted, and condemned by those around us.

How do we protect our reputations among those who hate us?

Jesus, of course, is our example. He suffered persecution constantly, but was always amazed at the *reasons* why He suffered persecution. His amazement was clear when once He asked, "*... are you angry with Me because I made a man whole?*"[15]

Perhaps we will find that it is not our sin or wrongdoing that angers those around us. Mostly, it will be the fact that we do good to those who do not love us or do good to us.

When we are constant to respond in love toward those who hate us, we are always in a position to ask our accusers the same questions Jesus asked, "*Many good works I have*

---

15 John 7:23

shown you from My Father. For which of those works do you stone Me?[16] Why are you angry with me because I've done good? For which good work do you stone me?"

These questions only fit into the life of a person who actually *does good*, who treats family, friends, and neighbors in a *good* way. They do not apply to those who are constantly squabbling and fighting to have their own way, suing those who wrong them, or making sure that no one cheats them.

Our lives, however, should be "full of good works,"[17] always abounding[18] in every good work. We only need to make sure that we are never accused for a good reason, and that when we do suffer, we suffer *wrongfully*.

Jesus asks, *"Which of you convicts Me of sin?"*[19]

Jesus' reputation could withstand scrutiny. It could withstand anyone examining His life by the Scriptures, and He felt no compunction at all to ask people to show Him where He had done anything wrong.

How many of us can stand this kind of scrutiny? Well, if our reputation has been as important to us as it should have been, this question should strike *no fear* in our hearts whatsoever.

You may say, "But, no one is without sin."

---

16   John 10:32 (NKJV)
17   Acts 9:36, "Dorca ... was full of good works and alms deeds which she did." Titus 2:7, "... a pattern of good works...." Titus 2:14, "... zealous of good works."
18   1 Corinthians 15:58, "... always abounding in the work of the Lord...."
19   John 8:46 (NKJV)

Don't get the two concepts confused. There is a state of being without sin (i.e., having never sinned). Then there is the person who says he does not sin as a matter of practice. This person can say that he "sinneth not" (as demands 1 John 3:6 and 5:18) without blasphemously claiming that he has *never* sinned. This does not describe a person who claims to be without sin, but rather, a person who has been born from above and been changed. Behavior displeasing to Jehovah is no longer a part of his or her daily life.

Of course, no one can say that they are without sin—or say that they have never sinned, but all who belong to the Family of God should be able to say that sin is not a part of their daily lives.

Nothing will destroy one's reputation faster than blatant outright sin. Get rid of it; get it out of your life.

Reputation

Upon hearing this concept, you may wonder about the neighbor that mistreats and persecutes you. How should you deal with him or her?

The Lord gives us no options here. *We are to love our neighbor.* We cannot find in the Scriptures that we should treat him or her as if he or she is *not* an enemy, but what we do find is that when we judge prejudicially, that is where the real sin enters the equation.

***

155

This is the morning the young man determined to hear Jesus speak.[20] Everyone has so much to say about Him. Many believed Him to be the Messiah!

This young man was a lawyer[21] and was sure that no Nazarene carpenter could trip *him* on the Law. He sees Him near the Temple. Moving through the assembly, he is able now to pick up the subject of this rather plain-looking man.

The One they called "Teacher" spoke of choices and repentance, of pleasing the Father and exercising power over the soul's sworn enemy. He spoke of promises to live forever and never having to suffer eternal death.

For a brief moment he forgets who he is and, like a hungry child, raises his hand and asks, "How do I inherit this eternal life?"

His own voice breaks the spell he is under, and he glances left and right to see if anyone noticed who had asked the question. Sitting down quickly and settling back into the mass of hearers, he tries again to blend in.

Now Jesus stands to find the source of the disembodied voice in the crowd. "Oh, no! Jesus is not simply answering the question, as I expected Him to do!" Their eyes meet and He casually points to the lawyer. With a twinkle in His eye and a smile He says, "You've read the Law; what did you find?"

---

20   Mark 12, Luke 10
21   *Nomikos* (in the Greek) is synonymous with "doctor of the Law or Scribe." These were men who were well studied in the Law of Moses but did not consider themselves to be theologians. They had the ability to argue the finer points of Law as evidenced in the story by the "loophole" he has found in the commandment to love his neighbor.

In the mental eternity known as an instant of time, a hundred thoughts run through this legal mind. "You've read the Law," He thought, "You've read the Law? I know the Law better than anyone is this city! He's making fun of me!" His heart begins to pound. "I'll show Him I *do* know the Law."

The sand sticks to his sweaty palm, as he scrambles again to lift himself in order to answer the Lord's question. Jesus is asking again, *"What is written in the law? What is your reading of it?"*[22]

As he smacks the sand from his hands he thought, "I know what He is expecting me to say. He expects me to list the Ten Commandments, but I know better." So he answered, "You shall love the LORD your God with all your heart, with all your soul, with all your strength, and with all your mind, and your neighbor as yourself." Then, to himself, "Now! What will He do with that?"

Jesus said to him, "You have answered rightly; do this and you will live."

Another flash flood of thoughts crossed the mind of the man. "What did He say? I am right? Is He tricking me? He must think that I don't live up to this ideal! I love the Lord with all my heart, soul, mind, and strength. I love my neighbor as myself (well, most of my neighbors).

Waving His hand back and forth, he speaks out, "And just who is my neighbor?"

Then Jesus answered by telling a story. He said:

---

22 Luke 10:26 (NKJV)

"*A certain man went down from Jerusalem to Jericho, and fell among thieves, who stripped him of his clothing, wounded him, and departed, leaving him half dead. Now by chance a certain priest came down that road. And when he saw him, he passed by on the other side. Likewise a Levite, when he arrived at the place, came and looked, and passed by on the other side. But a certain Samaritan, as he journeyed, came where he was. And when he saw him, he had compassion. So he went to him and bandaged his wounds, pouring on oil and wine; and he set him on his own animal, brought him to an inn, and took care of him. On the next day, when he departed, he took out two denarii, gave them to the innkeeper, and said to him, 'Take care of him; and whatever more you spend, when I come again, I will repay you.'*"

So Jesus finishes by asking the lawyer, "*So which of these three do you think was neighbor to him who fell among the thieves?*"[23]

Well, it went against the man's grain to say that the Samaritan was the one who was the neighbor (the Samaritans were hated so), but the answer was unavoidable, so he said, "He who showed mercy on him." There was no arguing the point.

Then Jesus really dropped the bombshell, "Go and do likewise."

Have you understood by this parable (as I once did) that we are being taught to go and do as the Samaritan did? Look again. The lesson that Jesus taught here was not to love our neighbor, but to judge our neighbor *without prejudice*.

---

23   Luke 10:36 (NKJV)

The subject of this parable was not "brotherly love." Rather, it is about *prejudice*. Who was the neighbor? It was the Samaritan. The neighbor was the *hated* one. It was the one against who was held *prejudicial* distaste, distrust, anger, and hatred.

Since I started to develop my lifestyle by taking my cues from the Spirit of God, I have found friends among some of the most unlikely people on Earth. Many of those people are not of my religious philosophy, skin color, or of my station and stature in life. But to do less is prejudice.

If prejudice is a part of evaluating our fellowman, we will shut off wonderful avenues of encouragement, enlightenment, and betterment of our own spiritual understanding. Sometimes the person that we least expect has a spiritual condition that is much better than our own.

We, as children of God, as children of His Kingdom and not children of this world, must be free from prejudice.

We may have developed a world around ourselves in which we hold certain positions or postures that cause us to be people who are held in high esteem among our peers. We may be considered spiritual people or leaders. We may hold stature in our congregations that, even at no desire of our own, have made us "above the average."

When this happens, whether knowingly or not, we may find ourselves looking down at others from time to time. We must recognize and resist this discrimination at all costs! This subtle, mental ranking of brethren is a form of prejudice that will cost us dearly in our Christian lives.

The first step to learning to suffer wrongfully is to stop injuring our fellowman by pre-judging him. Prejudice can make enemies where there are no enemies and it can convince us that we suffer for *good* reason when, in fact, we don't. We may even find another righteous brother suffering wrongfully because of us.

Simon, the Pharisee, had this kind of stature among his peers. He was, after all, a Pharisee, and he had learned, perhaps by the example of those around him, to evaluate certain persons as being "less" than himself.

In the Middle East, it is not uncommon to dine on the ground. While visiting in Israel a few years ago, my wife and I found an establishment that was designed to give one the experience of the Bedouin culture. We all sat on the ground with no table and we ate our meal in a reclined position. Some sat cross-legged on the floor, some reclined on their sides, but as was the custom, we all sat on the ground, as was the common practice in Jesus' day.

We can actually visualize the reclined position of Jesus when a woman of a lesser reputation made her way into Simon's tent where the Messiah was dining. With His legs folded behind Him, she was able to come and wash His feet and remain out of the sight of the dignified host.

The Rabbi spoke as if He knew her personally. He spoke of pardon and rebirth, of starting over, and power over sin. For the first time she felt hope of a new life rise within her. She walked the darkening streets of Nain, a town south of Capernaum. The calls of men and the lewd remarks flying from the darkened corners went unnoticed as she thought of the Rabbi she had encountered a few days before.

She remembered the peace that had flooded her as she unfolded her life to the sympathetic man who listened without condemnation. His words of love were not like the men to whom she had usually given her attention.

As she had done all day, she rehearsed the entire event in her mind. How she spoke of the snare in which her life was trapped—the never-ending circle of deceit and dishonesty, sex and sin, from which the only door of escape was repentance toward a God of purity—a God who would never accept a woman like her.

As she opened herself for the experience this new kind of man offered, a flood of peace, hope, and joy washed her clean and gave her a new life.

Everyone had heard of John the Baptist performing the *mikvah* upon repentant sinners. So, yesterday, forsaking her usual, late afternoon itinerary of seduction, she made her way to John in the wilderness.

She was intent upon being immersed in the waters of the Jordan River. Now that she could answer to God with a clear conscience, she was determined to start her life anew through baptism.

The hot sand beneath her feet turns to cool grass as she appears at the banks of the Jordan River. She found only John's disciples at the Jordan (for John was in prison for his righteous testimony against the king). Had she joined an insurrection? Had she allied herself to a group that was intent upon overthrow?

Her thoughts kept returning to her long-sought conversion and the new life that had been granted to her; she cared not a whit about the politics involved.

She told the awaiting disciples of John about her encounter with the Savior and was accepted with open arms. This time she was not taken into the arms of a man who was intent upon self-satisfaction. She felt as if her own father was holding her in safety and love.

She emerged from the water with ecstasy. As the water cleared from her ears, she heard laughter, but no one was making fun of her. They laughed with the angels who rejoiced from the sheer joy that a sinner had come to repentance.

From now on things would be different, and she knew it.

The night fell coolly on her clothes, which were now only damp at the seams, as she made her way back to Nain. She felt new. She felt clean. She had hope.

"What shall I do for the man who gave me such hope?" she thought, as she arrived home.

In her sparse dwelling there was nothing of any great value. All she had was her perfumed ointment that she used in her trade. Removing the stone in the wall (that only she knew was loose), she removed the expensive oil contained in the intricately carved stone bottle of pink alabaster.

Before she knew it, she was back in the streets again, and she was seeking the Rabbi. When she learned that Jesus sat at dinner in Simon's house, she felt a flash of hopelessness. How could she enter a Pharisee's house?

Arriving, she was encouraged to find many people there—so many, that she could probably blend in. Peeking into the tent with veiled face, she heard the precious voice of the Master speaking of John the Baptist!

Moving from side to side, she caught a glimpse of Him. She estimated His position and moved behind the tent where He was; she lifted the flap and crawled in low behind Him, out of view of the host and honored guests.

Jesus furtively glances behind Him and lets her know that He is aware that she is there. His encoded glance is returned by a bright smile that looks like that of a twelve-year-old girl. She almost giggles.

Suddenly, she looks down and sees the tired feet of many miles. She begins to rehearse her favorite thought again, and tears begin to fall. As her mind replays the beautiful story, her hands find water and towel, and she begins to wash her Master's feet.

Finally, she reaches into her bag and removes the precious oil. But, instead of merely opening it, she breaks the bottle and pours out all of the oil onto the feet of her benefactor in resolute determination of pursuing her new life: "This is all I have in the world," she thinks, but she brushes the thought from her mind as if it were a pesky fly.

No longer could she be hidden. The fragrance of the oil exploded in the room. People began to look about. There she was!

"… behind Him weeping; and she began to wash His feet with her tears, and wiped them with the hair of her head; and she kissed His feet and anointed them with the fragrant

oil. Now when the Pharisee who had invited Him saw this, he spoke to himself, saying, 'This man, if He were a prophet, would know who and what manner of woman this is who is touching Him, for she is a sinner.'"[24]

At last, it seems that Simon was not convinced that this dinner guest was indeed the Messiah. The question was still in his mind regarding whether he should believe this man and honor Him as the Christ.

Jesus answered and said to him, "Simon, I have something to say to you."

So he said, "Teacher, say it."

"There was a certain creditor who had two debtors. One owed five hundred denarii, and the other fifty. And when they had nothing with which to repay, he freely forgave them both. *Tell Me, therefore, which of them will love him more?*"

Simon answered and said, "I suppose the one to whom he forgave more."

Jesus said to him, "You have rightly judged."

Then He turned to the woman and said to Simon, "*Do you see this woman?* I entered your house; you gave Me no water for My feet, but she has washed My feet with her tears and wiped *them* with the hair of her head. You gave Me no kiss, but this woman has not ceased to kiss My feet since the time I came in. You did not anoint My head with oil, but this woman has anointed My feet with fragrant oil. Therefore, I say to you,

---

24 Luke 7:38-39

her sins, *which are* many, are forgiven, for she loved much. But to whom little is forgiven, *the same* loves little."

Then He said to her, "Your sins are forgiven … Your faith has saved you. Go in peace."[25]

Sometimes, in the questions of Jesus, we may answer, not realizing at first that our answers condemn us. This is one of the powerful things about His questions. When we finally are able to judge them rightly—even when we know the answer—the answer may condemn us. We must be honest and responsible enough to answer, take correction, and make the necessary changes.

Jesus was telling Simon, "I want you to know that this woman, whose sins are many, loves me because she has been forgiven. Compare her with yourself. When I came in, you made no overtures of love and care, but this woman, whose sins are many, has won forgiveness from God."

The disciples were not exempt from this discourse either. The story, told in another gospel, says that Jesus asked Judas, when he insisted that the breaking of such a costly bottle and pouring out of perfume was a waste, *"Why trouble you the woman?"*[26]

The question Jesus asked Judas is one we need to ask ourselves when we criticize acts of devotion that are different than our own. Why do we trouble those whose level of dedication, thankfulness, and gratitude seems to be different than our own? Perhaps we have inadvertently elevated ourselves to a higher level than we truly are.

---

25   Luke 7
26   Matthew 26:10

165

Prejudice, too, comes from a basic mistrust resulting from an insecure relationship with God. Consciousness of our own sin and shortcomings can purge the baser intellect of prejudice from us. Prejudice must be cleansed from us if we are to receive another word of revelation from the Lord!

Prejudice

Prejudice in our hearts requires some sort of measuring device. Whether that device is money, clothes, stature, occupation, or spiritual enlightenment makes not one bit of difference. However, prejudice involves measuring ourselves to be great and others less, or even if we measure others to be great and ourselves less, it is the measuring device that needs to be removed. The device is likely of our own making, and measuring is simply not our job.

Paul said, "Receive one who is weak in the faith, *but* not to disputes over doubtful things ... for God has received him. Who are you to judge another's servant? To his own master he stands or falls."[27]

It seems that money is the most common method of measuring a person's success and stature in life. Money is an unkind and harsh means of prejudicial evaluation that is utilized by almost every American. Every endeavor to better ourselves in this life has a monetary price tag attached to it; every day we are faced with new prospects that money can make available to us—while the lack of it can slam the door on opportunities.

---

27 Romans 14:1-4 (NKJV)

This daily enforcement of the power of money and our creaturely tendency to advance make *mammon* of money and *bigots* of us all. Citizens of the Kingdom of God have to properly respect the monetary system of the kingdom in which they find themselves, but we should regard the monetary system as *theirs* and not *ours*!

Faulty interface with the world's goods can greatly hinder our ability to handle spiritual goods.

I remember traveling in ministry to Nigeria, where a dollar of American money can be exchanged for a fistful of naira (their currency). As I walked through the marketplaces of Benin City, before making a purchase, I would ask how much the merchandise cost. Then I would look in my pocket to see how much money I had. Slowly I would have to look at the denominations on every bill and add them. When I did that, it became obvious to everyone that I did not know the value of naira.

The question in my mind was, "How much is this in 'real' money?"

This is not altogether a bad concept. To consider the cost of things in this life we should always wonder how much value it has in *real* money—in the currency of the *Kingdom*. If we are not careful, when money loses its assessment of value with reality, money ceases to be money, and then it becomes *mammon*.

The longer we stay "in country" the less we access *true* value. We start believing that the money in this kingdom is real and it is all that matters. So it is in our pilgrimage here.

While in Mexico, we met a man who chose to live there "because everything is so cheap!" He went there with only a modest amount of American dollars, but in Mexico what he had was a fortune in pesos. He lived like a king for a few years. As his money dwindled, however, he considered returning to the States in order to replenish his bankroll, but he found that he could not *afford* the return trip!

We must remember that we *will* return to our country one day. Have we forgotten the exchange rate? Have we forgotten the value of currency in our country? What will we have in store when we return?

Jesus asked a question to teach us how to deal with our money in this kingdom (in this life), *"This night your soul will be required of you; then whose will those things be which you have provided?* So *is* he who lays up treasure for himself [here], and is not rich toward God."* [28]

Living away from our home can warp our values and cause a person to consider his or her dream to be a reality and his or her reality to be a dream. Convinced that the Kingdom is delayed, prejudice begins to rule the individual's selfish heart. He or she may find his or her evaluations of purpose, money, and people skewed according to the world's value system. The eternal purpose for which he or she was born becomes slowly distorted and it degrades into ambitious survival; his or her money becomes mammon and people become like chattel.

"But if that evil servant says in his heart, 'My master is delaying his coming,' and begins to beat his fellow servants, and to eat and drink with the drunkards, the master of that servant will come on a day when he is not looking for him

---

28 Luke 12:20 (NKJV)

and at an hour that he is not aware of, and will cut him in two and appoint him his portion with the hypocrites. There shall be weeping and gnashing of teeth."[29]

Our value assessments in life should be realigned back to *real Kingdom values* in order to avoid this apostasy. Prejudice is the clarion indicator that we have not done that!

Whether a person is a pauper or a president, odious or opulent, we should consider *who* he or she is in the Kingdom of our God.

Jesus placed himself in the company of the undesirable and loathsome. He said that He was poor, thirsty, sick, in prison, and hungry.

It was said of Him that, "He eats (keeps company) with sinners." I am afraid the measuring stick we use today would put Jesus on the outside of our social circles.

Prejudice cannot be done without a measuring stick. A citizen of the Kingdom of God, who expects to hear the voice of God in guidance, cannot be involved in any kind of prejudice whatsoever.

---

29 Matthew 24

Faith

Faith will openly mark us as citizens and ambassadors of the Kingdom of God. Faith is the insignia, the flag, and the passport of every true ambassador from God's kingdom. Faith is what makes us different from all who are of this world.

We cannot muster faith on our own. It cannot be manufactured or successfully counterfeited. Faith is an endowment from our King, thereby marking us citizens from that *other* country, indeed!

Sadly, faith is not something that people of this generation have in abundance.

Abraham, the first ambassador, is known as the Father of all who are *in faith*. "Therefore it is of faith, that it might be by grace ... which is of the faith of Abraham; who is the father of us all."

Living by faith is not a new concept that started with the Book of Acts. Paul merely reiterated the Old Testament prophets when he stated that the *just shall live by faith*.[1] Faith has always been expected of Jehovah's children and it always pleases Him.

---

1   Romans 4:13-17

Philip and Thomas

Faith comes in all forms and intensities. When Philip discovered the Messiah, he ran to get his friend Nathaniel.

As soon as Jesus saw Nathanael, He said, "Behold an Israelite in whom there is no deception, no guile, and no deceit." (Wouldn't we be blessed to hear the Savior say this about us?)

Nathanael said to Him, "How do You know me?"

Jesus answered and said to him, "Before Philip called you, when you were under the fig tree, I saw you."

Nathanael answered and said to Him, "Rabbi, You are the Son of God! You are the King of Israel!"

Jesus answered and said to him, *"Because I said to you, 'I saw you under the fig tree,' do you believe? You will see greater things than these."*[2]

Jesus thought that Nathanael's faith was remarkable. "Do you believe on Me simply because of what I said?" The highest form of faith is faith based upon "Because *He* said!"

When we read the words of Jesus and believe what He says, it is a remarkable form of faith.

Poor "Doubting Thomas" receives a bad reputation. We should remember that even though Thomas had doubts, he ultimately *did* believe when he saw the nail prints in the hands of his Savior.

---

2   John 1:50 (NKJV)

"Seeing is believing," we say, but remember that Jesus required of Thomas that he should believe *before* reaching to touch His nail prints.[3] I believe he saw because he desired to believe, not the reverse. With us, therefore, it should be: "Believing is seeing!"

We, too, will see *if* we believe what He says! Then He said to Thomas, "Blessed are those who have not seen and yet believe."

Revelations will come to our spirits. Though we may have no reason to believe them, we will *know* them to be true! When we believe in the words that Jesus speaks, He said that we will receive even greater things. If we receive these greater things and have the ability to *see* them, we can place faith in those things, and by this build a foundation of faith that cannot be shaken.

The gospels give us more examples regarding how we are to believe.

There was a woman who believed the prophets' writings about healing being in the corners of the garment of Messiah.[4]

* * *

Her room smelled of potions and elixirs. Every thread of the fabric of her clothes was permeated with the smells of unsuccessful home remedies and the apothecary's attempts to cure her. Her health did not allow her to earn a living and her wage was not sufficient to restore her health. Her bloody flux made her despicable to the public; therefore, she lived alone.

---

3   John 20:27
4   Mark 5:30 - Luke 8:45

She had not been to the Temple since she was a child; for to approach a rabbi in her condition—well, she would have been stoned. But, she remained a woman of faith nonetheless.

As she lay upon her lonely bed, she thought of the lovely day when the Messiah would come and restore everyone, "With healing in the kanaph⁵ of His garment," she recited. Recalling the blissful memories of her youth, she could still hear the readings on the Sabbath echoing in the white stone halls of the synagogue. The memories would have to suffice, now that her physical condition had rendered her an outcast. Her only hope was in the Messiah's "healing wings" from a prophecy that Malachi gave long ago.⁶

It seemed by mere chance that the conversation of two men happened within her earshot. They were speaking of the new Galilean teacher *as if He were the Messiah.*

"Could it be?" she wondered. "I have heard of the rabbi Joshua of Nazareth, but can He be the Messiah? If He is, He will have healing for me in His kenaph!"

She strained to hear their conversation in the noisy street.

"The man was blind from his birth I tell you, and now he can see like a young man!"

Her mind calculated the possibilities. She thought, "If I could but touch his clothes … hmm."

---

5 Translated "wings" in many Bibles: actually it is the *tallis* or *tzit tzit* of a rabbi. They were the "fringes" commanded to be worn by the children of Israel. (See Numbers 15:38.)
6 Malachi 4:2

The next day, Jesus plodded along through the streets of a town in Galilee. He was being thronged by folks who were making demands on Him, asking for healing, asking for guidance, asking questions to gain His attention.

The crowds were pressing hard against Him; suddenly, He stopped. The clamor of people walking and talking and pressing in to hear, vanished so rapidly that only a few stones could be heard crunching under sandals.

He asked, *"Who touched me?"*

Mumbles, then silence again, as Jesus lifted His hand.

He asked again, "Who touched my clothes?"

Jesus was speaking only to the one who touched Him; only one person would know *why* He asked about *His clothes.*

His disciples said, "Master, everyone is touching You, what do you mean, 'Who touched Me?'"

Silence must have held for a while, as the crowd joined in the search for the accused.

As the dust was about to settle, our little woman, electrified with the excitement of being healed of a horrible plague, now felt wholeness in her body. She had received what she came for and her life was to be different from that day on.

When she came to herself, she only then realized the stillness that had replaced the noise and motion in which she had hidden herself. She heard whispers racing through the crowd, "Who touched Him? Who was it?" Not quite returned to reality, she did not hear their questions.

Then the voice of Jesus came booming forth in clear authority and undeniable request, *"Who touched Me—who touched My clothes?"*

The Scriptures say,

"And when the woman knowing what was done in her, saw that she was not hid, she came fearing and trembling, immediately and told him all the truth. Falling down before him, she declared unto him, before all the people, the reason she had touched him, and how she was healed."[7]

This touch was different than all the rest. In it lies some secret that is unknown to the theologians and the pious. Yet, it was a very natural act to this woman in need.

Her touch got the attention of Christ, not because it was odd, profound, or out of the ordinary, but because it drew from Christ what He usually had to exude as an act of His will, or in obedience to His Father's will.

This woman *took* from Christ that for which others begged. It impressed Him. It may have even disturbed Him a little. We are certain that it surprised Him, and, at last, pleased Him. You can almost hear a lilt in His response, as He comforted her and assured her that she had done well.

"But Jesus turned around, and when He saw her, He said to her, 'Daughter, be of good comfort: your faith hath made you whole; go in peace, and be whole of your plague.' And the woman was made whole from that hour."[8]

* * *

---

7 Mark 5:33 - Luke 8:47 (Combined)
8 Luke 8:48 - Mark 5:34 - Matthew 9:22 (Combined, edited)

Three Great Questions on Faith

As the disciples rigged the boat for a simple cruise to the other side of the Sea of Galilee, they had no idea that they were about to be called upon to rebuke the very forces of nature.

As the Master took a well-deserved rest in the hull of the boat, it began to pitch. The swells turned into waves and the breeze turned to a gale.

As an ice-cold wave slapped the breath from their tired backs, and their feet began to slide on the slanting deck, they realized that the storm had put them into a panic state. They ran to Jesus and awakened Him, saying, "Master, Master, we are perishing!"

When Mark tells this story he records the Savior's rebuke, *"How is it ye have no faith?"*[9]

To be faithless is a miserable existence for the Christian. Remember that the faith to be converted is a gift from God,[10] so it is entirely possible to be Christian and have no faith of your own.

The faithless Christian is doomed to push through his life with no communion, no guidance (except what he can glean from the advice of others), and certainly no intervention of Jehovah's power. *"How is it ye have no faith?"*

---

9   Mark 4:40 (NKJV)
10 Ephesians 2:8, "For by grace are ye saved through faith; and that not of yourselves: it [faith] is the gift of God"

Luke's account states, "Then He arose and rebuked the wind and the raging of the water. And they ceased, and there was a calm. But He said to them, *"Where is your faith?"*[11]

We have a tendency to look to *faith* only in times of trouble. Many of us wait to pray until things are out of our control.

Then, when we do have trouble in life, we may place faith in our bank account or our insurance policies, in our own wits, knowledge, or wisdom, or people in whom we have confidence. We may place our faith in assets of all kinds, *but we do place our faith in something!*

During this storm, when faith in God was absent, Jesus asked, *"Where* is your faith?" When faith in God is absent in our lives, it would do us good to consider *where is* our faith? When we find out *where* our faith is placed, we will be ashamed when it is not in the Messiah, His words, or His revelation. *Where* is *your* faith?

Frequently, doubt comes because we find ourselves in a troublesome situation with *very familiar elements.* Such was the case when Peter walked on the water. When he began to sink, Jesus reached, pulled him up out of the water, and asked him, *"Why did you doubt?"*[12]

I can almost hear the Savior imploring, "You were doing fine! You were walking on water! *Why did you doubt?*"

Now Jesus was not asking a *rhetorical* question. He did not, while shaking his head from side to side, think, "Oh, poor Peter; you are so stupid; oh, poor Peter, you don't have any

---

11   Luke 8:24-25 (NKJV)
12   Matthew 14:31 (NKJV)

faith." The Master was training Peter to consider this situation and determine *why* he doubted!

Peter was a fisherman. As a fisherman, he had grown up on the sea. He knew very well what waves and wind could do to a boat—and to a man *if he were not in the boat.* This *awareness* made Peter exceptionally vulnerable. The elements were familiar to him; in fact, he knew too much!

In Peter's experience, wind and waves were frequently severe problems for people out on the sea. On this night, that is exactly where he found himself—vulnerable to his well-known and frequent foes of wind and water.

The question, "Where is your faith?" *would not apply to Peter* because he had nothing in which to place his faith, *except* the Lord Jesus. In other words, if Peter had been standing in a boat and Jesus asked this question, Peter could have said his faith was in the boat, because he believed that boat would float, but there was no boat!

Neither would Jesus have asked Peter, "How is it that ye have *no* faith," because it is clear that Peter *had* faith, or he couldn't have walked on the water at all. No, the question that Jesus asked Peter was, *"Why did you doubt?"*

With these three questions we can analyze our own faith in God:

1) *"How is it ye have no faith?"* applies when we simply do not believe.

2) *"Where is your faith?"* applies when we do not have a solid faith in God, and we put our faith in temporal, physical remedies and any tools that may be at our disposal.

3) Finally, if we place our faith in the right things and yet we fail, we must ask ourselves, *"Why did we doubt?"*

By answering these three questions we can learn to have faith in God and learn what is causing us to fail. These steps, these questions, will help us repair the foundation of our faith.

People of faith will never be mistaken for citizens of the earthly kingdom. Rather, we will stand out as citizens of the Kingdom of God.

Testing Your Faith

The group of people intrigued by His teaching had grown to a multitude. They had to move to an open area in order to accommodate the throng.

They had followed Jesus to a remote location, and now evening was drawing near, and the people were getting hungry.

Philip took the problem to the Master. "This is a deserted place, and the hour is already late. Send the multitudes away, that they may go into the villages and buy themselves food."

But Jesus said to them, "They do not need to go away. You give them something to eat."[13]

The people were advancing toward them; Jesus looked at Philip and asked with a smile, *"Where shall we buy bread that these may eat?"*[14]

---

13 Matthew 14:15-16 (NKJV)
14 John 6:5 (NKJV)

Philip answered, "Two hundred denarii worth of bread is not sufficient for them, that every one of them may have a little!"

Philip was quickly moving into a panic mode, but notice what the Scripture says, "But this He [Jesus] said to test him, for He Himself knew what He would do."[15]

Let's further examine this question of Jesus.

When it comes to *living by faith*, invariably somebody will try to tell us about the devil and his role as tempter. They will tell us that the devil is tempting us, testing us, or trying us. They stress that we should not listen to the devil.

In reality, the devil is much more rarely involved in our battles of faith than we may think. We cannot be so quick to attribute our testing to the adversary; especially when we are fully engaged in conversation with the Lord Jesus. We cannot judge every challenging thought that comes into our mind as "of the devil." Sometimes the Lord himself will challenge us so we can objectively examine our faith in Him.

The words themselves are not sufficient to judge their origin. It is the *purpose behind the words* that reveals a good or bad source. Remember that a good solid doubt is better than any dishonest faith!

I meet many people who have a *dishonest* faith. When they find themselves in trouble, they just say with their mouths, "I believe that God is going to work everything out—all things work together for good to them that love God."

---

15 John 6:5 (NKJV)

Well, those thoughts may *seem* scripturally sound and pious, but in truth they ignore reality and do not show a *true* faith in God. If they hear in their mind the question, "How will you pay that bill?" or "Where will the money come from to buy groceries next week?" they may retort, "Get thee behind me, Satan!"

In truth, the questions that frighten us may very well have come from God himself—to test our faith and to get us to consider the *impossibility* of our situation, *because He is about to do something wonderful!*

"But this He said to test him, for He Himself knew what He would do."

This question became very personal to me one day when I first started the *Questions of Jesus* radio broadcast. To begin and establish the broadcast, it was going to cost well over $10,000!

This was money that we simply did not have, but the Lord had several times impressed upon me the need for this radio program to be on the air. Like Philip, I was miserable and afraid because I knew what the Lord wanted me to do, but I felt I had no way of accomplishing it.

One day, while driving down a highway in Oregon, this question of Jesus came into my head: *"Whence shall we buy bread that these may eat?"*

The best answer I could come up with was merely a modification of Philip's answer, "Lord, if I spent all I have, I could not supply enough that every man might take a little."

Then the story of Jesus feeding all those people on the hillside began to flow through my mind and spirit. I heard the next question, *"How many loaves have you?"*

At this, I cried out, "Why do you punish me? The facts show clearly that I *cannot* do this!" Then the rest of the Scripture came to me, "This He said *knowing what He would do.*"

The silence in the car was deafening. It continued until I got home. I fell to the floor and prayed and the phone rang— $11,000 to begin the radio broadcast! There was enough and fragments to spare!

Some would consider the challenging question that popped into my head, as the devil trying to break down my faith. We may struggle with questions that pop up about our faith, but we must not assign all such things to Satan. It very well could be that we are on the verge of a miracle.

The Lord Jesus asked this question because *He knew what He would do!* Without exaggeration, I can tell you that within forty-five minutes of this revelation, the means to initiate the broadcast was dealt into my hand by a single phone call!

Many times stories like this are told in order to generate or bolster faith and to give encouragement, but faith will not come to anyone by hearing my story! Faith will come only when we consider the situation in a frame of reality and not as an attack of satanic forces. When we are in reality, faith can then come by *hearing* (remember that word?) and hearing by the Word of God!

The Lord himself may be challenging us as He attempts to reveal to us, "I am going to make this impossible situation possible!" We need to be very careful that we do not consider the words of the Messiah to our own hearts as being the words of Satan.

* * *

Two sisters cried in each other's arms. Their lives had been in disarray during recent months. Ever since the new Rabbi, Joshua, came preaching through Bethany, Mary had tried to be in attendance, and left Martha to deal with the chores. Their brother, Eliazar, had become fond of the Teacher as well; in fact, they had become like brothers.

Poor Mary and Martha lost their brother, Lazarus, to death. Several days ago they sent for their Rabbi friend who spoke of the resurrection and the life; but He had not shown up. Oh, well, it was too late, for Lazarus was dead!

"So when Jesus came, He found that he had already been in the tomb four days. Now Bethany was near Jerusalem, about two miles away. And many of the Jews had joined the women around Martha and Mary, to comfort them concerning their brother. Then Martha, as soon as she heard that Jesus was coming, went and met Him, but Mary was sitting in the house."[16]

Martha ran toward the image on the road until it fully developed into the sad, but smiling face of the Messiah. He held her. Muffled by her cheeks pressed tightly against His robe in firm embrace, she uttered, "Lord, if You had been here, surely my brother would not have died."

Jesus grasped each shoulder and stood her at arm's length, as a father would do with a daughter in order to gain her

---

16   John 11:17-20 (NKJV)

full attention, "Your brother will rise again," He said with authority.

Martha sniffed and wiped her eyes; then she answered almost automatically, "I know that he will rise again … in the resurrection … at the last day."

Jesus said to her, "I am the resurrection and the life. He who believes in Me, though he may die, he shall live. *And whoever lives and believes in Me shall never die. Do you believe this?*"[17]

Confused now, she resorted to liturgical repetition, as if she were reciting from some responsive reading from the back of a church hymnal, "I believe that You are the Christ, the Son of God, who is to come into the world."

Jesus' heart likely ached at the realization of Martha's mechanical faith. The conversation broke off and she went her way, calling to Mary, "The Teacher has come and is calling for you."

Mary jumped from her fetal coil in the corner of the room that was now filled with guests and mourners. As she disappeared from the doorway, her guests said, "She is going to the tomb to weep there. Let's go with her." She followed her sister's instruction to find Jesus. He did not dare come into the town except secretly, but He was yet in the place where Martha met Him.

Then, Mary saw Him. She collapsed into a pile and clutched His feet, saying, "Lord, if You had been here, my brother would not have died."

---

17   John 11:25-26 (NKJV)

Jesus looked up and saw that a crowd had followed her. At first they were puzzled at the speed and direction in which she ran. Then it all became clear when they saw Jesus and Mary clinging to Him. Their next thought was, "Why couldn't this Man, who opened the eyes of the blind, also have kept this man from dying?"

Faith had fled. Unbelief was rampant. Sorrow had saturated the crowd. The situation was as disagreeable as it ever could have been for a miracle.

Unconsciously being guided by Mary, they arrived almost automatically at the grave, and Jesus took command of the situation. Lazarus was entombed in a cave, and a stone lay against its mouth. Jesus looked over at some able-bodied men, "Take away the stone." They scurried to do as He said.

Martha, now among them, said, "Lord, by this time there is a stench, for he has been *dead* four days."

Jesus said to her, *"Did I not say to you that if you would believe you would see the glory of God?"*[18]

His question to Martha is a question that we need to ask ourselves during our times of grief due to the death of a loved one in Christ (or even our own approaching death), *"Do you believe that you will never die?"*

Martha answered, "Oh, well, yes, I know in the resurrection that my brother will live again. I understand that."

Jesus asked again, as they continued their discourse: *"No, do you believe that you will never die?"*

18 John 11:17-40

"Oh, I know that *spiritually* we will never die."

"No," Jesus tried again, *"Do you believe that you will never die?"*

Sometimes we must take the words of Jesus, apply them and reapply them until they become a reality for us. As long as Martha believed that Lazarus was dead, she was destined to be despondent and sad; she would be destined to grovel in a "reality" that she felt was unchangeable.

When the words of Jesus are difficult, we must resist the temptation to turn them into something spiritual so that we can believe them. If He says that a person who believes in Him will never die, then that is what we must believe.

Even when all five senses say that there is a dead man lying in a grave, wrapped in linen, who had a testimony of faith in Christ—*are we still to believe* that whoever believes in Him will never die? Yes. *"Did I not say to you that if you would believe you would see the glory of God?"* Again, believing is seeing.

We must give no place to fear and sadness. We will see the glory of God if we believe what He says! Our faith separates us from everyone else in this kingdom. It is when we believe even though *there is no reason to believe* that we are shown to be citizens of another Kingdom!

When we don't believe what Jesus said, we place Him in a category *other* than the Messiah of God.

Many times, when people teach the story of Lazarus, they become confused or overly concerned about the fact that *Jesus wept.* Even the people who followed Mary looked at one another and said, "Oh, how He loved him!" But Jesus' tears were not for Lazarus. They were not for Mary, and they were not because "He did not want to bring Lazarus back from Heaven."

There are many explanations as to why Jesus wept. Look at the conversation with this woman who had sat at His feet and learned from Him every day. Even she had not arrived at the point of believing the words of Christ. I believe it was Mary's lack of faith that caused Jesus' tears and nothing less!

We must read the Scriptures and believe that what we read are accurate accounts. When the disciples feared not having any bread to eat, listen to the questions fire in rapid succession from a very frustrated Lord Jesus.

"Why do you reason because you have no bread? Do you not yet perceive nor understand? Is your heart still hardened? Having eyes, do you not see? And having ears, do you not hear? And do you not remember? When I broke the five loaves for the five thousand, how many baskets full of fragments did you take up? ...Also, when I broke the seven for the four thousand, how many large baskets full of fragments did you take up? ...So He said to them, 'How is it you do not understand?'"[19]

In Martha's situation He made her recall His promise. In this situation He called upon their memory of His past performance.

After the disciples had returned from the missionary journey with the seventy, He asked them a question, *"When I sent you with nothing, did you lack anything?"*[20]

---

19 Mark 8:17-21 (NKJV)
20 Luke 22:35

Jesus was reminding the disciples that He had been faithful in this past situation and, therefore, He will be faithful in the next. Many times it is the memories of our own experiences that allow our faith to grow from a mustard seed into a tree large enough for birds of the air to lodge in its branches.

As we progress in faith and believe God to bring about certain things in our lives and He faithfully answers, we will develop our own history of deliverance. We will be able to *remember*. Until then, as with Martha, we have His promises!

We must believe that He is the Messiah and what comes from His mouth is the Word of God. Then we can have faith in that Word. When we don't believe what He says, we tempt Him and we say with our actions and sometimes even with our mouths that He is not the Messiah and that His Words are not trustworthy—*but they are!*

There is a tempting, of sorts, that can take place when someone, even sincerely, asks the Lord to "prove" what He says or purports to be true. True faith makes no such demands. We seek revelation and await it patiently, but we do not make demands.

When they brought the coin to Jesus, with the question about paying tribute, He asked them a question. *"Why do you tempt me?"*[21] Let us presume that this question is for us, as well.

An honest answer to the question of why we doubt and tempt the Lord condemns us. If what He says is not true, He is not the Messiah, and we dare to presumptuously hold His

---

21 Matthew 22:18, Mark 12:15

commission in doubt because it doesn't make sense in our fallen minds. We must press further than the "reality" we see around us and believe His words. After all, we have **nothing** upon which to base our eternal salvation, except words printed in a book, spoken by someone we do not know, but merely promised to be true!

Don't let this thought distress you. This was (and *is*) the plan of Jehovah from the beginning. Redemption is to come by *faith*, so that it might be by *grace*, so that the promise of it will reach every person on Earth regardless of stature, ability, or education.[22]

We must believe those words are true! The gospel story is the door to faith in Jehovah. This is why we need to seek a revelation from Him, not a mere reading of the words or a memorization of them. Let the words in the Scripture become the Word of God and, be revealed to us so that it is *our* Word!

There is power in the realization when Jesus says, "Anyone who believes in Me, I will raise him up at the last day." He speaks not only to a group of people on a hillside 2,000 years ago, but, by revelation to us!

His words can transcend time and enter our spirits today. "You, I will raise you up on that last day!" Once that word has been spoken to our spirits, once it is received in our own hearts, we will never budge from faith—we will *know* that it is true! Not that a book is true but that He is true to His Word. Not that a prophet or scribe was faithful in copying the words book to book, but that He watches over His Word to perform it.[23]

---

22 Romans 4:16 (Author's interpretation)
23 Jeremiah 1:12

Your faith must be protected, and God must be respected.

Faith is not protected by willing ignorance of facts, but by dealing in reality *and* faith! Many times we pray, ask God for certain things, and we *do not receive them.* This is no secret, but it is treated like one. This is not something to be swept under the rug, pretending that it does not happen, or simply discounted due to "lack of faith."

When prayers are not answered or situations do not follow our requests, we need to analyze and examine our faith in full respect of the sovereignty of God and surety of His willingness to grant the desires of our hearts.

The apostle admonishes us that we ask and don't receive for a couple of reasons. One is that we may consume it upon our own lusts. We are still carnal beings—thinking like citizens of this world, not like citizens of the Kingdom of God. We are seeking and asking for the very things that He has already promised that He will give us, or things we should not want.

Our prayers are, many times, prayers of doubt, not faith. They need to mirror the scriptural examples; and if they do not, our prayers are muted in the halls of Heaven.

Jesus once asked, *"Shall not God avenge His own elect, though He bear long with them?"*[24] Do you *really* feel that you are going to pray for something that is good and worthy, just, holy, and right, and He is *not* going to give you what you ask for? He asked this question as if any answer, other than an affirmative one, would be ridiculous. *"Shall not God avenge His own elect which cry after Him day and night?"*[25]

---

24 Luke 18:7
25 ibid (Author's edition)

191

Faith in God is the coat of arms that we wear on this Earth. If we live like everyone else does, subject to the problems and uncertainties of life, fearing at every turn, with no faith in our Father above, who watches over us day and night, we look like fools to the world! We certainly don't look like we know anything about the Kingdom we claim as our home.

The world knows when faith is mustered, manufactured, misguided, and dishonest! It is the honest faith of the true Christian disciple that sets him or her apart as the *genuine* article. If we do not have an honest faith, our reputation in the world is sullied and made to be preposterous.

The world feels pity, not envy; they feel anger that no example of a true faith exists upon which *they* can lean for their own conversion. Many pitiful acts of "faith" become no more than "magic," or sleight of hand. Our "conversion" becomes some kind of behavior modification or brainwashing to them. These and other accusations that the world levels at the Church of God on the Earth are rightfully deserved if we display no true faith in God.

When we do not premeditate (conjure tales to convince) and we minister with a witness that is empowered only by the Holy Spirit, we engage the promise of the Messiah: "For I will give you a mouth and wisdom, which all your adversaries shall not be able to gainsay [contradict] nor resist."[26]

Our faith is to be protected. Our reputation is to be protected. Our citizenship is to be glaringly apparent, and the integrity of our sovereign God is to be preserved. If we maintain an honest faith, with no exaggerated tales of the supernatural, no lame excuses of failure due to arbitrary interventions of

---

26 Luke 21:15

evil spirits, it is then (and only then) that our lives of true faith will be irrefutable and inarguable to the whole Earth, and our citizenship is established to be *outside* this world.

Ministry

It is inevitable that anyone who has a relationship with Jesus Christ will want to share that relationship with those around him; however, Paul warns us about those who have zeal without knowledge. (I'm afraid that the Body of Christ is presently overpopulated with people who fall into this category.)

Zeal is good. Unfortunately, it comes at the *beginning* of the relationship when *knowledge* is at a minimum. Equally unfortunate is the fact that as knowledge *increases*, zeal seems to *diminish*.

When, with passing years, we become saddened and discouraged in our relationship with the Lord, when people want little to do with the life that we have found in Christ, we should analyze their reluctance accurately.

Perhaps the world wants nothing to do with the philosophy that guides the average Christian, because many of us who have attempted to coax them into a spiritual relationship do not deal with faith *honestly*. In view of this very serious problem, we should see the need to overhaul the common idea of ministry.

Ministries that are less than reputable and honest have not helped our reputation. By "less than honest" I do not mean crooked, but those who take liberties with the intangible and arguable aspects of faith. We may have to answer for the misguided and unscrupulous men we have consented to by our silence, for it seems that their reputations receive the majority of the world's attention.

More importantly, we should learn from these ungodly men what *not* to do!

The red-letter questions can help us here. The questions Jesus asked pertaining to ministry can help us avoid the pitfalls of illogical theology, vain and empty faith in God, and an impertinent, ridiculous gospel message.

Foundation

Whatever ministry we find ourselves in will undoubtedly have a "political" structure. The foundation upon which our ministries are built must be anchored upon the philosophy (the doctrine) of Jesus Christ.

As the Messiah's ministry was drawing to a close, He realized the disciples seated before Him would continue to be ministers. Jesus taught by a physical example exactly *how He wanted their ministries to be founded.*

He arose at the supper, His last supper, and girded Himself with a towel. Then He washed the feet of His disciples. When He was finished, He looked at them and asked, *"Do you know what I've done to you?"*[1]

Jesus was explaining by *example*: "I am a servant, and what I do to you, I expect you to do to others. You must mimic what I have done."[2]

---

1 John 13:12
2 John 13:14

If our ministries are not *serving* people, they are *outside* the framework that was established that night by the Lord Jesus. We are to be *servants*, not "shepherds" who reign over congregations (for there can be only ONE Shepherd).

In the example of our Lord, we must constantly pursue positions of lesser importance and promote others around us. Jesus never placed Himself above those to whom He ministered. Among His disciples, He made no pretense that He was anything but their Lord; and further demanded that it was to be so, but when it came to *actual* service, He was always found as the One who served. We, too, should always be found as servants.

When Judas became an enemy and a traitor, Jesus reverted to the position of a servant washing feet. In the Garden of Gethsemane, just a few hours after this lesson in ministry, Judas appeared with silver jingling in the bag on his belt. He stepped toward Jesus.

The Master looked at him and addressed him as if nothing had changed, *"Friend, why have you come?"*[3]

It is curious that He would call Judas "friend." Jesus easily could have said "Traitor, why have you come?" or "Enemy, why have you come?" I think there is a valuable lesson in His words—a lesson in humility, a lesson in *ministry*.

The Teacher, who taught that every idle word would be judged,[4] would not use words indiscriminately. When He called Judas His friend, He must have meant exactly what He said. Judas had been a part of Jesus' ministry. Jesus had

---

3 Matthew 26:50 (NKJV)
4 Matthew 12:36

been good to Judas. Now He assumed the role of a humble servant.

What a lesson in humility for us! We can see our example in the Lord's humility—even to those who are only a few minutes from planning His betrayal. He did not become indignant by exalting Himself even above His enemy. He did not condemn the betrayer, but rather, Jesus called him "friend." By His self-mortification, Jesus opened an opportunity for debate, but no argument came. It was indeed true that Judas was treated as a friend all the way to the end!

In the darkness Judas must have swallowed hard, but continued the treachery. He leaned over and kissed Jesus. In doing so, he confirmed, "No, Master, You have never treated me as anything other than a friend."

His conscience was burning within his breast, and his hands were likely shaking, as he had to stand there and listen to the next question Jesus asked, *"Judas, are you betraying the Son of Man with a kiss?"*[5]

It is unlikely that any ministry with which we involve ourselves will have a Judas-like member within the circle of influence; but, if there is, we will have neither right nor reason to judge that person or treat him or her any differently than anyone else. This is the mark of a minister who remembers the pit from which he was dug.[6]

A minister who has Jesus as his example is a servant who places his own interests *below* every soul within his influence. This is the foundation of true ministry. In many instances it would be very difficult to point out and identify many of the

---

5   Luke 22:48 (NKJV)
6   Isaiah 51:1

leaders of today's conventional Christian congregations by comparing them to the altruistic, self-denying, servants of the people we are commanded to be.

Remember the words of the Lord Jesus. For it is still true today that many leaders "… love the best places at feasts, the best seats … [they love] greetings in the marketplaces, and to be called by men, 'Rabbi' [Pastor, Father, Reverend]. But you should not be called 'Rabbi'[7]; for One is your Teacher, even Christ, and you are all brethren. Do not call anyone on earth your father; for One is your Father, He who is in heaven. And do not be called teachers; for One is your Teacher, the Christ. But he who is greatest among you shall be your servant."[8]

By His own exemplary life, the Lord taught us that we must be different! We have been given revelation. We are being shown by way of this revelation that servitude is primary and utmost in ministry. When this revelation begins to falter, our ministries begin to fail.

No doubt, we will be tested on this! The people to whom we minister *will* attempt to elevate us beyond our servant role.

Integrity

My God has been good to me. He has saved me from heartache and misery countless times. One particular time in my life came to mind as I considered these words of Jesus.

Many years ago, I was headed down a path that, I am convinced would have led to my destruction. I was a young pastor who seemed to have the right doctrine and the right

---

7   Exalted, teacher
8   Matthew 23:5-11

faith, and was becoming more and more firmly ensconced in mainstream Protestant religion.

Through a series of events, God showed me what my future would be if I chose to continue down this path. *He showed me the inside of another man's ministry.*

When brought into the inner circle, I became a major part of this nationally known ministry. It was headed by a man I respected, and I saw no perceptible differences between us. By his life and ministry, God showed me my own future.

Most people (including myself) would have considered mine a bright future. I would have had a respectable vocation with no real worries, but I was always on guard and defensive for my station in life. Paranoia reigned and hung over every conversation.

The part that sickened me most was the deception. It was rampant toward my fellowman, my colleagues, and my family. It was always at hand, especially in the presence of visitors and contributors, before the television cameras rolled or the radio microphones connected.

Deceit was required to keep good people giving their hard-earned money. White lies, embellishments, and facts omitted made testimonies more interesting and poignant in order to wring the hearts of the contributors.

Before long, I began to practice self-deception. I started to believe the stories! Secrecy became a part of my day-to-day life.[9]

---

9 Excerpt from *The Questions of Jesus*—© 2003–2007 Think Red Ink publications www.ThinkRedInk.com

A Pattern of Destruction

I escaped this experience and added knowledge (and much gratitude) to my life; however, I was not yet relieved of my "education." I witnessed the experiences of friends and other members of my family who were among world-famous ministers. Many times, I was made privy to the internal meetings of these ministries. Through the years I watched the disintegration of their ministries and reputations, one by one.

In considering their problems, I was able to see the pattern of secret behavior. Before the love of money, women, power, and the desire for fame took over the hearts of these men, secrecy was abundant—secrecy in the form of distortion of facts, willing ignorance, second bookkeeping ledgers, and selfish and wasteful usage of contributions.

The hypocrisy was considered a customary part of "ministry." More than the clothes changed in the dressing rooms of these men, there were new faces worn before the public. The families and close friends of these men hardly recognized them when they were in front of the cameras. Wives cried, children despised them, and every problem was covered with money.

Their guilt (although I did not witness guilt in all the men of whom I speak) was covered with the self-deceiving belief that *they were different.* They were "special men" who had been called of God for a grandiose purpose, while the truth of their wretchedness was held in *secrecy.*

During my days of involvement with these ministers and ministries, paranoia reigned over every action and word. Management of information became top priority. Espionage and damage control became a part of "ministry," when an embarrassing breech occurred.

Secrecy is a natural outgrowth of wickedness. Hiding actions indicates that we have determined that what we do is disagreeable—or we would not hide them. The gospel ministry has no components that should be hidden. Secrecy is not a part of evangelism and never has been.

According to Paul, even *our sins* are not to be kept secret. "Them that sin rebuke before all, that others also may fear."[10]

And James, too, instructs us, "Confess your faults one to another, and pray one for another, that ye may be healed."[11]

Secrecy offers a destructive power of "truth evasion" that can devastate the noblest Christian and topple the most sincere minister. Secrecy has no part in the justification of our actions, our ministry, or even our reputations as children of God.

Jesus stood in the doorway of the palace of the high priest of Israel. Bedraggled and tired from his long time of prayer in Gethsemane, He had, no doubt, been dragged out, through the Kidron Valley, and into the palace to appear before Annas.

Peter stood outside and he sidled up to the wall to hear what he could. There were echoes and parts of words, but he could not make out what was being said. Suddenly, he heard the unmistakable crack of a hand landing a stinging blow upon the face of his Friend. What had prompted such treatment?

Jesus was being questioned by the High Priest. Annas wanted to know all about His disciples and His doctrine. "Let

10   1 Timothy 5:20
11   James 5:16a

me in on Your secrets," he may have asked. "Tell me about Your plan, what is the scope of Your mission? I am a leader of men like You—*let me on the inside.*"

When questioned about His ministry, the Lord Jesus was able to look the High Priest in the eye and say, "I spake openly to the world; I ever taught in the synagogue, and in the Temple, where the Jews always resort; and *in secret have I said nothing.*"

His ministry was clear of any duplicity, deception, or mental manipulations. Our ministries must be also. We should always be able to speak freely about what is said in private.

Christians should not do anything that requires secrecy. We should be like open books to any inquiry into our purposes, strategies, desires, goals, finances, and indeed anything about ourselves. We should have clear and pure motivations for everything we do. We should press to the fore with our missteps, mistakes, and even the sins over which we stumble. Instead of justifying or hiding them, we should admit them.

The world is ready to receive, not perfect people, but honest ones. The beautiful gospel story of Jesus Christ suffers from its intemperate messengers who are either people who think they are perfect (and maintain that "perfection" through deceit) or they are foolish enough to believe that they are arbitrarily forgiven for every sin committed and that their lascivious lives should be overlooked.

Even our homes are havens for private meetings with ulterior motives and strategies. Our children should have license to speak freely about what and who was discussed at their dinner tables. Secrecy is a cloak of maliciousness. We should be wary of its power to mask undesirable conduct and language.

What we say in private should be EXACTLY what we say in public. Only then can we answer any who ask about our secrets, with the unaltered words of our Lord, *"Why do you ask me? Ask them which heard me ... they know what I said."*

Direction

Once we develop the foundation of our ministry (what our ministry *will* include and what it *will not* include), then we must decide its direction. Where are we going with this ministry? What are we going to do?

In order to develop the proper scope of our ministry, we must see with the eyes of Jehovah. It is very easy for ministry to take directions that have little to do with His purposes, simply by mimicking others.

Someone who noisily slurps the last drop from a cup can be considered ill-mannered. The sound of many guests doing it at once will send chills up the back of a hostess who, at the start of a wedding reception, has just discovered that there is nothing left to drink.

The mother of Jesus found herself at a wedding in Cana with just such a problem. The vessels were dry. With the lone exception of Jesus, this was a catastrophe to everyone in attendance.

Here we witness a metaphor of a common scene; what was very, very important to everyone else was of little concern to Jesus. His mother came to Him and said, "We have no wine!"

Jesus asked her, *"What have I to do with thee?"*[12]

Sometimes in the course of ministry, we, too, can find ourselves involved in things that are of little or no concern to our Father. When we implore His power to deal with these things, He may well ask why we are concerned about things that do not concern Him?

What we *should* do is find and move in the direction in which *He* wants to go! He may not care one whit whether we have new choir robes, a paved parking lot or padded pews. When we pray as though He *does* care about these things, and an influx of money facilitates the acquiring of them, we *assume* that God has answered those prayers. Worse, we will tend to think that the receipt of those funds proves He *wants* us to have these things! This is nothing short of covetousness that has gone to seed.

Within ourselves we can falsely feel as though our ministry is going *toward* what He wants to see accomplished. At the wedding in Cana, Jesus actually answered His mother's request, though we see by His answer that He did not really care that they were out of wine.

I believe that, in some cases, we are given what we pray for, *even though it is not necessarily His will*. When we cry about the things we do not have and then go about to acquire them, we are actually moving farther and farther from *His* ministry, while we attribute our success to His blessing!

How does this happen? How do we get into this situation that feels as though we are going forward when in reality we are going backward? It is because we have lost focus and communication. An honest evaluation may reveal that we have replaced the leadership of the Spirit with our own ambition. Good intentions, coupled with ambition exacerbated by poor communication, end with *confident* ministers proceeding in the *wrong* direction.

***

Two disciples fell far behind the group, as the rest of the disciples walked along with Jesus. Their falling behind was not because they were tired or merely slower. Ambition had risen and shown itself in their discussion, and they were ashamed for the Master to hear their conversation.

In the back of the pack, they had begun to discuss the new kingdom that Jesus was going to establish. "I wonder who is going to reign with Him? I wonder who is going to lead the new kingdom? Maybe I could be a leader?" One pointed at the other, "Maybe you could be His chief minister!"

After they had settled in for the evening, Jesus asked them, *"What was it that you discussed among yourselves?"* They looked back and forth at each other silently.

* * *

Our motivations and conversations can be very embarrassing when the Lord questions us about our secret ambitions. When we think we are out of earshot of the Lord, what thoughts arise? What is it that we secretly want?

I assure you that these motivations and thoughts will present themselves in your ministry. The truth will be apparent when the Lord questions you about your thoughts. It will be embarrassing to answer His questions about your goals and ambitions, if you have not developed the *attitude of a servant.*

Our goals should be centered upon those lost sheep that are out of the Way. Not just to add them to our congregational numbers, but to rescue them from destruction. If we have not learned *to whom* we minister, if we are merely involved in church building, we have not developed the mind and the heart of our Savior or His ministry.

Jesus asked, *"If a shepherd has one hundred sheep and one of them is lost, does he not leave the ninety-nine and go and search until he finds that one lost sheep?"*[13]

Jesus asked this question because He was attempting to establish a fact. When a man's concern is for the sheep, he *will* go after the one that is lost. When his concern is for numbers, he is satisfied with the flock that's left.

Why *would* a man risk his ninety-nine sheep and go and look for only one? Because he cares for that sheep! Not a number! Not a missing part of a whole! *That* sheep!

So, who are the sheep? To whom are we ministering? Let us never be guilty of not caring about the *one* simply because we have secured ninety-nine others! This would be shameful!

We are not commissioned to build "churches," denominations, or any kind of congregation. That is *His* business. All who are called the children of the God of Abraham, Isaac, and Jacob are commissioned by our Lord to be ministers to the *one*. We must always keep this task utmost in our mind.

---

13 Matthew 18:12, Luke 15:4 (Author's interpretation)

Ambition rears its hideous head at every opportunity. It is in the heart of fallen mankind to make a name for ourselves and to want to do bigger and better things. Ambition can only be honorable when it is the *Lord's ministry* that we are trying to build.

Jesus sat on the seashore as He gave Peter his commission. The wickedness of his ambition was exposed when he asked the Master about the job of another man (John). "... and what shall this man do?"

Jesus asked Peter, *"What is that to you? You follow me."*

It doesn't really matter what the Lord is doing in the lives of others. We are to fulfill our own commission. We must keep this utmost in our minds. It is very easy to look from side to side, but, if we do, we cannot simultaneously look ahead!

As I stood on the shore of the Sea of Galilee, I wondered to myself what this shoreline must have looked like every morning when the fishermen came back from their nights of fishing.

Peter was a fisherman and, as a regular part of his day, when the boats came back to the beach, he would sit on the shore with the rest, count his fish, and mend his nets. As a competitive fisherman, he would naturally look to one side and then the other. He was looking to see how the other fishermen were doing. All of his life, Peter had been *conditioned* to look side to side and be curious about how his fellowman progressed.

Jesus made it clear that in our ministries there is no room for side-to-side evaluation. It does not matter what the other people do or what they think. We are to do what we have been commissioned to do—that is to minister to the *one*!

**

The Feast in Jerusalem had come to a close. All the families had packed their belongings and started their treks homeward. Jesus' family was no exception, except that their twelve-year-old son was not walking along with His parents. He was thought to have joined another part of Joseph's family and was expected to come home with His cousins.

When the travelers arrived in Nazareth, they found that Jesus was not among them and they went back to find Him. They searched and searched and finally found Him in the Temple discussing the Torah with the doctors of the Law.

The boy looked at Mary and Joseph and asked them the very first of His questions that are recorded in the Scriptures, *"How is it that you sought me? Did you not know that I would be about my Father's business?"*[14]

It is interesting that Jesus used the term "my Father's business." Isn't that the "business" that we as ministers should be engaged in—our *Father's* business? The worried parents wrongly assumed that Jesus would be involved in things other than *the Father's business* or they would have found Him quickly, knowing exactly where He would be!

As we spend our time searching for the Christian life, truth, and things pertaining to godliness, many times we become distracted, because we assume that Jesus should be in *certain places*, doing *certain things*. Like Mary and Joseph, we may find ourselves disappointed when we don't find Jesus where we *think* He should be.

---

14 Luke 2:49

The Father's business was laid out in no uncertain terms on the day when Jesus stood in the Temple to read. He opened the scroll and read aloud His own mission from Isaiah:

"The Spirit of the LORD *is upon Me, because He has anointed Me to preach the gospel to the poor; He has sent Me to heal the brokenhearted, to proclaim liberty to the captives and recovery of sight to the blind, to set at liberty those who are oppressed; To proclaim the acceptable year of the* LORD. *"*[15]

In this Scripture we find the Father's business. Listed among the concerns of Jehovah, you will never find church constructions, development of softball teams, or all- night gospel sings. Although these things may be wholesome activities, they are inarguably *not* listed in the mission of Messiah.

We can easily find our lives taken up with *good* things; thus leaving the *best* things forgotten and undone. More importantly, we poorly reflect His light to the world when we merely attempt to clean up creaturely and sensuous entertainment and attach His name to pastimes and the things we categorize as "ministry."

It is time for us to go to work! It is time for us to *work in His vineyard*, not just invite Him to play in our playground. People are searching for a relationship with their Creator, and they are starving for real examples of conversion. They do not want to be better ball players or be merely entertained for an evening; they want to see *real examples* of *changed lives.* They want healing for their broken hearts, they long for their blind eyes to be opened, and they want no longer to be held captive in their prisons of habit and self-loathing.

---

15   Luke 4:18-19 (NKJV)

Is it the least bit coincidental that when these seekers come to our fellowships searching for Jesus (just as Joseph and Mary did two thousand years ago), they find no one "about the Father's business?" They most certainly surmise that they have looked in the wrong places and go home severely disappointed.

Jesus has come "to seek and to save that which was lost." When our ministries do not focus on the problems of society, we are useless to the purposes of Christ.

Our ministry is to display *to the world* the truth that Jesus changes lives! He changes lives because He, as the Messiah, has been commissioned to do so; and just like He said, "… as my Father hath sent me, even so send I you."[16]

The people of the world need to learn of the Messiah and apply His lifestyle to theirs. Then, when they have truly encountered the Christ, they will be known by the Father. Joy upon joy will be ours in eternity if, through our ministry, the lost have received revelation from the Father that Jesus is indeed the Messiah!

It is time to evaluate our ministry. It is critical to see how effective we are. Perhaps we could do this like Jesus did—He asked a question.

The disciples were gathered around the fire. As it grew quiet, Jesus asked them, *"Who do they say that I am?"*[17]

The people in the communities where we live and minister "see Jesus" because of *our* testimony and ministry. Do they say that Jesus is just "a really nice guy that died for our sins?"

16   John 20:21
17   Matthew 16:13, Luke 9:20

Do they think that because He died, they get to go to Heaven one day? Do they say that He is a fictional character who weak people use as a crutch? They only know what they see in us. Do they see us panic and experience fear when death touches our families, as they do, "... even as others which have no hope"?[18] These examples are not attempts to merely oversimplify. The lives of us who call ourselves "Christian" portray Him to the world.

When we meet a person who is truly seeking and wants to please God, and we witness a true desire for change, are we guilty of saying (either by our life or our words) that everyone "must sin every day?" Do we pass on the idea that all he or she needs to do is to ask for forgiveness even when the Scriptures clearly teach that *repentance* is needed?

We cannot answer properly, because we have no answers for ourselves. Many have misspent their Christian lives in churches singing songs, learning liturgies, and studying dogmas. They have never set upon the task of *preaching the acceptable year of the Lord*. The Messiah's ministry was to usher in the *Jubilee*, and we who have been counseled to avoid the Old Testament, do not even know what that means.

Does our ministry prepare people to receive revelation or does it merely attempt to educate them?

Jesus asked the disciples, *"Who do they say that I am?"*

"Well," Peter said, "Some say that You are John the Baptist. Some say that You are Elias."

---

18 1 Thessalonians 4:13, "But I would not have you to be ignorant, brethren, concerning them which are asleep, that ye sorrow not, even as others which have no hope."

Then Jesus asked Peter, "But, who do you say that I am?"

Peter answered, "Thou art the Christ, the son of the living God!"

Undoubtedly, we have heard numerous sermons on this discourse, but let's look at it again. Did Jesus say, "Oh, good for you, Peter; you must have learned that in Sunday school?" or "Oh, you must have learned that in seminary."? No! His response should bring great revelation to us. Jesus said, "Simon, *the Father has revealed this to you.*"

So Peter received a revelation! He did not receive an education! He did not simply deduce by the words of another, nor just hear in the lyrics of a song that Jesus was Messiah; it was *revealed* to him!

The fact that Jesus is the Christ must be *revealed*. It cannot be told by proclamation, taught by education, or caught by contagion. Our ministry is not to go around *proclaiming* Jesus to be the Messiah. We are not to simply *say* that Jesus is Lord. We are not to *teach* people that He is the Christ.

The overall lesson of this book is that we are to make *disciples* of all nations so that they will learn to follow Jesus Christ. Only the Father can reveal to them that He is the Messiah![19]

It is up to the Father to give revelation. It is not our job to cram truth into the heads of people. Frankly, we *cannot*. This Scripture reveals that it was never Jesus' intention to *tell anyone that He is the Christ*, for He looked straight at Peter

---

19   John 6:44

after his confession of Jesus being the Christ and charged him in no uncertain terms to tell no one![20]

Now, why would Jesus tell Peter not to tell people that He was Messiah? Isn't that what we are supposed to do? This message to Peter makes it clear that this is the work of the Holy Spirit. What we are to do is to teach people how to be *disciples*. To do this we must discipline ourselves and live in such a way that the Spirit of God can reveal to us and others that He is the Messiah.

Those who have been *told* that He is the Messiah know nothing! If we have merely deduced that He is the Messiah, we know nothing. It must be revealed to us by the Father!

The fact that Jesus Christ is the Messiah is something that is revealed to each person individually. It is revealed only by the Holy Spirit. When it was evidenced (when Jesus performed a miracle) He would always say, "Don't tell anyone! Don't tell anyone that I am the Christ." He knew that revelation *is His Father's business;* otherwise, no one will truly know Jesus Christ as the Messiah. *People do not seek revelation when they think that they already know.*

While standing before Pilate, Jesus heard the ruler profess suspicion that He was indeed the King of the Jews, the Messiah, and asked him *"Sayest thou this thing of thyself or did others tell it thee of me?"*

This is the very same question the Savior asked Peter: "Is this something that has been revealed to you or is this something that somebody has told you?"

---

20 Luke 9:21

Jesus knew that the answer to this question would make a great difference. If this had been revealed to Pilate, then Jesus knows the Source of revelation. But if this were something that had been told to Pilate, then, of course, the ruler was just mouthing something that somebody had said, revealing nothing about his own beliefs.

There are many people who believe that Jesus is the Christ because they have deduced it. Some believe because they are afraid to believe anything else. Some believe because they *have been so educated*. Our purpose and ministry need to be focused on helping people reach a certain stage in their lives in which the Father can reveal this truth to them.

This is done only through discipleship. "Go ye therefore, and *teach* [make disciples of] all nations … *Teaching* them to observe all things whatsoever I have commanded you …"[21]

A disciple is a student, a student of the true, living Word of God—Jesus, the Christ. "And the *word of God* increased; and the *number of the disciples multiplied* in Jerusalem …"[22]

Ministry requires wisdom, for, "… he who wins souls is wise."[23] To win a soul is to win a person to discipleship. If we make obedient and astute disciples, we open communication between the disciples and their Father.

If *the Father* reveals Christ to a disciple, if *He* heals a broken heart, if *He* delivers him or her, we have helped to bring about a true conversion. We have actually won a soul *in reality*. We can know that this is no longer a lost soul, because that soul

---

21 Matthew 28:19-20
22 Acts 6:7
23 Proverbs 11:30 (NKJV)

is now open to receive the revelation of God the Father--that His Son is indeed the Christ!

The Message

Now, having thoroughly discussed our ministry's structure and foundation, and determining the direction our ministry is to take, we must consider our *message*.

In having decided what our message is *not*, we now face the question of what *is* our message to the world--and *how will we deliver that message?*

It can be an emotional encounter for a person who is lost in sin to come to Christ. We must be careful that our message does not evoke emotion for the sake of emotion. The "ends" (the actions related to Christian living) are not our goal. Even the "means" (the reason and motivations, the empowerment and purpose) are not to be pursued in and of themselves.

Our mission is to help those who are seeking a relationship with their Creator set up an obedient lifestyle that will *facilitate that relationship.* Obedience is a natural outgrowth of discipleship and revelation.

Emotion

Emotion as a means to conversion is a cop-out. It is a lesser grade of motivation.

Emotion can induce obedience, but it is short-lived and subject to change. Dedication to personal revelation is lasting. It is an effective motivation to Christian living. It creates a tie to the Source that is not subject to circumstances or mood, personal priorities, or distresses.

If we consider our emotions candidly, we will be hard-pressed to determine a difference between the tears in our eyes when we hear our country's national anthem or when we sing "O How I Love Jesus."

We must remember that theology is not poetry and poetry is not (necessarily) theology. By the word "poetry," I do not mean the metrical writings or the production of a poet, per se. For clarification, I offer a *secondary* definition of the word, "The language chosen and arranged to create a specific emotional response through meaning, sounds, or rhythms."[24]

This should not even have to be said, but, regrettably, evoking emotion is a preferred form of teaching and preaching that should be extricated from the syllabus of the man *of faith* and those who have been endowed with the grace of the gospel message.

Emotion is a major factor in the reverting of the sinner to his prior state (backsliding) and the overpopulation of denominations with less than dedicated persons of no real conviction. (It does, however, keep 'em comin' back for more!)

Jesus once asked His disciples, *"Why are you so sad?"*[25]

To ascertain the *cause* of our emotions is a most valuable endeavor. However, we must never resort to *evoking* emotion as a sign of the movement of the Spirit.

The Stranger on the road to Emmaus found that the disciples were sad on what should have been considered the happiest day of their lives. Because their emotions had

24 ©2000 Merriam-Webster, Incorporated
25 Luke 24:17

taken control of them, they were not present to witness the Resurrection of the Lord Jesus, nor were their minds open to receive such a supernatural event.

Some may argue that the disciples had *reason* to be sad. If this is true, why did just a few sentences from the Stranger change their sadness to ecstatic joy? They simply lacked *knowledge* of the facts. Knowledge has a very difficult time breaking through emotions.

Many people are locked into a circular Christian experience because of emotions. They feel that they have experienced repentance simply because they are "sorry" for their sins. The circle is completed as they continue to seek this sorrow to assure themselves of their salvation. This emotional merry-go-round is *not* a tool that is suitable for use in ministry.

When supernatural experience causes emotion, it is fine; however, it is absolutely *backwards* to attempt to evoke a spiritual revelation by way of emotion. Our message is a simple truth about faith and obedience.

After bringing a soul back to life, Jesus asked the man, *"Do you believe on the Son of God?"* This is a very simple question, but it required a soul-searching answer.

Jesus did not ask how he *felt* about the Son of God or ask him to emotionally evaluate his condition before God. Nor did He demand that the man should be sorry for his present status of sin and/or lack of repentance. His pointed question was, "Do you *believe* on the Son of God?" For Jesus, emotion was *unimportant*--it had no bearing on the question or its answer.

Simply put, your message can only be: *believe and obey*; nothing more, nothing less. If true faith is placed in the Son of God, that life will reflect that belief. *If* he or she believes in the Son of God, it will be seen in his or her works; it will be displayed in attitude, language, and philosophy of life—*every* day!

Unfortunately, many ministers in whose hands the charge of the gospel has been placed have not come to terms with this concept of *believing* on the Son of God. You and I are required to share the gospel with those who do not believe. This can easily include those who are in this emotional circle--those who have never really believed, but only hoped, and, therefore, seek the weekly recurrence of sorrow (or joy) to bolster that hope. Their bellies are empty of the Bread that fulfills for a lifetime. They thirst for the water that springs up from within to everlasting life.[26]

Loaves of Life

In order to make a feasible and sincere offer, *we* must have the Bread of Life in our possession. If we do not have the Bread of Life ourselves, how can we offer it to others? How is it possible to feed others with bread that we do not have in our possession and have never tasted ourselves?

Jesus taught that *He is the Bread from Heaven*.[27] In ministry you must first examine your own cupboard. Jesus asks, *"How many loaves do you have?"*[28]

26 John 4:14
27 John 6:48
28 Matthew 15:34, Mark 6:38, Mark 8:5

When it came time to feed the multitudes, and because it would be their commission to deliver the bread to those who were hungry, Jesus looked out over the multitudes as if to count them, and asked His disciples, "How many loaves do ye have?"

Even so, as those attempting to distribute the Bread, we must ask ourselves two questions: Do we *have* it? Do we have it to *spare*?

When Jesus asked how many loaves were present, He was given a number that was well below the requirement. The answer came back, "Five loaves and two small fishes." They *had* the bread, they just did not have it to *spare*.

If we have not settled the matters of our own faith in Jesus Christ within ourselves, we *do not* have bread to spare. Unfortunately, in the modern-day scheme of things, ministers who have no bread of their own (much less bread to spare) are offering food to others.

Today's minister will often claim, unashamedly, that he or she *struggles as much as anyone*. If this is true, *what*, then, does he or she have to offer? Some even come close to bragging that they *sin every day*. If they have this much trouble with their own sin, then what hope can they offer?[29]

Some ministers claim that they *hunger and thirst to know Him*. If they don't know the Bread of Life, then what bread *have* they encountered and, more importantly, what bread are they offering to the multitudes of the hungry?

---

29 Hebrews 7

They insist that we are to just do as they must do--get their bread from the Savior. This concept within itself is not wrong, but if we are to be *ministers of the gospel*, we must have that bread within our possession, and in abundance!

If you do not have it—if you have not encountered the Bread that forever satisfies,[30] if you have not drank from the well that quenches thirst forever,[31] you must leave the ministering to someone else. When the hungry can do nothing more than commiserate with others who starve, we witness the classic situation of the *blind leading the blind*.

Jesus asked, *"Can the blind lead the blind?"*[32]

When Jesus asked this question, there is an overtone of impossibility in His words. (Not that it is impossible for the blind to lead the blind, for the blind lead the blind every day.) Nevertheless, He continues, *"Shall they not both fall into a ditch?"* Such a situation is as if someone with cataracts is leading another who is suffering with myopia.

Can this method ever be successful? If you intend to "minister" as a vocation, these warnings are not for you; however, if you want to win souls, if you want to set at liberty those who are captives, if you want to open blind eyes, you must have the ability to *see!*

Supernatural revelation gives us sight. We have received this outlook from the Bread of Life himself. We have, by obedience, ingested it and have forever satiated the longing within us to worship *Who we know*. We have engaged full

---

30   John 6:35
31   John 4:14
32   Luke 6:39 (NKJV)

deference to our God's commandments and find our lives perfected more and more every day.

If these concepts are not familiar to you, and these words do not describe *your experience*, you may stand, as a minister, in a position where "food" that you do not have will be demanded of you.

Jesus was puzzled many times by the religious leadership because they lacked the basic understandings about salvation, repentance, redemption, the Kingdom of God, and the general ministry of the Messiah.

In order to *have* a ministry, we must *be ministers*. We must have settled within ourselves all of the facts and established within ourselves that we do indeed **believe** in the Son of God.

Humanistic leadership fails in this regard over and over again. Our leadership, our guidance, and our teaching must come from *The* Teacher. Jesus said it like this, "*One* is your teacher"; "*One* is your master." He said this to *me*. He is saying this to *you*. He says this to us *all*.

❊❊❊

The Pharisee Nicodemus peers at the camp of Jesus and His disciples from across the valley. He can see the firelight, and the wind carries faint laughter and conversation to his ears.

As he approaches their camp, he wonders whether he'll have the courage to ask the Messiah the question his young lawyer friend had asked, "*What does my life lack?*"

His image now appears from the black backdrop surrounding the fire. A friendly hand waves high above the firelight. Jesus recognizes him and beckons him to join them. After a few simple pleasantries, Nicodemus, unable to contain himself, can only blurt out an awkward compliment, *"Rabbi, we know that You are a teacher come from God; for no one can do these signs that You do unless God is with him."*

Upon first glance, a person may think that Nicodemus had a faith in Jesus and believed in Him to be the Messiah. You might say that he actually *believed* in the Son of God. But did he?

Jesus knew why Nicodemus was there. He was not put off by the accolades offered to Him. The Master responded, *"Most assuredly, I say to you, unless one is born again, he cannot see the kingdom of God."*

It seems that Nicodemus's idea of Christ is not much different from the thinking of many modern Christians. Certainly we believe that He is the Christ and that He speaks the Word of God truly. Of course we do! No one can do the things Jesus did without the help of the Father--*but do we believe on the Son of God?*

Had Nicodemus believed on the Son of God, he would have been filled and infused with the Holy Spirit. There would have been a *spring* within his soul, the *living water*, which he could have then offered to other people. But Nicodemus had only "lack" in his possession. This is why Jesus did not respond to his compliments.

Isn't it curious that Jesus did not say, "Why, thank you, Nicodemus; that's very kind of you to say so, and you, too, are a wonderful man." Instead, Jesus responded, "Nicodemus, you must be born again."

* * *

The experience of being *born again* has taken a thorough battering in recent years. People who have no idea of what this statement means claim to possess it for themselves.

To be *born again*, or more correctly as the Scriptures say, "born from above,"[33] means to have taken on a new life from the realm above.

When we have been born again and have taken on new life--when we are filled with the Spirit of God from above--we have received the vital bread and water from Heaven, and we will never be thirsty or hungry again!

"… My Father gives you the true bread from heaven. For the bread of God is he who comes down from heaven and gives life to the world. I am the bread of life. He who comes to me shall never hunger, and he who believes in me shall never thirst."[34]

How would you attempt to reconcile these words of Jesus with the words of most Christians who, when dissatisfied with their "church" experience, will often say, "I'm not *fed* there," or "That sermon was as *dry* as dust"?

These and many other statements that are heard far too often confirm that the Body of Christ at large is hungry and thirsty. There can be only one conclusion to draw from this fact: these people (and perhaps you, too, my friend, if you feel hunger and thirst in your soul) have *never received* the Bread from Heaven nor drunk from that spring that He offers.

---

33   The word "again" was translated from *anothen*, Greek, meaning "from above."

34   John 6

How else can you explain the promise of the Messiah? Was He merely exaggerating? Was He speaking in unwarranted hyperbole? His promise was that if you *ever* eat of this bread you will *never* hunger again; if you drink of this water that I shall give, you will *never* thirst again.

Nicodemus was concerned because Jesus had said that if a man is *not* born again, he will *not* see the Kingdom of God. He was confused and probably a little scared.

"If a man is not born again, he shall not enter the Kingdom of God," Jesus continued.

Nicodemus, in his apprehension, asked questions like, "How can I be born again? It doesn't make any sense. It is a physical impossibility."

Jesus retorted, "You do not understand spiritual things. The spirit is not like the physical realm; you don't have to enter into your mother's womb to be born again. Look at the wind; can you see the wind?"

You may want to answer, "Of course we can see the wind!" but, in reality, you *cannot* see the wind. You can only see its effects on the Earth--the movement of the grass and grains in the fields.

Jesus said that that wind blows where it wants; no one knows where it comes from or where it's going.

Just because we can see the *effects*, feel the *effects*, or hear the *effects* of the Kingdom of God does not mean that we can *see* the Kingdom of God!

Then Jesus asked Nicodemus a very probing question that should have prompted introspection in him, *"Are you a master of all Israel and don't know these things?"*

Are you a teacher, a respected leader, pastor, seminary professor, etc., and don't know these things?

Jesus was *astounded!* How can a man to whom others look for guidance and direction have no idea about the Kingdom about which his students inquire? Is that possible? Yes. It happens every day. How can students (disciples) accept guidance and direction to the Kingdom from a man who cannot even see it? If we intend to minister to a lost world about the Kingdom they cannot see, we must be able to see it ourselves!

Is Jesus still astounded today? Probably not. It's been going on for about 2,000 years!

When John the Baptist appeared on the scene, he was rejected by the conventional religious leaders and organizations of his day and was fully accepted by the sinner. The reason he was rejected by the leaders is because they could not see the Kingdom of God or any of its citizens.

They had no idea that John the Baptist was born at a very precise time during the Passover/Feast of Unleavened Bread. They did not know that the Messiah's birth followed six months later at the Feast of Tabernacles. They did not understand the Father's way or His schedule of events, so they could not *see* the Kingdom of God.

The religious people of the day did not understand the calendar by which the Kingdom of God operates; therefore, they rejected John's commission. When they rejected his commission, they automatically rejected his *message* as well.

Jesus did not ask the Pharisees how they *felt* about what John the Baptist had to say. He said, *"Let me ask you a question, did the Father commission John the Baptist or not?"*[35]

In order to answer Jesus' question *accurately*, they had to understand the message *and* the prophesied presence of John the Baptist. In order to answer it *honestly* they had to be able to *see* the Kingdom of God, something they were not able to do!

Jesus was constantly saying and doing things that were very hard for religious people to digest. He just didn't fit into their frame of understanding. Likewise, many Scriptures today do not fit into the frame of denominational understanding. Compensation is made for misunderstanding, and His words are changed somewhat or interpreted differently in order for people to accept them.

They do not have the right to do that. Just because a certain Scripture offends us, we cannot arbitrarily change it to say what we *want* it to say.

There was a time when Jesus had thousands of people following Him. One late afternoon a hungry crowd stood on hillsides far from their homes. They had heard that Jesus was prone to serve a nice free meal after preaching, and they were wondering if He would feed them, too.

Jesus understood their intentions and said, "Most assuredly, I say to you, you seek Me, not because you saw the signs, but because you ate of the loaves and were filled." He

---

35 Matthew 21, Mark 11, Luke 20

was pointing out to them, "You only follow me because you want something to eat."[36]

Later He added a question, "If you really want something to eat, then why not eat my flesh and drink my blood?" This was absolute pagan heresy! Jews are forbidden to ever taste blood. If they were to accept these words of Jesus, it would go against everything they ever understood as being right and pure before God.

Jesus, knowing their thoughts, asked a very strange question, *"Does this offend you?"*

What will *you* do when the words of Christ offend you? Consider the final question of the Messiah to this hungry crowd, *"What, then, if you should see the Son of Man ascend where He was before?"*

And finally His summation, "It is the Spirit who gives life; the flesh profits nothing. The words that I speak to you are spirit, and *they* are life. But there are some of you [my disciples] who [yet] do not believe."

Do you see in this discourse that when our concept of the Kingdom of God is distorted, we may have no place in our minds for His words? If we could see the Kingdom of God, if we knew everything that He knows, everything He has ever said would make perfect sense!

What if we cannot understand? What if we cannot yet *walk by sight*? This is our opportunity to walk *by faith*!

---

36 John 6:26

If we only would *believe* on Him as the Messiah, we would change our thinking to accommodate His words, not change His words to accommodate our thinking.

If we would *walk by faith*, we would change *our* theology to accommodate His doctrine, not change *His* doctrine to accommodate our theology.

In my present understanding of theology, I must admit that certain words in the Scriptures are very difficult for me. I would prefer that some things in particular had never been said by Jesus.

This mental process of reducing the words of Christ into our thinking while conveniently leaving out certain passages we do not like or understand is nothing short of wishing our Lord would just go away!

This is not a bit different from what the Pharisees decided to do in the physical realm. They decided to make this "trouble-maker" go away! The words of Jesus and Jesus Himself are *inseparable*. He is, after all, the *Word of God*.

The Word of God knew the heart of man. He asked the Pharisees, *"Why are you conspiring to kill me?"*[37]

At first, they denied His accusation, and they asked Jesus, "Who goes about to kill you?"

It is not recorded that Jesus ever answered them, but He could have easily responded, "You do! Every time I turn around you are trying to discount what I say, what I teach,

---

37 John 7:19

or my philosophy of life. It is obvious that you really would rather I just go away."

When we are guilty of changing His words to fit our theology, He could ask us the same question, "Why are you going about to kill me? I thought I was supposed to be the main character here?"

Paul, also a Pharisee, was asked this very same question on the road to Damascus. *"Saul, why are you persecuting Me?"*[38]

Paul's response was, "Who art Thou, Lord?

This was a very good response! When Jesus accuses us of going about to "kill Him," change His words, philosophy, or doctrine, we could very well respond like the Apostle Paul, "Who *exactly* are You?" because it is obvious that we don't know Him!

When we *know* the Word of God, we find the Man and His words are inseparable!

In order to accept the Word as truth we must change our thinking. There should be places in our minds where His words fit perfectly without changing, rearranging, or redefining them.

The gospels are a gift given from Jehovah. They are the fulfillment of the prayer of Jesus in John 17, that all "those who believe on Him through their word ..." so that God would make us all as *one*.

---

38 Acts 9:4 (NKJV)

The gospels were written by apostles and disciples of Christ, and their words are the basis for what we *believe*. All who have received Jesus Christ are *believers*, and they are included through the apostles' words (the gospels).

The incidents in Jesus' life were called to the minds of the disciples by the unction of the Holy Spirit.[39] We are to *believe* what they say and accept them as truth--not changed, not altered in order to be palatable to theologians, and not ignored by those who have trouble fitting them into their doctrines.

We must be very, very careful that we understand the *unadulterated* words of Christ. He knows that this would be difficult for some, and this is evident when He asked the question, *"Why do you not understand My speech?"*[40]

This question does not need an answer—for the answer is given directly afterwards, "… even because you cannot *hear* my word" (KJV). The great Teacher was saying, "You don't understand the words I say, because *you don't understand the Word of God*."

In this verse we find yet another reference that the Word of God is *not* a Bible. It is *not* a written series of words and sentences that create a thought. The *Word of God is none other than Jesus Christ.*

Can you see that if we understood the *Word of God*, we would understand the *words* of God? Remember? If you do not understand this parable, you will not understand any parable. "The sower sows *the Word.*"

---

39   John 14:26
40   John 8:43 (NKJV)

The Word of God

The Word of God may come from many spouts, but only *one* source. The Scripture says that Jesus Christ Himself is called (or named), the *Word of God*.[41]

However, Paul does use the same term for the supernatural communication of Jesus Christ to spiritual ears.

"... because when you received the word of God which you heard from us, you welcomed *it not as the word of men*, but as it is in truth, *the word of God*, which also effectively works in you who believe.[42]

Jesus asks, *"Is it not written in your law, 'I said, "You are Gods"'?"*[43]

Why would He ask such a thing? Are we gods? Should we attempt to change this Scripture or shall we explore it as it is written? Let's look at the rest of the verse with our new understanding of the Word of God.

Jesus continues, "If they were called 'gods' unto whom the *Word of God* came, then why do you take umbrage with the fact that I [merely] said I am the *Son* of God." (His message is an interesting study but, sorry to say, it is outside the realm of our present concern.)

Look at *His understanding* of the words He used in His proposal. *If* the Word of God comes to a person, that person changes into something more, somebody different. The Word

---

41 Revelation 19:13, John 1
42 I Thessalonians 2:13 (Emphasis added)
43 John 10:34—Jesus quoting Psalm 82:6 (NKJV)

of God can come to a man or woman only as he or she places himself or herself in a position to *receive* that Word!

This is the position in which *we* want to be! We must be able to hear within ourselves the Word of God so that we will not only *taste* of that Bread from Heaven, but have that Bread to spare in our ministry to others.

We must have the Word of God coming from our mouths in power just as He promised Moses that he would *speak the words I tell you!* See, I have made you a *god* unto Pharaoh!"

You see, there is no need to change the words of Jesus, His reasoning, or His vocabulary (unless you believe that the Word of God is only a book). When our vocabulary matches His, everything you read makes perfect sense.

If we do not have a basic understanding of the Word of God and how we need to *hear* it, then how will we receive the words? How *will* we hear it?

We are far too fond of mechanizing the spiritual realm. We like to believe that if we happened to be standing under a particular tree when the Lord spoke to us, the next time we stand under that tree, we will hear from Him again. (Some people have these misguided hopes when they visit the "Holy Land.")

It is common for a person who has heard the Word of God while listening to a sermon by a particular pastor, teacher, or preacher, to return to that source in order to hear the Word again. This system is applied whether the Word is heard in congregations, denominations, books, lectures, through fasting, and even when praying at particular times and places.

If one hears the Spirit speak while reading the Bible, he or she may mistakenly consider the Bible as his or her source. We are pitiful creatures! Why do we think this way?

The Lord does not need a pastor, nor does He need a tree or a particular piece of real estate in order to speak to His people. I concur with the Apostle Paul who said, "I perceive that in all things ye are too superstitious."[44]

What Things?

Two despondent disciples were joined by a "stranger" while they were walking on the road to Emmaus. When the stranger inquired about the reason for their sadness, these downhearted men looked at Jesus as if He were crazy, and asked, "Are you a stranger in Israel? Have you not heard about the things that have happened in the past few days? Why haven't you heard about these things?"

Listen and hear within your own spirit (as if Jesus may ask you personally) the question Jesus asked in response: *"What things?"*[45]

We know that Jesus was fully aware of what had transpired in Jerusalem during those past few days. So why did He ask this question?

I understand that people who manage large department stores or franchises across the country are forever concerned about how their company *looks* to the public. Are their employees representing them well? Are the products displayed and promoted as they should be? Are the stores stocked

---

44   Acts 17:22
45   Luke 24:19 (NKJV)

properly? Are they advertised well? What is the look of their employees?

Many are the concerns of the owners of these companies, so they develop a list of guidelines by which they want their franchisees to operate. They know that a list of regulations is not enough; the guidelines must be implemented, and the owners want to be assured of this. Frequently, they hire "shoppers" to travel from store to store in order to make sure of its conformity to the rules and expectations of the owners. The reputation of the company and its owner is at stake!

This is what Jesus was doing on the dusty road to Emmaus on that famous first-day afternoon. When He asked His disciples, *"What things?"* they began a monologue about exactly what had happened.

They talked about the Messiah who had come. They had had great hopes that He was going to change the world for the better. They told about how He had been despised and hated by the religious leadership and eventually had been crucified and entombed.

Still unaware of the identity of the man to whom they spoke, they explained, "… and now it is the third day and we don't know what has become of Him. We heard some rumors about Him being raised from the dead, but we have not checked them out to see if they are true."

Jesus wanted to know if the disciples knew indeed what had transpired during those last few months. Did they have an understanding of what had happened at the execution? Had they figured out that Jehovah Himself had visited the Earth in human form? Did they comprehend that the Creator had tabernacled among men?

The Messiah had been with them and had answered questions and revealed secrets that had been kept since the foundation of the world! He had fulfilled prophecies from Genesis through their present-day prophet, Johannan ben Zechariah (John the Baptist)!

Jesus had fulfilled the prophecies perfectly and had been killed as the Lamb of God—on Passover—for the redemption of the world!

The Savior had been in the grave now for three days and three nights—perfectly fulfilling the *sign of Jonah!*

Still, the disciples (though they had been there and seen it all) were still quite unsure of *exactly* what had happened, and they were ill-prepared to answer His question—just as many of us who minister are ill-prepared!

Do *you* really understand what has happened? Do *you* really recognize who Christ is? Do *you* comprehend His purpose, His message, His mission? Do *you* realize what things transpired that day?

This "Stranger" *is* that Bread from Heaven that you must first receive yourself and then have enough to spare when someone asks you for the Bread of Life. This *is* your mission, and this *is* your message. Everything else is unessential.

We can spend our time teaching *Seven Ways to Prosperity* or *Three Steps to Healing.* We may hold studies on different books of the Bible, pursue our denominational lessons, and read our quarterlies (or whatever else we have occupied ourselves with) but, what we need to know is the answer to the question our Savior asks, *"What things?"*

PART 3

Jesus' Questions
Challenge Our Theology

Our Concept of the Messiah

The appearance of the Son of God on the Earth has given us unprecedented insights. It was the Earth's opportunity to understand who God is, His attributes, and His characteristics, in human terms. Even so, many still misunderstand.

Many who read the Old Testament see Jehovah as demanding and exacting—a God who is acquainted with death and destruction in order to have His way on the Earth—a God of little mercy.

But, I assure you, that idea has been given to us *outside of divine revelation*, and does not come from the pages of Scripture. The Father shows Himself as being merciful many, many times throughout the Bible.

In the *Person* of Jesus Christ, we find a picture of the Father that, if missed, we will have missed 99 percent of the mission of the Messiah! Let's face it; redemption could have been carried out in a day. Why would Jesus spend such a long time with us? *He wanted us to know His Father!*

He asked, *"Have I been with you so long, and yet you have not known me, Philip? He who has seen me has seen the Father; so how can you say, 'Show us the Father'?"*[1]

Separating Jesus Christ from the Father in character, personality, and purpose is not only a regrettable thing to do, but religion's history shows us that it is a blasphemous thing to do, as well. It is not a new idea!

Pagan theology taught that there was an evil god who created the Earth. He was an evil and wicked being. Since that creation, his son came and has redeemed the world to himself and now is the new king of the world. This new king reigns with mercy and kindness in the place of his cruel and exacting father.

Unfortunately, this sounds very familiar to much modern-day theology, doesn't it? Our idea is that Jesus has come and *repaired* the mess that His Father left behind. There is only one problem—it's not true.

Jesus asks, *"Do you not believe that I am in the Father, and the Father in me?"*[2]

Ask yourself this question—and answer it honestly. Do you see the Father and the Son as two different beings? Do you see the Father as having a certain severe and stern agenda, while Jesus has a mild and more lenient one?

If you do, you have missed the ministry of the Messiah! You have somehow mentally bypassed the very purpose for which He came!

---

1   John 14
2   Ibid.

His very intention was to introduce us to the Father. This He did in every word He spoke and in every action He took. On many occasions He said, "I don't do what I *want* to do; I do what the Father *tells* me to do. I see Him work; therefore, I work. There is no difference between Me and the Father. If you have seen Me, you have seen the Father."

Hopefully, this concept is not difficult for you, but I assure you that it *is* difficult for some. Many have been taught that Jesus has come to *undo* or *fix* what had been done, when in reality Jesus was a part of the Creator's plan from the foundation of the world.

Sometimes I think that Jesus Christ is perceived in as many different ways as there are people who believe in Him.

We learn Who Jesus is by the *testimony of the Scriptures*, but it is by *revelation* to our souls, our hearts, our minds, and our spirits that we *know* Him. We can be taught what He said, but not Who He is. We can read studies on the "historical" Jesus, but He must be *revealed*.

Jesus was amazed that John the Baptist was not received as the great prophet that he was. John was ridiculed, cast out, and despised by the conventional church. These folk knew all about John (after all, he practically lived in their backyard), but he was never revealed!

Let's listen in as John the Baptist was revealed to the disciples.

Jesus asked a series of questions about John the Baptist. (Many of the people He addressed had followed John before Jesus appeared.) *"What did you go out into the wilderness to see? A reed shaken by the wind? But what did you go out to see? A man clothed in soft garments? Indeed, those who wear soft clothing are in kings' houses. But what did you go out to see? A prophet?"*[3]

Then Jesus answers His own question, "Yes, I say to you, and more than a prophet." He says that John the Baptist was "*The* greatest prophet ever born of women."

Jesus is teaching us to be suspicious of our viewpoint and our stubbornness in that position. I assure you that many in that day *did not* consider John to be the greatest prophet ever born. I don't know that anyone in our day says that either. Yet Jesus made that fact unequivocal. If our viewpoint is unlike Christ's, what shall we do?

We are in danger of the same selfish influences with regard to our appreciation of the spiritual. We must be very careful that our preconceived ideas are not "written in stone," and we need to be sure that we are not so stubborn in our traditions that we miss His revelation.

We must be very careful that our concept of who Jesus Christ is conforms to the Scriptures and the Scriptures alone. Otherwise, we will be asking people to believe in a God *they cannot discover in the Scriptures* and that is something you do *not* want to do.

Many of our ideas are assumed to come from the Bible, but they do not.

Here's a good example of this: If you were to ask the Christian community at large why Jesus asked, *"My God, my God, Why hast thou forsaken me?"* the vast majority would

---

3   Matthew 11:7 (NKJV)

say that God turned His back on Jesus because He could not look upon sin. You've heard this, haven't you? Do you realize that there is no scriptural evidence whatsoever to support this? Since when can't Jehovah look on sin? As ridiculous as that is, it is commonly understood. Even doctrines are built on it as a premise.

If Jesus did ask, "Why hast thou forsaken me?" why can't the explanation of this be that He simply was quoting the Psalm?[4] The psalm *does* describe His death: "And as the people stood watching Him die they said, 'Let God come and save Him.'" It's very likely that this Psalm came into His mind, and He quoted it during His passion.

It never did make sense to me that He would hang there wondering why His Father had forsaken Him. The saddest part is that Jesus' doubting His Father never needed to be dealt with, but because of meddlers adding fiction to facts, we are left with what seems to be a theological paradox.

There is plenty of baseless teaching that ceased to make sense a hundred years ago. It still continues, confounding and clouding the minds of those who hear it. Therefore, you will have to research everything you hear, and especially everything you say.

So many of our traditions do not come from the Scriptures. Similarly, so much of our perception about the nature of God does not come from the foundations of faith. Many ideas have been developed by men and women who, perhaps, while well-intentioned, were unfaithful messengers of the obvious words of God.

---

4   Psalm 22

Why don't we just *do* what He says and *say* what He says? Why don't we quit inventing these religious ideas that only confuse the issues and create perplexity? Why use words that He didn't use? Would the mission of the Messiah have been more successful if He used the word "Trinity" to describe the Godhead? If He had only taught that the Father was omniscient or omnipresent—yeah, that would have really helped!

Yet these are words and concepts that we *insist* that converts should own and use; otherwise, he or she will be unorthodox, dissenting, and heretical.

Let's just *do what He says* and *say what He says* instead of spending time pleading false traditions and manufacturing our own ideas! There is great simplicity and power in the message of Christ to do what He does, not to add to it or make it "better," not to trim anything from it—just do what He says!

Jesus wants to know the answer to His question, *"Why is it that you call me Lord and don't [simply] do what I say?"*[5]

I feel responsible for my part in this mess. I preached my share of opinions, too! I called Him Lord *and did what I said.*

I had to decide that if it is not in the Scriptures, I'll not preach it. If it IS there, let's shout it from the housetops!

Doctrine

Sadly, it seems that "doctrine" is a "dirty word" among many people in modern Christianity, but it need not be so.

5   Luke 6:46

Permeating through contemporary congregations, when faced with doctrinal differences, is often heard the mantra, "Why can't we all just get along?"

Doctrinal **unity is not** *spiritual* **unity.**

It is not *doctrine* (or a lack of it) that divides congregations and builds walls between relationships. It is a lack of freedom that allows each individual to grow in the family of Christ, *as truth is revealed by our Father.* Families, like no other institution on Earth, can tolerate differences of opinion and philosophy.

We see the call for familial love throughout the Bible, "Be kindly affectioned one to another with brotherly love; in honor preferring one another"[6] and "By this shall all men know that you are my disciples, if ye have love one to another."[7]

It is lack of love, not doctrine, that divides us.

Doctrine is the philosophy upon which we build our lives. It is something that we share and teach, as we are asked and led to do so.[8] (They *will* ask when doctrine becomes something that we *live*.)

The fruit of *authentic Bible doctrine* is a true, sweet, and harmonious life. In another word, it is joy. The life of joy may even be in outward turmoil, riddled with persecutions and trials, but inwardly it is deep joy. Joy is the strength that comes from "knowing."

---

6   Romans 12:10
7   John 13:35
8   1 Peter 3:15, "… be ready always to give an answer to every man that asks you the reason of the hope that is in you with meekness and fear."

As ministers of His gospel, we must be very careful to teach only the doctrines that are found in the Scriptures. As servants of the Lord, we must certainly live only by those same doctrines.

So how did doctrine become a nasty word?

The first source of doctrine is Scripture, but sometimes religious leadership becomes adamant about biblical doctrines that are vague and vague in the areas about which the Bible is explicit. So translations, interpretations, and personal motivations begin to obscure the pure message.

You may offer, "So let's bypass the men and go directly to the source!" I would agree, but many times, a "subject-verb-direct object" approach to Scripture will not always prove to be sufficient either. By this method it is possible to read words that clearly state a particular idea—word for word, subject, verb, direct object—but many of the truths of Scripture may remain hidden. For the most part, doctrine is not written as commandments in the Bible.

Don't be discouraged. What you have to realize is that these things are not hidden *from* you, they are hidden *for* you. This is where the second step in determining doctrine comes into play.

Revelation. Many students of the Bible neglect this second step. When the Spirit of God speaks to the heart and reveals the depth, scope, and breadth of the Scripture we are reading, this is the *Word of God* to us!

If we take the "subject-verb-direct object" approach to the Scriptures, we may end up proving that the way we live is okay with God (no matter what the state of our consciences may be). Or we may condemn ourselves, neglecting His abundant mercy! We cannot have an all-encompassing understanding and life philosophy that is based only on what we have *read* from the Scriptures! We must also know that there is much more to be *revealed* to us.

Semantic arguments about doctrine muddy the waters of life. The joy of living inside of inviolable doctrine is overlooked because of the public misuse of the Scriptures.

Many times in order to prove a doctrinal position we use the words of Christ or the words of the prophets to "prove" our contentions. Too often cited are examples of people in the Bible doing or saying things to make our points valid.

An example is, "Jesus drank wine; therefore, it is all right for me to drink wine." The scriptural "proof" gives a basis for one's own alcohol consumption.

Next, they may proceed to "prove" that the wine Jesus made at the wedding in Cana was indeed fermented. Then they sum up their position by stating that Jesus was accused a being a "wine bibber" because it was a well-known fact that he drank wine, etc.

Is this the approach we are supposed to take?

Once a man came to Jesus to "use" Him for a "proof text."

What? Yes, he wanted to get his brother to share more of his inheritance. Obviously Jesus' opinion held some sway in his brother's life, so he thought, "I'll get Jesus to settle this! I hear Him teaching, 'It is more blessed to give than receive.' This will work out perfectly!"

Now, this seems like a really good idea! If we can go to Jesus, and His words justify our position, wouldn't that bolster any argument? I mean, if the Savior says that it's okay, then it's okay!

So the man scurries up to Jesus and whines, "Master, tell my brother that he should share his inheritance with me." Jesus' response was totally unexpected, *"Man, who made Me a judge or an arbitrator over you?"* [9]

This man wanted Jesus to give him a word of *license* to continue his malicious, covetous, and greedy acts toward his brother. Remember, he could have received his "justification" from the Scriptures with *no* argument. He could have quoted from a hundred sources on being kind, lending to your brother, being generous, and how "... the liberal soul shall be made fat!" But he went to Jesus. He got more than he anticipated from the great Teacher!

Though a crowd could hear, the Son of God spoke to *one* man. He told the famous story of the man who took literally the advice, "Eat, drink, and be merry, for tomorrow you shall die." Jesus said to the greedy brother, "Take heed--beware of covetousness, for one's life does not consist in the abundance of the things a man possesses." His story ends with, "You fool! This night your soul will be called for!"

Our lesson, however, is not about *greediness*; our lesson is in the Lord's question, *"Who made Me a judge or an arbitrator over you?"*

We should hear this question within *ourselves* when we summon Jesus' written words into our petty arguments over

---

9   Luke 12:14 (NKJV)

our selfish beliefs. When we spout His words, (usually quite detached from their context), sometimes we do so in order to *prove* our positions, doctrines, and theories. "Go on! Tell 'em Jesus! Tell 'em I'm right!"

As ministers, we are not to *prove* anything to anyone. Jesus is neither our arbiter nor an erudite lawyer who serves to prove our position. The only honest thing we can do is let our lives stand as examples. We *should* direct people to the words of Scripture, but teach them to *hear* the voice of God in their own spirits, as well. Let *them* decide within their own consciences.

Some would counter, "Oh, no, if we do that, then they are liable to fall into error! We must *insist* that they follow the Bible and denominational doctrine!"

We have to understand that people who *are* in error *were* in error before you condemned *or* justified their position with Scripture. Nothing has changed just because we may have coerced them to accept a certain doctrine.

Sometimes people merely concede. This does *not* mean that within their hearts they are honestly compliant. Concession can only be compliance *to your doctrine* and not the Holy Spirit. This is why we must teach people to listen to and obey the Spirit of God.

Remember, He said, "I will send [the Holy Spirit] to you. And when He has come, *He* will convict the world of sin, and of righteousness, and of judgment … when He, the Spirit of truth, has come, *He* will guide you into *all truth*."

Not answering the question of this covetous man, Jesus took the opportunity to expose his hidden covetousness.

When we take Jesus' words to prove our positions on our pet indulgences, we risk such exposure as well! Chances are, we make demands on His words so that we can continue in our ways and enjoy our selfishness with "license."

Doctrines regarding behavior (morals) are easy to analyze because of their root in covetousness. Theological doctrines, however, are a little harder to ascertain. Sometimes we just want to prove that we are right in what we believe.

I had to admit that for me to engage in this behavior is absolutely wrong! It is not for me to justify myself, the leaders of my particular group, the founders of a denomination, or even honored men and women of the past. Chances are, the founder of any great work (no matter how great) *did not know everything* and at times said something that falls squarely into the category of *false doctrine.*

Likely, there is within the pages of this book some false doctrine, as well! That is not easy for me to admit, but anything short of confessing that is purely dishonest. It has always been and will continue to be up to *you* (and no one else) to find what is true.

We have been commissioned to "Prove all things; hold fast that which is good."[10]

Prove *all* things *within yourself—to yourself!* I have come to the conclusion that attempts to prove my position to groups or individuals by citing and rehearsing the words of Jesus or the Torah or any other Scripture is unacceptable behavior for me.

---

10   1 Thessalonians 5:21

Jesus alone has license to open these arguments. Only He is to be our spiritual leader. He is the sole Head of the Church.[11]

Traditional Doctrines

Jesus found a fatal flaw in the Pharisees' doctrine. They were convinced that there was one God and there would always be only one God; therefore, anyone who claimed to be the Son of God makes Himself to be equal with God, making two gods, and, therefore, He is a *heretic*.

When the Pharisees heard Jesus claim to be the *Son of God,* according to their understanding and commonly held theology, they were justified in rejecting Him as a false Messiah.

Understanding their mindset, Jesus asked them a series of questions, *"What do you think about the Christ [Messiah]? Whose son is he?"* They quickly answered, *"The Son* of David."

Then He asked, *"How then does David in the Spirit call him 'Lord'...? If David then calls him 'Lord,' how is he his son?"*[12]

His question scrambled their theology. Their minds raced to make sense of it and their mouths opened to speak some words of retort, as their thoughts continued to whirl, but no words came forth. I can see the Son of God with a smile on His face reach over, put His finger under the man's chin, gently close his gaping mouth, and then say, "Go and think about that one for a while, boys." The question was so theologically devastating, the Bible says that from that day on they asked

11   Ephesians 5:23
12   Matthew 22:43-45

Him no more questions! They had learned that the questions of Jesus would *expose them for who they were.*

The questions of Jesus can expose error in doctrine and theology. His questions can expose lifestyles as being licentious, covetous, and sinful. Just like the Pharisees, *if we desire to remain in error, we will quickly learn not to ask, and certainly not to answer any more of Jesus' questions.*

Mark's account of this event records Jesus' question this way, *"How say the scribes that Christ is the son of David?"*[13]

It's curious that Jesus asked *"How say* the Scribes ...?" He wondered *how* they were able to say that.

The answer to this question may shake you a little. The Scribes *say* it because the Bible *says that!*[14] Of course, *it was first filtered through their own understanding, but it can be found in the Bible.* Yet Jesus questioned their conclusions. Is it possible to get a doctrine from Scripture that the Lord will find questionable?

Jesus teaches us that the message *behind* these words was not the message they received. So we must presume a question of our own. Is what the Bible *says*—in subject, verb, direct object—exactly what the Bible seems to be *saying*?

---

13 Mark 12:35

14 The Old Testament references to the son of David as the awaited King of Israel are extensive. The most well-known is Jehovah's promise in Isaiah 9:7, "Of the increase of his government and peace there shall be no end, upon the throne of David, and upon his kingdom, to order it, and to establish it with judgment and with justice from henceforth even for ever. The zeal of the LORD of hosts will perform this."

Now, this thought may put fear in your heart. Remember, it is only when we do not trust our *relationship* with our God that we will have a fear of misunderstanding the Bible.

It is preached from coast to coast and around the world that we can trust what the Bible *says*, but no one ever tells us how to find the *message* of the Bible. They may read the words, but its message is only heard through *revelation*.

Revelation comes when we understand that the Word of God is none other than the *person* and *revelation* of Jesus Christ. The Word of God is the *supernatural communication* between God and His people, which is made possible by the Spirit of His Son. *The Word has become flesh and now dwells within us.*

This concept is *key!* We must make this important distinction! A Bible could be destroyed by fire, but no one can throw the Word of God into a fire! Pages can be torn from a Bible, but words cannot be removed from the Word of God! A person can distort what they read in the Scriptures, but no one can distort the Word of God. *Every word of God is pure! (Because it is purely communicated.)*

If we desire to find the will of God for our lives, so that we will be effective Christians and effective ministers, we must understand this differentiation. If we do not understand *this concept*, Jesus said we would not understand *any* parable--for the sower sows the *Word*.

If you do not understand what the sower sows, how will you know what to reap? If the sower sows the field with the Word, then "whence hath it tares?" If you do not know what the seed is, or how it is sown, you will not understand the Word of God when you hear it, the Scripture when you read it, or their rightful place in your life. Your ministry will suffer, your message will be ineffectual, and your doctrine will be faulty.

Remember, it is only by *tradition* that we call the Bible the Word of God. The prophets never did. The apostles never did. Jesus never did. Even the early church called the Bible you have in your hand (or at least their portion of it), "the Scriptures."

The Word of God, referred to in the Scriptures, has always been either the supernatural communication of a divine message or a *name of Jesus Christ Himself*.

Doctrinal Traditions

Our traditions often get in the way of understanding.

When I find that my tradition is made false by the words of Christ (or the word of Christ is made false by tradition), I am no longer at liberty to continue in it.

So, my friend, when your tradition contradicts your own conscience and you know within yourself that something is wrong with your practice or idea or theology, what will you do?

Jesus asks, *"Why do you transgress the commandment by your tradition?"*[15]

How sad it is when we find ourselves in transgression of God's commandments simply because it is our *tradition* to do so.

---

15   Matthew 15:3

A perfect example of this exchange of commandment for tradition concerns the Sabbath day. There is no *scriptural* reason to honor the first day of the week and disregard the seventh day of the week—it is merely our *tradition* to do so. This fact is admitted and undisputed by almost every Bible scholar. Keeping Sunday as the "Lord's Day" is widely held as an unquestionable truth, yet it is done with no precedent or historical evidence.

Do we believe these words of Jesus, "Therefore the son of man is Lord of the Sabbath Day"?[16] Can we simultaneously believe that the first day of the week is the "Lord's Day" while He claims to be Lord of the seventh day? Are we to believe He is now Lord of both days or *no longer* the Lord of the Sabbath Day? Why, then, would we hold Sunday as the Lord's Day?

It is our tradition to do so. "My grandmother and grandfather held Sunday as the Sabbath; therefore, I hold Sunday as the Sabbath." Your congregation and your denomination may hold this day by tradition, but Jesus asks, "Why do you transgress the commandment (the fourth commandment) by your tradition?" This is a very difficult thing to justify in our Christian existence.

The truth is that if you decide to keep this particular commandment of God and ignore tradition, you will stand in opposition to (literally) millions of good, well-meaning, and lovely people who profess a faith in Christ. This is why so many people find a rationalization that enables them to continue their tradition and ignore the commandments.

Remember the leaven of the Pharisees? (Refer to Warning Two.)

---

16 Mark 2:28

The Bible

Many believers today consider themselves to be "New Testament Christians," and thus, they virtually ignore the rest of the Bible, including the Ten Commandments. We must properly place the earlier testimonies into our own Christian faith. Without them we are ripe for heretical influences.[1]

To many, the Law is perceived as contradictory to faith and faith is seen as being contradictory to the Law, but this was not so in the mind of our Lord Jesus Christ. To Jesus, the words of Moses were *indispensable*. They are needed in order to have a basis upon which to place our faith. He said that a man who "... is instructed unto the kingdom of heaven ... brings out of his treasure, things [both] *new and old*."[2]

"And he said unto him, 'If they hear not Moses and the prophets, neither will they be persuaded, though one rose from the dead.[3] For had you believed Moses, you would have believed me: for he wrote of me.'"

Then the question, *"But if ye believe not his writings, how shall ye believe my words?"*[4]

---

1   Isaiah 8:20, "To the law and to the testimony: if they speak not according to this word, it is because there is no light in them."
2   Matthew 13:52
3   Luke 16:31
4   John 5:46-47

Can a man, ignorant of the words of Moses, claim to truly believe in the Messiah?

The modern church now wrestles with the consequences of 2000 years of "Torah neglect." We wrestle with questions like "Does life begin at conception?"[5] Should there be a death penalty?[6] Should a modern man believe in evolution?[7]

The Old Testament gives unequivocal answers to these and many more questions, but, sadly, it is not a part of the study of many "New Testament Christians."

The Old Testament, and its role of importance, if improperly appreciated and understood, can lead a person to believe erroneous things about the Messiah, as well. The Pharisees, with their literal and extended interpretations, believed that the words they read were "magical" or at least very "mysterious." They believed that the words (and even the letters) held within them certain messages from God. They took upon themselves the responsibility of deciphering these words.

Unfortunately, the results of their conclusions and the doctrine created from their revelation did not allow them to recognize John the Baptist *or* the Messiah while both passed through their towns—and ministered—for years! Their Bible *and* their system of interpretation let them down.

At every Passover they were taught that one day Elijah would come. Because of this practice, they looked for Elijah to

---

5   Exodus 21:22-23, "If men strive, and hurt a woman with child, so that her fruit depart from her ... he shall be surely punished,... then thou shalt give life for life."
6   Deuteronomy chapters 13 and 17, et al.
7   Exodus 20:11, "For in six days the LORD made heaven and earth, the sea, and all that in them is, and rested the seventh day: wherefore the LORD blessed the sabbath day, and hallowed it."

precede the Messiah. All Jews expected Elijah to come first. It had been believed by them ever since they were children; and it was *"proven"* to them by the Scriptures. The disciples, too, had been raised in the Jewish frame of reference.

At the scene of the Transfiguration, we can see that Peter, James, and John were very excited when they saw Elijah with the Messiah. To Jesus they exclaimed that it had been prophesied that Elijah must first come. The three disciples thought, "This must be who we have been looking for!" Where did the disciples get this idea? Why was this so important to them? They were *taught* by the Pharisees.

Although we do not know the words of their conversations with the Pharisees, I believe that the disciples *were* counseled in private about exactly *who* they thought Jesus was. They were likely discouraged to believe in Jesus as the Messiah because, they said, "Elijah had not yet come!"

You see, it had become obvious to the Pharisees that the people of Jerusalem were beginning to believe that Jesus was the Messiah. *"And many of the people believed in Him, and said, 'When the Christ comes, will He do more signs than these which this Man has done?'"*[8]

The Pharisees likely attempted to "prove" to the disciples, by Scripture, that Jesus could not possibly be the Messiah because (as everybody knows) Elijah must first come. They began to doubt.

This explains why they were so excited to see Elijah with Jesus on the Mount of Transfiguration. Have they indeed seen

---

8   John 7:31 (NKJV)

the sign that they, and their fathers before them, sought every Passover?[9]

They must have really been baffled when Jesus said to them, "No, Elijah has come already—and you missed him." His disciples were more confused than ever.

The transfiguration was surely the very *sign* that the Pharisees *said* should be first, but Jesus said that it was *not* the sign and emphasized that *Elijah had already come.*

Jesus was incensed that these Pharisees had so manipulated His friends. He took the opportunity with the Scribes, *"What were you discussing with them?"*[10]

The Lord's question pointed a finger at the Scribes and Pharisees and accused them of confusing His disciples. It was a statement to the fact that the questions they asked the disciples were only adding to their *confusion* and not to their *faith.*

Jesus was compelled to straighten out the thinking of His close companions and followers and point them to truth. He must do this with us from time to time, as well. (Have you ever heard that the Bible is so plain you have to have help to misunderstand it? We have a lot of help!) Sometimes a single, well-timed statement by the enemy can cost us hours of realigning of our thinking.

We must realize that well-meaning students of the Bible can produce some very compelling arguments. At the same time, we must not develop theology by what someone *says* that the Bible says. The Scriptures themselves are accurate and

9 John the Baptist was actually born on Passover. So close, yet so far away!
10 Mark 9:16 (NKJV)

blessed. The Spirit will speak to us *if* we understand the proper role of Scripture and are open to its Author to guide us.

First of all, we should understand that the Scriptures are of no *private interpretation*.[11] Unfortunately, this phrase is used to prove the very opposite of what it actually says, which is that we should not take the *conventional* understanding of the Scriptures to ourselves as *revelation*. It may be considered, but it is not *revelation*.

The Scriptures are *revealed* to us. This revealing is the ministry of the Holy Spirit, "However, when He, the Spirit of truth, has come, He will guide you into all truth …"[12]

The Scriptures will be and must be fulfilled. We must know *exactly* what they say and hold them in the light that God has shed abroad in our hearts—not by exegesis or semantic scrutiny, definitions of words, or, as Paul said, "doting about words." We must understand these things from *revelation* in our hearts.

Again, we often fear being misled by *our own understanding* of Scripture. Remember, the fear of being misled comes straight from the insecurity of our own *relationship* with our Creator.

We must be sure of our relationship with Jehovah. We must not live in violation of the commandments. We have to live in all good conscience. When we do, we can trust the Holy Spirit to reveal the meaning of the Scriptures to our hearts. If we do not, our consciences are untrustworthy and even dangerous. The mind of Christ was filled with Scripture—*Old Testament*

---

11   2 Peter 1:20, "Knowing this first, that no prophecy of the scripture is of any private interpretation."
12   John 16:13 (NKJV)

Scripture. How will we have the mind of Christ[13] if we shun the very contents of these very important Scriptures?

When Jesus informed the disciples that He would soon suffer many things and that He would be crucified and lifted up on the pole in the sight of every person, their first reaction was horror. Peter's response was, "Be it far from thee, Lord!"[14] They cried, "We do not want this to happen to you!"

Even after the execution had become reality, on the road to Emmaus, they still had not learned that He should die for every man. They continued to neglect the Scripture's sure fulfillment and reasoned only within their unregenerate minds.

In response to the reaction of His disciples (who in the shock of the moment had forgotten all they had learned about their Messiah), Jesus asked the question, *"How then will the Scriptures be fulfilled?"*[15]

The Scriptures must be fulfilled.

One time, when Jesus was speaking to a group of Pharisees, He was trying to show the fallacy of their viewpoint. He asked, *"If the ... Scriptures cannot be broken, then how can this be?"*[16]

He accused the Pharisees of believing that the Scriptures cannot be broken, yet developing their own doctrine that *requires* the Scripture to be inconsistent. He was trying to

---

13   1 Corinthians 2:16, "For who hath known the mind of the Lord, that he may instruct him? But we have the mind of Christ."
14   Matthew 16:22
15   Matthew 26:54
16   John 10:35

show them the dichotomy in their own minds; and He is trying to show us ours, as well. Do we do this?

Today, the average Christian ends up living comfortably with many convoluted and even contradictory thoughts. This happens when we learn doctrine from others—opening our minds to whatever doctrine tickles our fancy. Being trained to only memorize Bible verses, *we nearly never consider the whole picture given in the Scriptures.* We then compartmentalize our beliefs—never letting one doctrine near the other in any fluid thought lest the dichotomy is discovered.[17]

A great example of this phenomenon concerns the doctrines surrounding the sin penalty. The Scripture is clear, "The wages of sin is death."[18] It says only "death," but we *add* to it, "… death … without dying; an eternity in a burning fiery torment forever and ever." In another compartment we hold that Jesus paid this "sin debt" (although the Scriptures say nothing of a "sin debt").

Do these two ideas correspond? Jesus did not burn in hell, nor is He still there, to remain for eternity, yet He paid "in full" the sin debt? How's that?

We say that "It is finished," the words cited at the execution of Christ,[19] referred to the plan of salvation (thereby proving there are no other works necessary for salvation). But, at that point, He hadn't even *died* yet. Death, burial, and resurrection hadn't occurred yet. How can all these doctrinal ideas (and fifty more just like them) all be true? They can't, but no one seems to care.

---

17 Proverbs 18:2: "A fool hath no delight in understanding, but that his heart may discover itself."
18 Romans 6:23 (NKJV)
19 John 19:30

When speaking to people, I have been known to quote a Scripture or two. I am constantly amazed when their response is "I've never read that!" or "Where does the Bible say that?"

The reason certain Scriptures are not recognized could very well be because they have been denounced, left aside, deemed as unimportant; and what is left is misquoted or misapplied. Usually, the Scriptures that are doubted are in the Old Testament.

Remember when the rich, young man came to Jesus and asked Him what he must do to inherit eternal life? Jesus answered him, *"What is written in the law? What is your reading of it?"*[20]

How about you? What's your reading of the words of Moses? Could you answer this question?

This young man had read Moses—he had designed his whole life around the Torah. The result was that his purpose and intent was to keep the Law—*to the letter.*

Many people have speculated that this rich, young ruler really did not keep the Law. Some say that he only *thought* he kept the Law. But, think about to whom he was speaking—the Lord Jesus Christ! Jesus was never shy about telling people when they were wrongly assuming a fact. When anyone tried to justify himself or herself before Him, He was quick to point out the ways that they had offended the Law. Do you remember when He asked, *"Did not Moses give you the law, yet none of you keeps the law?"*[21] He was not shy about accusing people who did not keep the Law!

---

20   Luke 10:26 (NKJV)
21   John 7:19 (NKJV)

Jesus was never reticent to contradict what someone said; but in this case, He *did not say* that the young man *did not* keep the Law. On the contrary, He accepted that this man *did indeed* keep the Law. I submit that it is also likely because the Father's blessing was on him for keeping the Law (he was both young and rich at the same time)!

With both men in agreement that the youth had indeed kept the Law, they entered into another stage that was suggested by the man's final question, "But, what lack I yet?"

In modern Christianity, many are very impatient about the Christian life. We want to move toward perfection *before* we begin to keep the Law! However, when we get these things out of order, it will greatly hinder our progress toward perfection.

May I ask you, "How did you come to Christ?" The Bible teaches that "the Law is a Schoolmaster … to bring us to the Messiah."[22] I can remember thinking, "I didn't come by the Law! I came straight to Jesus."

So, did I come to the Messiah by way of the schoolmaster, the Law, the way Paul described? Did you?

The Times

As you stand in the higher regions of Jerusalem, looking toward the top of Mount Moriah, where Abraham offered Isaac nearly four millennia ago, you can see a wall created by the excavation of rock that supplied the stone for the Temple and the walls of Jerusalem. When the rock became unusable,

---

22 Galatians 3:24

they stopped cutting, and over time, large chunks of soft sand and gravel fell from the cliff side. It formed a jagged, foreboding image that is still recognized today as Golgotha, "the place of the skull." (Now this image of death looms over the parking lot of a Jerusalem bus station.)

* * *

This warm, spring day, the whole town of Jerusalem prepared for Passover. The fusion of anxious and angry voices near the Damascus gate was becoming a roar. "What is it?" the women wondered, as they shifted their bundles from arm to arm. "They are taking Joshua of Nazareth to the place of the skull," someone shouted.

The women knew exactly where Jesus was going. As the crowd passed, they looked at His marred and battered face. Fright and sorrow surged inside them. They sorrowed for His misfortune and passion, but as any woman would, they ached in sympathetic rhythms with His mother who observed from a distance.

What is on a man's mind who is being tortured? What was on Jesus' mind this afternoon? The women wailed audibly now as they went closer to comfort Mary. He looked over at them and said, "Do not weep for me, but weep for yourselves." He asked, *"For if they do these things in the green wood, what will be done in the dry?"*[23]

In this question we find a metaphor that illustrates the subject of Jesus' thoughts about the Church of God in the Earth.

---

23 Luke 23:31 (NKJV)

When Jesus was on the Earth, the Church was the "green tree." It was transplanted from Heaven as a seedling in the Earth. The sin-tainted soil, the seasons which are not quite right, and an environment so totally different from where it was born and sprouted, it seemed destined to wither and ultimately die.

In the end, the Messiah will return, raise it up, and save the last vestige of life in it. Today, the modern Church of God is not at the *beginning* of its existence; we are not beginning a "New Era," as some are saying, we are at the *end!* We are not in the green tree stage; we are in the dry. After suffering for so long, the tree is starting to feel its age.

The Church has suffered from a lack of living water and real sustenance, but it is still alive and continues to live. In the beginning, the more we were persecuted, the more we grew. But the Church of Jehovah is no longer a persecuted newborn. It is a drying tree that is awaiting redemption through the return of the Messiah.

So, "What *shall* be done in the dry?" Where is the persecution of which Jesus warned?

The true Church is not worthy of persecution today. We must realize that the Church is much different from when we were first established. In the beginning, we had power; we had influence, strength, and stamina. Persecution only made us bigger and stronger. The enemy knew this and he adjusted his schemes and plans accordingly.

Starting with Constantine, deadly compromise prevailed in the Body, leaving us to constantly resuscitate the anemic cadaver we have today. As we await the Bridegroom, we wallow in compromise. As we compromise, our lives become more at ease and more confident. The Church is confident and comfortable in its apostasy. While we dry, while we die, we thank our God for the wonderful lives we have, lives that are free of persecution.

At one point, early in the history of the Church, the disciples of John the Baptist had a concern about the disciples of Jesus. They asked Him, "Why don't your disciples fast?"

Jesus attempted to aid their understanding by asking a question, *"Can the friends of the bridegroom mourn as long as the bridegroom is with them?"*[24]

He knew that at the beginning of the Church, while the Bridegroom was with them, there would be no fasting, but His question indicated that there was coming a day when the Bridegroom would be taken away from them, and then they would fast.

My friend, *we now live in those days!* We are waiting for the Bridegroom to return. If living in this Earth requires faith; it may also require fasting. Perhaps fasting should be incorporated into our daily lives of dedication and prayer because we await the Bridegroom.

We should be *prepared* for ministry. The true earthly congregation of Jehovah is the world's door to the Kingdom of God. In order to enter this Kingdom you must be a part of *the* Church. Not a church, but *The Church*. Again, Jesus asks us to examine our criteria, *"What are you looking for?"*

Why do we look to a "church" for fellowship, communion, and feeding? The congregation of the Lord is not a place to

---

24 Matthew 9:15 (NKJV)

feed, but a place for people to come together to worship in spirit and in truth. We are to be fed by our Pastor, the Lord Jesus, and by Him alone. Once He feeds us, we will never again hunger!

Inclusion

People want to be included. They want to be assured. They do this by forming groups. The only way to develop a group of "included" people is to define the "excluded." What a terrible, sinful, and unjust practice this is on the part of mankind! Whether consciously or not, we form lists of people we deem to be "unacceptable" and "exclude" them from our "fold."

Exclusion

Jesus addresses the topic of exclusion in a couple of different ways. One time the disciples came to Him saying, "We met people who were casting out devils, but they walked not with us so we told them to stop."

Jesus said, "Don't forbid them, because if they are not against me, they are for me."[25]

When we make lists of "the included" and "the excluded," there is a great danger of excluding those whom the Messiah may count as His friends!

On another occasion, the Pharisees said that Jesus was not a part of their group because He cast out devils by Beelzebub.

Jesus said, "Wait a minute, guys. You just said that I cast out the devil. How do you figure that I'm not part of the household of God? *How can Satan cast out Satan?*"[26] And *"By whom then do you sons cast them out?"*

---

25 Mark 9:40
26 Mark 3:23 (NKJV)

God can actually work *outside* of our denominations! Here is where it becomes very difficult for those readers who have denominational mindsets. But, when you see good occurring, and lives being changed, even though they are outside of your denomination and perhaps a part of a group that you repudiate, you must consider Jesus' question, *"Would Satan cast out Satan?"*

We need to see denominations as exclusionary and not as just a way to name our group. When we cannot rightly judge whether a person is truly in the Church, why would we judge him or her as being "excludable" from our group? Unless, of course, we are admitting that our group is not the true Church. If we admit that, why would we be a member of it for even ten seconds longer? This goes back to our basic and very *human* problem. Very seldom do we know the difference between what is *truly* good or evil.

If you are honest (and have come this far in reading this book), it should have occurred to you that we frequently do not see things as we should. We should all be less judgmental about things we simply don't understand; and the list of things we do not understand takes in a lot of doctrine and theology! In time, Jesus will judge us all!

Names
Nearly all of this kind of judgment would be totally eradicated if denominationalism was not a part of our Christian experience. I submit that denominationalism is *not* a part of the Spirit of Christ within us. We don't know what Spirit we are of when we denominate ourselves and exclude others.

I have visited denominations and groups within denominations all over this country (and in several others).

I have found "good" and "bad" attributes in *every* one of them.

I have been in Baptist congregations, Catholic congregations, Presbyterian congregations, and Lutheran congregations. I have attended the Kingdom Hall of Jehovah's Witnesses and the Church of Jesus Christ of Latter Day Saints. I have found "good" and "bad" people everywhere.

Our purpose should be to *do good*. We are to strive to perfect *ourselves* (not others) on a daily basis. If we make *doing good* our purpose, if we strive toward perfection, this will keep us busy for the rest of our lives!

Building churches, growing denominations, making larger and larger structures, can only take time away from the more necessary and important task of perfecting of ourselves. Everything else should be of lower priority! What should denominate us is not who's who, or who's not—neither should it be names, words, and articles of "What We Believe …" Rather, it should be our *purposes*.

Salvation

It is not very popular to talk about the *cost* of our salvation, but the questions of Jesus deal with it; therefore, we must deal with it, as well.

Many insist that salvation is a gift. They feel it is blasphemy to say that works are warranted, necessary, or an integral part of salvation in any way.

In the depths of our own spirits, we are sure that there are requirements that must be met in order to be saved, that there are tests of faith we must pass, and there is a cost that we choose to default upon or pay. What then must a person do to earn His salvation? What must a person do to make himself or herself worthy of saving? What may we do to justify ourselves in the sight of God and earn His love and redemption?

The fact is that there is nothing that will earn this gift. Faith in Christ alone is all that can effect the grace of God on our behalf. There is no sacrifice we can make; no good work that we can do that will accomplish redemption in our own soul or the soul of any other person.

Are the thoughts of the last two paragraphs in contradiction? Those who can hear their hearts know that coming to Christ is a *costly* gift. Though it sounds like a contradiction in terms, salvation is a *costly* gift.

Let us look at an example of a costly gift. A child and an adult see totally different things when they look beyond the sign that says, "Free Puppies." The "gift" of a puppy is vastly different than a gift of a simple, inanimate souvenir. The maintenance costs, the care and feeding, and the responsibilities of its care must be factored into the *cost* of any gift. We acquire salvation as a gift from God, but to say salvation is *free* is misleading. A gift cannot be considered free *based on its acquisition costs alone.*

Jesus said this in a question, *"For which of you, intending to build a tower, does not sit down first and count the cost, whether he has enough to finish it? Or what king, going to make war against another king, does not sit down first and consider whether he is able [to do so]? So likewise, whoever of you does not forsake all that he has cannot be my disciple."*[27]

---

27 Luke 14

Who is it that does not consider costs? Many people have "signed on" to Christianity by accepting it upon the condition that it is a free ride. When they became aware of the costs, they sought out and settled into faiths, denominations, and teachings with no challenges in order to minimize the demands placed upon them. But has the requirement been paid? Have they endured?

We must count the cost in order to be honest and just in our dealings with men, money, *and with God.*

Who is it that starts to college and then just waits for the bills to come in? Do we not first sit down and count the cost of a full degree to see if we have sufficient funds to finish it?

Who is it that builds a house and never asks, "How much will it cost" and "How much do I have?"

Who is it that doesn't consider costs?

Who is it that sets out on a trip and doesn't look at a map to calculate the costs?

Have you ever wondered what your faith in Christ may cost you? Jesus made lists of things on several different occasions. Let us look at them in brief.

It may cost the peace in your home. *Matthew 10:35-39, Luke 12:53, "... And a man's foes shall be they of his own household."*

It may cost your possessions. *Matthew 19:29, "And every one that hath forsaken houses ... lands, for my name's sake ..."*

It may cause you to have to choose between your faith and your family. *Luke 14:26, "If any man come to me, and hate not his father, and mother, and wife, and children, and brethren, and sisters ... he cannot be my disciple."*

It may even cost your life. *Luke 14:26, "Yea, and his own life also...."*

This "free gift" of salvation can run up quite a tally! Who is it that doesn't consider costs? Perhaps you? Perhaps me?

To honestly and properly consider costs, we must not only consider what it will cost us to attain and remain in the Kingdom to come, but we must also consider the cost of default and failure. Who is it that doesn't consider costs?

The subject of eternal security is bound to come up in almost any conversation dealing with religious matters. I happen to be one who believes in the security of the believer.

In my study and understanding of the Scriptures, I have found that there is a place in Jesus Christ where we do not have to worry or concern ourselves with whether we will be *safe* on the Day of Judgment. Where I differ from so many others, however, is that I don't think that this *place* is so quick and easy to attain.

The Apostle Paul "weighs in" on the subject of salvation. He was under no delusion that his salvation was "paid in full" and that he need not worry about gaining eternal life. "But I keep under my body, and bring it into subjection: lest that by any means, when I have preached to others, I myself should be a castaway."[28]

28   1 Corinthians 9:27

Perhaps Paul was reflecting on a question that had been asked by Jesus, *"What does it profit if a man gains the whole world and loses his own soul, or is 'cast away'?"*[29]

If we are to accept the words of our Savior as they are written, we must concede that it *is* possible to be cast away! If our Father looks at our lives and sees nothing worth saving, we will be deemed to be unworthy and cast away. (If these words disturb you, we could change the words of Jesus to mean something else, but we would have to ask ourselves why He would warn us about something that is not possible!)

Jesus taught that there were *unprofitable* people in hell, people who are not necessarily *wicked* people. These unprofitable people always do their "own thing" and do not really care about the things of God.

We *cannot* be satisfied with the faith we had as a six-year old child. (A lot has happened since you were six!) We *cannot* feel safe because we were baptized when we were twelve.

This is why striving for perfection is so important to a Christian. A person who pursues perfection is a person whose desire it is *to please his God (not simply miss his judge's hell!)*. Pleasing God requires faith and *perfection!*

We must admit that our faith in God comes and goes. It can also grow to a stage of perfection so that it comes and stays! We can stop this cycle of dedicating and rededicating if we will simply settle upon what we *believe.*

***

---

29 Luke 9:25

The disciples were at a high point in their faith. They had just understood a story that Jesus unmasked by removing the parabolic language, and they remarked, "By this we believe that You came forth from God."

Jesus was not impressed by their "faith." Why? Listen to His response, *"Do you now believe?"* Indeed the hour is coming, yes, has now come, that you will be scattered, each to his own, and will leave Me alone."[30]

Let us settle this question once and for all. Once a man or a woman repents and becomes at peace with God (and He with him or her), can he or she then lose this state of salvation and revert to his or her old condition?

There are those who will tell you that the Bible emphatically says *once saved, always saved.* Then there are others (who read the same Bible) who say that the possibility of losing salvation after it is given *does indeed exist.*

One side of this argument seems to rely on strained perspectives and definitions of words. Clever arguments and empathetic reasoning are used to give assurance to those who are lukewarm and less than motivated. The other, more stringent position uses sharp warnings of hell and burning to backsliders.

Unless we are willing to do a lot of mental calisthenics and redefinition of common, everyday words, what else can we conclude from the following words of Peter?

"For if after they have escaped the pollutions of the world through the knowledge of the Lord and Saviour Jesus Christ,

they are again entangled therein, and overcome, the latter end is worse with them than the beginning. For it had been better for them not to have known the way of righteousness, than, after they have known it, to turn from the holy commandment delivered unto them. But it is happened unto them according to the true proverb, The dog is turned to his own vomit again; and the sow that was washed to her wallowing in the mire."[31]

Can we wring some other meaning from this Scripture, or are we going to live honestly and adapt our faith to the Bible record? The Scriptures clearly show that it is the *present* condition of a person that is most important, not some vague, faded history of a decision that was made long ago.

What we *were* is of little import. Whether we are a sinner who was a saint or a saint who was a sinner, according to the Prophet Ezekiel,[32] it is what we are *now* that counts.

With that background laid, read again Christ's question, *"Do ye now believe?"*

What was the concern of the Savior at this point? He must have been remembering the time when He was doubted even by His own disciples, but *now* they believed. Jesus was well aware that these disciples, *now* faithful, would later depart and forsake Him.

Poor Peter has the bad reputation of being weak and a deserter, but the Scriptures indicate that Peter was not the only one to promise and renege. "Peter said unto him, 'Though I should die with thee, yet will I not deny thee.' *Likewise also said all the disciples.*"[33]

---

31   2 Peter 2:20-22
32   Ezekiel 33
33   Matthew 26:56

And later we read, "… Then *all* the disciples forsook him, and fled." Knowing this, Jesus asked, "Do ye *now* believe?"

There is likely a time coming when we will be called upon to take a stand that will be uncomfortable. We may even find that this stand will be one we have to take alone. For no reason that will be readily apparent to those around us, this stand will be based on only our faith.

Or, there may come a time when a quiet denial of Christ will be more convenient, or when we could gain ourselves an advantage by not being so "straight-laced" in our convictions. Will you have what it takes to take that stand and refuse to deny Him?

Don't answer too quickly, for "likewise said all the disciples," and *all* the disciples "forsook him, and fled." When we face the possibility of failure and couple it with the knowledge that we may lose all we have gained, we should be humbled and respectful of the kindness of the Lord to this point in our life.

Could Christ become an outdated and irrelevant motivation in your life? Could the same Jesus you responded to so eagerly in the days of your youth become impertinent or inapplicable to your present manner of life?

Could "mammon" exercise its influence on you and your family until the benefits of being an up-to-date sophisticate of the world far outweigh the illusive and intangible benefits of being a dedicated Christian?

Don't answer too quickly, for "likewise also said all the disciples."

I do not intend to cast doubts upon the power of faith, nor to cause doubt where God's faithfulness is concerned, but we need not think that we have in our hands paid, first-class tickets. Just because we believe *today* does not give us an assurance that we will believe *tomorrow*.

We must strive to enter in through the straight and narrow gate. We must work while it is day. We must run the race. The New Testament is replete with messages requiring us to press forward, strive, work, follow, and hold fast.

Many will believe the "strong delusion,"[34] many will fall away in the apostasy;[35] many will say to Christ, "Lord, Lord, open unto us, did we not do many works in thy name?"[36]
Still, He asks us, *"Do you now believe?"*

* * *

The motor in my little airplane quieted as I pulled the power back to end my long cross-country flight. I had everything under control. The landing checklist had been completed, and I was in "base" to land at Dayton Airport. Rolling back to level after "final," all was well. It was a cool evening, and there was essentially no wind, so I cut the power some more and felt the pleasing descent to the runway. Just as the wheels chirped, announcing their contact with Earth again, I felt the relaxing peace of having arrived come over me. The long, instructional solo flight was over. I was glad to be home.

Whoa! UP! DOWN! ROLL RIGHT! Correct! Correct! Bang! What was that? Suddenly, it was airborne again, then it went down, bounced up and over, and hit a landing light on

34 2 Thessalonians 2
35 Ibid.
36 Luke 13:25; Matthew 7:22

279

the runway. The light punctured and ripped the fabric belly of the plane as if it were filleting a fish. I had wrecked my favorite little Piper.

I was explaining the mishap to my instructor and said, "I don't know what happened … it all happened so fast!" He said, "I know what happened. You *thought* you had landed! You relaxed. You can relax when you get to the hangar!"

* * *

Nothing is more dangerous to any achievement than the fantasy of having already attained it.

We do not have crowns on our heads. There are no medals around our necks. We have not yet finished our course!

It is possible that we could cast off our faith. Many will fall from grace, and fall back to their lives without God. Let us keep on pressing toward the mark. For, he that endureth to the *end* shall be saved.[37]

Jesus knew that in only a few days everyone would forsake Him. They would run. They would fear. They would doubt. He also knows how we will respond in the time of our temptation.

Let His question forever pierce your heart, *"Do you now believe?"*

Judgment to the unbeliever is sure, but many of us do not understand how judgment works or upon whom it is exacted.

---

37 Matthew 10

How will the next tragedy (and there will be one) be received? Will it make us better or worse?

Jesus was asked about a couple of stories that had been floating around Jerusalem. Of concern were two tragedies. A company of Galilean men, traveling to Israel to make sacrifice, were persecuted and eventually killed in the process of giving their sacrifices in the Temple. Jesus was asked, "What happened there? Why were these people destroyed?"

As we have come to expect, Jesus replied by asking a question, *"Do you think the reason that they were destroyed is because these men were sinners above all the rest?"*[38]

He didn't stop there. He continued, *"And those eighteen upon whom the tower of Siloam fell, do you think that they were sinners above all Galileans?* I tell you nay, but except you repent you shall all likewise perish."

Jesus speaks of a *perishing* that takes place in the life of a Christian *before* death. Many times the above Scripture is applied to eternal damnation, when this is not at all what it is saying.

Now, in the case of this particular illustration that was described by Jesus, there was a *self-condemnation.* The tragedy that befell these people was not brought upon them because they were sinners; it came on them (as the preacher in Ecclesiastes says) just as tragedy comes upon everyone.[39]

Tragedies befall human beings living in this Earth—whether by death, fire, flood, or natural disaster. Whatever is

38   Luke 13
39   Ecclesiastes 2:4

experienced by one person is experienced by us all. So, why did Jesus say, "Except you repent, you will all likewise perish"?

It is a different matter to *perish* from these tragedies than to simply be *harmed* because of them. We are all harmed by unfortunate problems and accidents in this life, but we need not perish because of them! The troubles need not take our souls!

The Secret

If we live in constant fear for our own salvation and if we live wondering constantly if we will be worthy enough to be redeemed, when these problems in the world come on us, our first thoughts might be: "Why are these things happening to me?" or "This must be happening because I am a sinner and God is punishing me." The reason our trials cause us to perish is because we are never *sure about the way we live every day.*

How can we prevent these misgivings? How can we remove this fear from our lives? It can only be done by keeping God's Law every day we live! This is the secret to a joyous and happy life—no matter what our situation—and it leads to a clear conscience.

When we are *right with Jehovah*, we do not view destruction, mayhem, and disaster as if they are being pointed toward us. We can see these things as they really are—things that happen to all people. This life need not make us *bitter* people, but rather, the experiences of our lives can make us *better* people.

Give this idea some thought: think about the power you would experience in death, or a financial collapse, a tragic loss of everything you own, *if* the Lord Jesus appeared to you and whispered in your ear, "This is not because you have sinned. Your sin has not caused this. These things happen to everyone."

With this kind of communication you could endure almost anything!

You *can* hear within yourself, the Savior speak these very words to *you*—but *only* if you live in such a way that the commandments of God are not violated, and you have no blatant sin in your life. Our Lord wants you to know that He will keep you and protect you in every situation so that you can come out of it victoriously.

The secret to a joyous life is not living without tragedy! It is to experience all tragedy and all blessing in a state of sinlessness. We can face anything if we have no offense toward our conscience, no offense toward the commandments, and no offense toward our God!

What has all this to do with salvation? The fear that many people feel thrives because *they live every day violating their consciences.* They need to be convinced that they are safe, because they know within themselves that it is not true.

Everybody needs assurance that He will save us in the end, but we cannot just make trite, unsubstantiated sayings or memory verses to convince ourselves of it.

Stop violating your conscience. Stop justifying sin. Stop sinning every day.

If this were not possible, Jesus would not have looked at the adulterous women and said, "Now, go and sin no more!"

Habitual sin must be removed from our lives. If we do not turn from our sin, that is, if we do not repent, the inevitable tragedies in life will take us down and *we will all likewise perish!*

Balance

It's amazing that while I ministered among various denominations, it was easy to find groups that believed we are saved by works and other groups that believed we are saved by faith; however, in all of my travels, I never found a single congregation that believed we are saved by faith *and* works.

Yet, the Bible says that we are saved by both faith *and* works! We must have proper behavior to show our faith and we must work in faith in order for our proper behavior to be honored by God. Works without faith are *dead works*, just as faith without works is dead!

When we take this concept to heart, and believe that it takes both faith and works to be perfect, then look through the Scriptures, we will be amazed that no passage denies this fact. To the contrary, Scripture *proves* it to be true!

If while we are reading, we see a verse that seems to say that we are not saved by works, but are saved by faith, does it also say that we are saved by faith *alone*? Why add the word *alone*? Where did the idea of faith "alone" come from? The Bible *never* teaches that we are saved by faith *alone*. We are saved by grace.

Does the Bible say that grace without works is dead? The faith that invokes the grace is coupled to works. All of the warnings of Jesus make no sense otherwise. Blessed is he that does (not believes in) the will of my Father. *Faith* has an undeniable inclusion of works.[40] How did "works" become a dirty word?

The words of Jesus are: "He that believes and does ..." "Believes and does ..." He that doeth ..." "He that hears my word and doeth it ..."

I have to apologize to those I told differently, but you must have works that show your faith for your faith to be able to save you.

Born Again

There is nothing instant in nature. Just as being born of water (in the flesh) is a progression, so is regeneration of the soul a *progression* for every believer.

The Savior chose the word "born" for a reason. Being born requires several, sequential, and timely occurrences. There is nothing *instantaneous* about birth, or the salvation of our souls. If we do not understand this, we will miss a great question of Jesus.

The concept of Christmas has so clouded the gospel narrative regarding the birth of Jesus that we have missed an integral part of the doctrine of salvation. Why was this story placed in Scripture?

I believe that within the beautiful story of the birth of our Savior there is a metaphor. It portrays an example of what

---

40   James 2:20, "But wilt thou know, O vain man, that faith without works is dead?"

happens when a person is visited by the Holy Spirit—the "Seed of God" is placed within him or her!

Jesus was sitting in a house teaching. When His mother and brethren came to the house, some of the people from the outside came in to give Him a message, "Master, your mother and your brethren are outside desiring to speak with you."

Baffling them (and theologians for centuries afterward) Jesus asked them a question, *"Who is my mother and my brethren?"*[41]

What an odd question! I believe that its message was revealed to me, and now I will attempt to share it with you.

The story of the conception of Jesus shows that the Holy Spirit came to Mary.[42] This was her "visitation." Just as the Holy Spirit visits, overshadows, and tugs at our hearts, and calls us to repentance, the Spirit came to Mary and explained to her that within her would be placed the *Seed* of God.

Do you remember that Jesus said, "If you do not know this parable, you cannot know any parable"? When Jehovah calls a person, it is His desire to place within that person the *Seed* of Christ (the sower sows the Word of God).

Do you remember when Paul said that we *grow* up *in* Him?[43] And, "Christ in you, the hope of glory"?[44] We hear Paul speak of "... travail of birth ... till Christ is *formed* in you"?[45] These are all expressions of the process of salvation.

---

41   Mark 3:33, Matthew 12:48
42   Luke 1
43   Ephesians 4:15
44   Colossians 1:27
45   Galatians 4:19, "I travail in birth ... until Christ be formed in you."

When we consent to the purposes of our visitation by the Holy Spirit, as Mary did, "Be it unto me according to your word," Christ is placed within us as a *seed*. The proper conditions, willingness, and timing all culminate in a successful conception and the seed of the Word, Jesus Christ, begins to *grow* within us.

Following the metaphor, there is a time of pregnancy, a term of gestation, and finally a bringing forth, or the *born-again* experience. When the believer reaches this state of being *born*, all things have become new; everything *old* has passed away.

Why do the old things seem to remain and *not* pass away? Why do we still struggle with *old* ideas, habits, sins and desires and are even now afraid to admit this to ourselves? Why does the *old* flesh continue to give the same *old* problems? Could misunderstanding this process (or unawareness that there even *is* a process) be the reason? If all these concerns are true, have we been *born again*?

Read these Scriptures with your new understanding of the "Word," the "Seed." and being born again, and see if it happens for you like it did me.

1 Peter 1:23-25, "Being born again, not of corruptible seed, but of incorruptible [seed] by the word of God, which lives and abides for ever ... the word of the Lord endureth for ever. And this is the word which by the gospel is preached unto you."

1 John 3:9, "Whosoever is born of God doth not commit sin; for his seed remaineth in him: and he cannot sin, because he is born of God."

Perhaps our *doctrine* about salvation is lacking. If we believe that salvation *is* an instantaneous thing; if we think that on the day we came to Christ we received *all* there was to receive from Him, we will likely become severely disappointed in our experience with Christ.

How many times has a new convert said, "I don't feel like I'm saved. I don't feel like anything has changed." If the pregnancy metaphor is correct, this could explain a lot! (My wife tells me it is a very rare experience for a woman to know the instant she has truly conceived.)

Please consider that just because a person doubts salvation, does not mean that he or she is being spoken to by Satan. How does God bring a person to perfection if it is not to condemn his or her present condition? God's Spirit could very well be trying to communicate that the instantaneous salvation they hoped for is actually still in process!

He will then be instructed to nurture that Seed and *create an environment for it to thrive and grow*. All of this is done through *repentance* and *perfection*.

"Now I pray to God that ye do no evil; ... that ye should do that which is honest ... and this also we wish, even your perfection."[46]

So, if you, like a new convert, feel within yourself that you may not be *saved* yet, that conversion has not fully taken place yet, you *must* consider this to be the voice of God. I assure you that when repentance has been fully engaged and redemption has taken place, you will know it and nothing will shake your confidence!

---

46   2 Corinthians 13:7-9

Aside from some who may be shocked by this doctrine, many others will feel a sense of comfort. To know that God is really not finished with you; that there is a Seed within that will bring forth life; that you can bring this Seed to the point of being *born again*; that this is not going to happen accidentally; that you need to add works to your faith; that you are, *without any doubts*, part of the family of God.

After all, when Jesus asked the question, *"Who is my mother and my brethren?"* He gave us the answer, "He who *hears* and *does* the will of God, the same is my *mother* and my brethren." No, works alone cannot save you; yet, according to the Apostle James, neither can faith.[47]

Because our conventional ideas about salvation do not line up with the Scriptures, many have no idea how the "plan of salvation" works, or *if* it works! Because we have been woefully inadequate as Bible scholars and have ignored the clear truths printed in the Scriptures, we have taken a shortcut regarding our responsibilities and misguidedly sought (or at least have accepted) signs, wonders, and miracles as affirmations.

Because "He got me a parking place when I prayed," He must love me; and if He loves me, He'll save me. These statements fall short of the mark.

By these insignificant and meaningless happenings in our lives, we try to *establish* an *active* relationship with God. All the while, *we know within ourselves that many of these occurrences are not supernatural at all!*

We seek assurances because *works* are absent from our Christian life. Will supernatural evidences in our lives give us

47   James 2:14

assurance? No! Will signs and wonders give us peace? No! Do miraculous occurrences assure us of proper doctrine? No!

We do not know the doctrines because we do not know, nor do we keep, His commandments.⁴⁸ We seek after signs because our *relationship* is lacking. Our relationship lacks because our *doctrines* are sagging from lack of support.

Jesus recognized this problem in us and asked, *"Why does this generation seek after a sign?"*⁴⁹

Our ideas of salvation being instantaneous, free, and costing us nothing—the concept that salvation is simply a decision— the idea that Jesus waits for us to *accept* Him—all these ideas have created crippled, unsure, and doubting Christians by the millions!

We are unsure and doubting; therefore, we quietly seek signs and little intrusions into our lives in order to prove to us that Jehovah cares, but true assurance can only come with obedience.

The Apostle John was under no delusion that signs and supernatural intervention would be how we would know that we are children of God; rather, he said emphatically, "And hereby we know that we know him, *if we keep his commandments.*"⁵⁰

Does that mean that if you *do not* keep His commandments, you *do not* know Him?

---

48 John 7:17, "If any man will *do his will*, he shall know of the doctrine…"
49 Mark 8:12
50 1 John 2:3

If we understood the costs and processes of salvation *before we started*, we would not be the forest of half-built towers of incomplete salvation—monuments to our own improvised, unscriptural salvation.[51]

We would not be under any delusion that Christ has been *added* to our life. Rather, we could enjoy a lifetime of faith and works to show ourselves thankful to Him for calling us to enjoy His Kingdom! "Ye have not chosen me, but I have chosen you."[52]

The Kingdom

Jesus spent so much time defining Heaven, yet I sure did get the idea of Heaven wrong!

Jesus spent much time asking one question and answering that same question over and over. He asked, *"To what shall we liken the kingdom of God? Or with what parable shall we picture it?"*[53]

His answers began, "I'll tell you what it's like …," and then He would go on with figurative parables like, "The Kingdom of Heaven is like *leaven hidden in meal; it's like a mustard seed … it* is near to you, it is within you," and so on.

Why was the definition so difficult for the Master orator? Why couldn't He just tell us *exactly* what the Kingdom of God is like?

If I ask you, what is the Kingdom of God like, can you answer? We claim to live in it every day, but we do not know

51 Luke 14:28
52 John 15:16
53 Mark 4:30 (NKJV)

what it is like. I had to face the fact that I can't describe it, because I have never seen it. But that little detail did not stop me from teaching all about it!

Many of my ideas were borrowed from paganism and the foolish ideas of world religions. By this method, I created a *Heaven* that is populated with ghostly spirits, half-man and half-angel beings or, in some cases, creatures that sprout wings, float on clouds, and play harps. I believed that we will go "up" to Heaven (strictly pagan) and that we will be there watching what happens on Earth. Does any of this sound familiar?

Wow! It is no wonder that the world wants nothing to do with religion! Heaven sounds like a fairy tale—because that is exactly where it originated. Shame on us for not getting our facts from the Scriptures! When Jesus asked, *"To what shall I liken the Kingdom of Heaven?"* He never mentioned any of the things I just listed. So where did I get those ideas? I didn't just make them up, for millions of people believe those very things (or some of them, at least).

Our ideas about Heaven are not much more than a hodgepodge of Gnostic fables and paganism. If we got our clues from the Scriptures and taught others what we read in the Bible, our lesson to our brother would be that, one day, our King is coming and will subdue the kingdoms of this Earth. He will rule and reign over them and we will reign with Him—*on the Earth!*

I have no desire to float around in an ethereal Kingdom, leaving the Earth I was created to inhabit and enjoy. I was pleased that when I looked into the Scripture, the life He promised will be here (at least for the Millennium), minus evil influence, minus my sinful propensities, and always with my King! Now, that's Heaven!

Our ministry will go absolutely nowhere unless we have an understanding of the reward that we offer to the lost. How can we offer reward of a place that we don't understand?

Jesus *is* the way, the truth, and the life. We have no need of *fairy tales*. Jesus came to *show* us the Father, and reveal eternal life.

Symbols, Rituals, and Sacraments

The Protestant churches of today have been spawned from the Catholic church. They brought with them two means of divine grace or sacraments: Baptism and the "Lord's Supper" (also known as Communion or the Eucharist). Few self-respecting Protestants will admit that these are "sacraments." Instead, they are renamed "ordinances." In both Catholic and Protestant circles, participation is required in these ordinances in order to be considered a part of their *body*. (It becomes easy to infer from this, therefore, that these ordinances are required to be included in the Body of Christ.)

Some "Statements of Faith" dictate that, although baptism doesn't *save* us, we *must* be baptized because ... (insert the reasons you have been told here). They state that although the *Lord's Supper* does not save us, we *should* partake in it, because ... (again, insert the reason here). Why all the fuss about outward rituals, signs, and symbols?

Jesus asked an applicable question, *"Foolish ones! Did not he who made the outside make the inside also?"*[1]

The Pharisees came to Jesus to ask Him why He did not wash His hands before He ate. Jesus quickly explained

---

1   Luke 11:40

to them that there was *no commandment* to wash His hands before eating. He stated that the practice was only due to their *tradition*.

His answer also seems to say, "Furthermore, your *symbol* of hand washing doesn't make any sense. You must realize that my Father made what is *inside* as well as what is on the *outside*. You can't clean what's inside by cleaning the outside! Your hand washing is only a symbolic form."

One of the most damaging characteristics of symbols is that the symbol begins to displace the *reality* it was intended to symbolize. There is a grave danger when we allow *symbols* to compete with *substance!* Or, as Jesus puts it, "The outside vs. the inside."

Every one of us must be *baptized in the Spirit of God*. We all need *communion with Christ*. If we go about to accomplish these things through *baptism* and *communion*, we will be in worse error than before. Do you see the danger in the symbols replacing reality?

Jesus once asked, *"Where is the guest chamber?"*[2] This was where the "Lord's Supper" was to take place.

Let's attempt to answer His question and, in doing so, we may understand a deeper meaning about our subject. We will concede that in first-century Jerusalem there was a *real* guest chamber. But perhaps the story is told for another reason, as well.

For us, the *guest chamber* is not a physical room in a house somewhere, where we partake of communion, but our guest

---

2   Mark 4:14, Luke 22:11

chamber is *within ourselves.* If it is within, it is a quiet and personal time of reflection and dedication. If it is without, it is necessary to determine a time to do it, a place to do it. We will need bread and wine! We need rules and form!

Now, we may start to understand better, *"Did not God make that which is inside as well as that which is outside?"*

We will never come to perfection if we are constantly adding to our temporal lives; that is, if we are constantly adding to the *symbology* of our Christian exercises and neglecting the *true* Christian relationship. So, *"Where is the guestchamber?"*

The idea of us being the temple of God is neglected in much modern theology. These symbols, these "sacraments," are of man's making. Unfortunately, they often tend to carry more weight than the symbols of reality that are given to us by the Scriptures.

The symbols of Scripture are things like the Passover, the Temple of God, and the Feasts of the Lord, and the calendar of the Creator. In fact, all of the Feasts of the Lord, in symphony with His calendar, are prophetic indicators that teach us truths that are past, present, and truths yet to come.[3] However, in conventional Christianity these are virtually non-existent.

Still, most people place more emphasis on their outdated and pagan-oriented symbols, such as crosses, buildings, candles, and stained glass. There is a great danger in the use of these symbols, especially when we neglect the symbols we were given.

---

3   More information on these fundamental truths can be found at www. ThinkRedInk.com

I've said it before, and it bears repeating: we have a tendency to attach ourselves to the conduit from which our experiences come—whether it is right or wrong.

Nehushtan

There is an Old Testament account of God sending serpents among His people to punish them. After thousands had perished, He told Moses to put a brass serpent upon a pole and hold it high above the heads of the people. Anyone looking on that serpent would live.

Now, it does not take a whole lot of seminary education to see Jesus Christ in *that* symbol! By His own testimony, He *is* that serpent that was lifted up on a pole.[4]

Unless you are very familiar with the Old Testament, though, you may not realize what later happened to that brazen serpent. It was kept for many years and, finally, that very same brazen serpent that saved the people that day in the wilderness, became an object of devotion! The children worshipped it as a molten image, "... and they called it 'Nehushtan.'"[5]

It is very common for us to attach an affection to any symbol that was involved in our deliverance, but this is a *very dangerous practice* and accounts for the reason we have crosses, hundreds of different denominations, certain reverential artifacts attached to our worship, the instruments of the Lord's Supper, and even the church buildings themselves.

We need to be very careful to shun these symbols and any others that replace *truth* in our lives!

4 John 3:4
5 2 Kings 18:4

The holiest object that we will ever encounter in our lives is the next person we see before us! They should be respected, not simply because they may don white gowns, or wear crosses around their necks, or because they wear a three-piece suit, and not because they carry a Bible or call themselves a "preacher," but because they are made in the image of God himself.[6]

Can you see that too much importance and meaning has been attached to symbols? Do you understand that reverence of symbols flies in the face of the life and teaching of Jesus Christ, who came to deliver *grace* and *truth* to us? We have miserably degraded Him when we look for plastic fish symbols on bumpers in order to determine if a person is a brother or sister in Christ instead of loving our fellowman.

We are to worship Him in *spirit and in truth*, not in symbol. Symbols should be rejected and the truth they represent must be sought, so that we don't make the deadly mistake of seeking easily acquired emblems and symbols instead of the illusive Truth they symbolize.

Again, too many get this important point wrong. Why do we get it wrong? It's because we are pitiful, fallen creatures. We must understand that we *do not* understand. We must know that we *do not know.*

We must be especially careful when we are dealing with those who are yet in sin. Never make them think that baptism will do anything, except wet them. Never allow the Lord's Supper to become something of substance to them. It is truth and the power of the Father that sanctifies any symbol and He should be the only object of our worship.

---

6   James 3:9-14, "Therewith [with the tongue] bless we God, even the Father; and therewith curse we men, which are made after the similitude of God.... My brethren, these things ought not so to be."

To accomplish this in others, it is necessary for us to make these changes first in ourselves. Perhaps this next question of Jesus can help us with our perspective regarding symbols and the truth that makes them authentic.

Jesus asked the Pharisees, *"Fools and blind! For which is greater, the gold or the temple that sanctifies the gold? And ... which is greater, the gift or the altar that sanctifies the gift?"*[7]

---

7   Matthew 23:17 (NKJV)

PART 4

Conclusions

Who Is a Faithful and Wise Steward?

Jesus asked, *"Who is that faithful and wise steward?"* He gave an example in the gospel accounts:

"Let your waist be girded and your lamps burning; and you yourselves be like men who wait for their master ... Blessed are those servants whom the master, when he comes, will find watching ... And if he should come in the second watch, or come in the third watch, and find them so, blessed are those servants. But know this, that if the master of the house had known what hour the thief would come, he would have watched and not allowed his house to be broken into. Therefore you also be ready, for the Son of Man is coming at an hour you do not expect."

He also gave an example of *bad* stewardship:

"But if that servant says in his heart, 'My master is delaying his coming,' ... the master of that servant will come on a day when he is not looking for him, and at an hour when he is not aware, and will cut him in two and appoint him his portion with the unbelievers. And that servant who knew his master's will, and did not prepare himself or do according to his will,

shall be beaten with many stripes. But he who did not know, yet committed things deserving of stripes, shall be beaten with few. For everyone to whom much is given, from him much will be required; and to whom much has been committed, of him they will ask the more."[1]

From these examples, it is not difficult to see the great difference between the two stewards. The good steward waited patiently for the return of his master, which he believed was imminent. The bad steward, convinced that the return was distant (perhaps soon, but not today), had not prepared himself *by doing the will of his master.*

The good and faithful steward was prepared; the bad steward was not. The good and faithful steward *did* the will of his master; the bad steward *did not. The difference was readiness (faith) evidenced by actions (works).*

Jesus also gave us insights into the world to come. He spoke of how conduct and beliefs held in this life will dictate either a *position of "least" or "great"* in the coming Kingdom.

The Savior says, "Whoever therefore will break one of these least commandments, and shall teach men [to do] so, he will be called the least in the kingdom of heaven: but whoever will do and teach them [to be done], the same will be called great in the kingdom of heaven."[2]

He also spoke of how our willingness to stand for Him in this world will affect His willingness to stand for us in His Kingdom.

"Whoever therefore shall be ashamed of me and of my words in this adulterous and sinful generation; the Son of man

---

1   Luke 12:35-48
2   Matthew 5:19

will be ashamed of him, when he comes in the glory of his Father with the holy angels."[3]

How sad it will be to be known to our heavenly Father as unwise, to carry the title "least" for all eternity. How terrible it will be for the King of Kings to be ashamed of us in His Kingdom.

How absurd to be known in this world as successful in business, a faithful spouse, a dependable parent to your children, and a trustworthy friend to your companions; yet known to your God as an *unfaithful steward.*

Modern theology has so encouraged the idea of "accepting Jesus" that the average Christian today has nearly no concern whether he will be *accepted* by Him. David prayed for acceptance.[4] Paul *labored* to be accepted.[5] Peter, too, understood that works of faith were necessary to be acceptable.[6]

As painful as it would be to find that we missed the mark of His acceptance by our reluctance to work according to His commands, it would be ecstasy above delight to be known by our King as faithful and wise. A wise and faithful steward is one who has built his house on the rock foundation of "hearing *and* doing."[7]

Modern Christianity is not answering the needs of modern man. Battles are lost daily by unprepared and faithless people who have no allegiance to truth. A great deal of contemporary

3   Mark 8:38–Luke 9:26 (Combined in paraphrase)
4   Psalms 19:14
5   2 Corinthians 5:9
6   Acts 10:35, "But … he that fears him, *and* works righteousness, is accepted with him."
7   Luke 6:47-48, "Whosoever … *heareth* my sayings, and *doeth* them.… He is like a man which built an house … upon a rock."

preaching is not bringing about permanent changes in contemporary lives. There are few evidences of power!

The answer to this recession of power is more complex than the commonly heard slogans, "We must get back to the Bible!" or "We must return to Hebrew roots!" These ideas, though excellent within themselves, *will simply not work* if they are received into hearts that are prejudiced by family and church traditions or applied around pre-existing religious convictions that are rife with paganism and influences of false religions.

There is no revival coming to the "church." There is a new birth coming to those individuals who will "come out of her"[8] and listen to The Shepherd.

If we determine to go "back to Bible," yet fear being found *outside of convention*, we are destined to emerge from all of our efforts with the same lamentable and powerless lives, starting all over again with a new name for the same efforts. (I've been there. I've done that. It is a waste of life!)

The early, untainted believers found truth *outside* of human understanding. This can only happen when the Father *wills* the revelation of His truth. Truth cannot be filtered through *our* own understanding or denominational guidelines.

Judgment is coming on the Earth. It has already started, and we, upon whom the ends of the world are come, are being called now to speak *truth* to His chosen ones, to the great harlot, and to political powers.[9] If we do not possess more truth than the average believer, we will likewise fail.

---

8   Revelation 18:4
9   Revelation 17:1

Burning Beliefs

It is the desire of our Lord Jesus that a fire of judgment be kindled.[10] *"What will I, if it already be kindled?"*

However, it *is* possible to kindle a fire in which we can destroy even ourselves. If His consuming fire of judgment came today and destroyed all the pagan influences in pure worship, what would you do next Easter or next Christmas?

When He suddenly appears as a sworn enemy of the great harlot church, will you be able to explain where you acquired your doctrines of the immortal soul, Sunday Sabbath, or your pagan symbols of worship?

When He comes and pulls up the tares, will it disturb your personal root system?

If He requires that you *mikvah* before that final Feast of Tabernacles[11] that we are to spend with Him, do you have any idea what to do or when to do it?

If He were to tell you that the world as you know it will come to an end on the fifteenth day of the seventh month, would you have any idea when exactly this would be? (Hint: It would *not* be July 15!)

Hearts of men are far from Him. Religion is even farther. *Now* is the time to work and be faithful. *Now* is the time to listen to our Guide and hear His revelations. Now is the time to *love truth.* Now is the time to lay down our lives, take up our burdens, and *follow Him.*

---

10   Luke 12:49, "I am come to send fire on the earth; and what will I, if it be already kindled?"
11   Zechariah 14:16

"Have you understood all these things?"[12]

Jesus spent a fairly large amount of time during the last part of His life explaining that judgment is coming!

Excuses such as, "But that's the way I was taught," "That's the way we've always done it," or "But that's what I understood to be the truth" will not go very far on the imminent Day of Judgment.

The disciples were being warned that they *may not* understand. Jesus tried again, "Again, the kingdom of heaven is like unto a net, that was cast into the sea, and gathered of every kind: Which, when it was full, they drew to shore, and sat down, and gathered the good into vessels, but cast the bad away. *So shall it be at the end of the world*: the angels shall come forth, and sever the wicked from among the just, And shall cast them into the furnace of fire: there shall be wailing and gnashing of teeth" (Matthew 13:47-50).

Then Jesus looked into the unblinking, wide eyes of His disciples. As they shook themselves back into this world, they heard Him ask (perhaps for the second or third time), *"Have you understood all these things?"*

They nod their heads slowly and automatically and say, "Yes, Lord."

Friend, have *you* understood all these things? Do you understand that one day you will stand to be judged and give an account? The analogies, parables, and metaphors (interpreted any way you like) will lead even those slightly motivated to understand that one day, we will all stand before the One who

---

12 Matthew 13:51

made us, and we will face judgment for how we conducted ourselves while living here on this Earth.

The fish in the net, the sheep in the cote, the ready and waiting bridesmaids, the ten virgins, and the house built on sinking sand are all meant to be applied to the coming judgment of mankind. During this time of judgment, we will not be asked questions to which there will be right or wrong answers. There will be no quiz requiring a passing grade. By all accounts, we will not be asked what we believe, what doctrine we accept as true, or which Bible we read.

We *will* be called upon to give an account of our *works*— what we did—and what we did not do. That account alone will prove what we believed during our lifetimes.

Have you understood all these things?

Judgment Day will be an irreversible event in our future— a day in which we will be determined to be chaff or wheat,[13] a sheep or a goat,[14] faithful or unfaithful.[15] It will be a day in which we will be found ready or not ready,[16] wise or unwise,[17] walking on the straight path that ends through a narrow gate entering life, or walking the broad road terminating at the wide gate, which leads to destruction.[18] Judgment Day will be a day when all the choices we ever made in life, all the paths we may have chosen in our journey, will be held in the piercing light of His pure and holy judgment.

---

13   Luke 3:17
14   Matthew 25:32
15   Matthew 24:45
16   Luke 12:40
17   Matthew 25
18   Matthew 7

For some people it will only then occur that it was not a string of various choices that directed them; it was the little daily choices, made all through life, that add up and divide out to be the *one great choice of eternity!* Faithful to our selfish philosophies, we make the *same choice* again and again.

You make that choice today! You will make the same choice tomorrow! You choose only between life or death, your way or His way, over and over and over again. Indeed, *you have already chosen*, by your very life, one of two roads, one of two destinations, one of two eternities. You have already chosen between two rewards and between two lords.

All choices culminate in *one last great choice* that has already been made—by *you! Have you understood all these things?*

Finding Real Faith

How can something as simple as faith be so misunderstood by so many Christians? How can the Bible be so available as to exist in almost every household in America, yet its words and content be totally unknown to the people in residence there? How can something as grand as redemption be so squandered in the minds and hearts of mankind? How shall we escape if we neglect so great a salvation?

Something is wrong in the world, and *you* have the ability to change it! You have the ability to hear the voice of God within you, enabling *Him* to teach you! Do you understand how important this is? Are you going to do it?

The "church" at large has essentially failed in our century. Having begun well, we seem to be finishing as fools. There was a time, even within our present generation's memory, that a different Jesus was preached on the street corner. Lives were changed, bars were closed, cheating was stopped, and people repented.

It may be argued that those were the days when people were ignorant, but I don't believe it. Someone may make a case that people in those days had different problems than we have today, but I don't buy it. Those were the days when real men, full of the Spirit of God, stood and preached in His power and preached a real gospel of repent or perish, and real men and women believed it! It was a real faith in a real God that really changed real men and real women.

The "gospel" today in many cases runs the gamut from weekly theological seminary regurgitation to motivational pablum that is on the scale of a pyramid-scheme sales meeting.

How does "having a winning attitude" keep me from striking my neighbor or my wife? How does "Seven Steps to Prosperity" help me overcome the sin in my mind's eye? How does "understanding the Trinity" break the drug addiction that has me bound to sin until the day I die? If our sermons and lives don't start speaking in the power they have supposedly encountered, we are doomed to destruction and those in our tow are hopeless.

Judgment is nearer now than ever! How much time is there for you to stop your foolishness and get busy? You don't know? "You have the ability to look at the sky and decide that it is about to rain," Jesus asks, *"How is it that ye cannot discern this time?"*[1]

Time is pregnant with eternity! Imminent is the birth of forever and ever. Our world is coming to a close, and we must understand these things and seek after them as we would seek after gold.

We must strive to enter into that narrow gate through which few will go! Only your revelation will get you there. Your perfection will simplify your journey, and your faith and works will remove all your doubts. This is the doctrine of the

---

1   Luke 12

Lord Jesus, not mine. He claimed further, "My doctrine is not mine, but his that sent me. If any man will do his will, he *shall know of the doctrine*, whether it be of God ..."[2]

Judgment is an awesome thing, but one day you will stand to be judged for what has been revealed to you! Not what has been taught you, or what you learned as an act of your own will, but what has been *revealed*.

One day you will give an account as to why you did what you did, believed what you believed, acted the way you acted, and said what you said. You must have some foundation for doing whatever it is you do. And believing whatever it is you believe. How embarrassing it will be to stand before God and have nothing to show for your Christian faith other than your trust in the words of another person within your own sinful generation!

There is coming a day when the words of Moses (the words of the Old Testament) will judge us for how we lived in this Earth.[3] Do you have a reason for not obeying His commandments? Contrary to what we have been taught, the commandments of God are easy to live within, and we must accomplish this task.

I believe in the mercy of God. I believe that He will forgive us for what we do not know, but by that same token, I believe that we *will* be held accountable for what we *do* know and what He has revealed. We must follow our consciences and the promptings of the Holy Spirit; otherwise, we cannot look forward to a merciful judgment.

---

2   John 7:16-17
3   John 5:45, "... there is one that accuses you, even Moses, in whom ye trust."

You will not stand in judgment with your denomination, nor will you stand with your Bible teachers or preachers, but you will stand *alone*.

However, standing judgment, enduring before the Father's criticism, is not what being a child of God is all about. Although to many, merely escaping hell is enough, I am persuaded of better things for you. Our Messiah's heart is broken in the question we read now:

"... Nevertheless, when the Son of man comes, will He find faith on the earth?"[4]

For many years, I read this question of Christ with great interest. It was indeed the motivation for the creation of my first book, *The Questions of Jesus*, and its theme held throughout my study. The distinctive language in this particular Scripture created curiosity in me. It led me to doubt that the question can be answered *affirmatively*. It left me fearing the worst. *"Nevertheless when the Son of man cometh, shall he find faith on the earth?"* Will He find people who really *believe* in Him?

Why would He ask such a question? Doesn't He know that the United States of America, the supreme world power, is a Christian nation? There are more Christians alive today than ever lived before combined! Doesn't He know that better than ninety percent of our population celebrates His birth every year? How can Christmas be celebrated without the existence of faith? Will He find faith on the Earth? Look at Sunday morning television. Listen to Christian radio. See all of the steeples popping through the skylines of every rural

---

4   Luke 18:8

community, small town, and city of the world! Will He find faith? Of course He will!

Or maybe He is talking about a faith that is altogether different from anything any of us has ever encountered in our lifetimes.

Your flesh (and likely that of your peers) promises you realization of true faith by pursuit of a spotless church attendance record or by gaining respect as a religious person in your community, by tallying a long roster of good deeds for your eulogy, or even by becoming a dedicated Bible student.

In reality, church and its proponents are part of the *problem* and not the *solution* in all too many cases.

To this point in life you have lived by worldly intellect, the physical accomplishments of life, and the comfortable foundation of agreeing friends and family. You have interpreted the health and continuance of your life and fortune as God's blessing, and, thus, His condoning of your decisions. In these confidences you have lived and moved and had your being.

Continuing this course of action will eventually destroy your *true* faith while subtly replacing it with religious hypocrisy that is motivated by ego, to the ultimate, singular goal of gratification of your flesh.

You may make an admirable presentation in the church world, granted, but you will end by knowing your *pastor* better than your *Savior*, your *denomination* better than your *Bible*, and your own *good* better than your *God*.

315

A New Basis—Faith

I must apologize at this point. Throughout this book I've used terms like "*True* Faith" and "*Real* Faith," but it was only to distinguish it from the examples that are so prevalent in our society. I talked of "*Real* Christianity," as if there were something else. There is not, however! This is why Jesus *did not ask*, "Will He find '*real*' faith on the Earth?" He asked "Will He find *faith*?"

There is no kind of faith but "*real*" faith! The next question is, "Do we have it?"

All who have experienced the invitation of Jesus and have repented are now being led into new life and must discover this *new basis* for that new life. That new basis is faith.

Faith is more than believing, more than receiving goodies from God. Faith is a way of life. If the just shall live by faith, it would behoove those of us who claim to be justified by faith to know what it is. This question of Jesus continues to haunt anyone who professes faith in Him: "*When the Son of man comes, will He find faith on the earth?*" If *faith* is absent (or near absent) what does that say about those of us who claim to have it? Perhaps we don't have it after all.

Many will be ultimately discouraged by my admonition because they have equated faith *in Him*, with their faith, which is based largely in the *institution*, in the *clergy*, in the *church machine*, and in the *form*.

My experience has been that a person will never discover whether he possesses the faith the Messiah desires until he or she comes out of "the incubator" and tries it on his or her own. Compromise and fear of what others think keeps him or her in the "church machine."

Most everyone I meet does it this way. We want to be around others who believe like we do. The truth is we all want to be a part of a group. We *all* want to be right! No one wants to be wrong!

But *most of us* would rather *belong* than be right!

My friend, you can't belong to two churches at the same time! There is only one church where you can belong *and* be right, and that is His Church. We all fancy ourselves as members of His great Church, but membership is by faith—faith that is based in truth, not truth based in faith.

Why would the Apostle Paul say, "For there must be heresies among you …"? Why would we want divisions, factions, and heresies? He continues, "[So that] they which are approved may be [recognized] among you."[5] The divisions will deliver you to be the man or woman your Creator wants you to be!

He longs for the faith of men and women who believe and, therefore, fear no truth, *or lie!*

Do you know the difference between searching for truth in your faith and struggling to develop faith in your truth? Truth is not something you must *believe* is true.

When you stand as a member of the invisible and universal body of the Messiah, The True Church, you stand with Him. From the world's viewpoint you appear to be alone. You may

---

5   1 Corinthians 11:19

even *feel* alone without your support group, but you will never truly be alone.

Our journey through the **Red-Letter** questions has redefined words that we have used for years. The questions have realigned our thinking in so many areas. Now we can read the words of Jesus and the prophets and the apostles with clarity. We can articulate our faith with the unvarnished and unaltered words from Scripture, in honesty and understanding.

His questions have revealed to us secret things from the foundation of the world.

So my appeal is this:

Come on, join the *real* Church, join hands with the *real* Pastor, be baptized in *true and living water*, enjoy communion with *real bread*, and experience the Savior who *really* changes *real* men and women!

But do we need to qualify every word with superlatives and modifiers? No, not when *real* faith is present. Oops! There I go again.

Now let me write that challenge again, avoiding the qualifiers that are needed only for the lukewarm, the apostate, and the superficial. Now that you understand, my appeal can be in plain and simple language, with no fear of misunderstanding:

Come on, join the Church, join hands with the Pastor, and enjoy communion with the Savior who changes men and women! And that is just the beginning!

To this point you have considered more than 150 of the **Red-Letter** questions of Jesus. Perhaps this one is the most important yet, *"When the Son of man cometh, shall He find faith on the earth?"*

***

Index

A

ambition 15, 57, 206, 208

B

baptism
  by fire 90
  in water 161, 295, 296, 299

C

calendar 226, 297
Christmas 307
clothes 175, 201
conscience 127, 128, 161, 198, 254, 261, 282, 283

D

decision making 315
delusion
  the strong 279

E

Easter 307

F

forgiveness 4, 21, 36, 79, 80, 81, 107, 123, 126, 165, 203, 313

G

grace 21, 72, 93, 113, 116, 171, 190, 217, 272, 280, 284, 295, 299

H

hatriotism. *See* patriotism

K

kingdom
  hidden 39
  of God 46, 56, 63, 71
  of heaven 66, 150, 308
  of the Earth 150, 168
  to come 113

M

mammon 48, 49, 56, 60, 74, 167, 168
meditation xv, 127
mikvah 161, 307. *See* baptism

P

paganism 228, 292, 297, 307
pastor 100, 226, 315
  as teacher 135, 199, 233
  Jesus as 103, 269, 318
patriotism 150

321

R

reputation 106, 151, 152, 153, 154, 155, 160, 172, 192, 195, 235, 277

S

Sabbath 6, 7, 48, 103, 174, 255, 258, 307
stewardship 59, 303
symbolism 85, 295, 296, 298, 299

T

Trinity 244, 312

W

worship 115, 119
improper 34, 111, 113, 114, 298
proper 112, 221, 269, 299

The Questions Jesus Asked

p. 2   "What wilt thou?"

p. 4   "Will you be made whole?"

p.8   "Why are you crying?"

p.11, 12   "Children, have you caught anything?"

p. 13, 15   "If you then are not able to do the small things, why do you take thought for the rest?"

p. 17   "Are you inquiring among yourselves about what I said?"

p. 20   "Now how is your vision?"

p. 29   "What do you think?"

p. 33   "Why are you fearful, O you of little faith?"

p. 36   "Why do you think evil in your hearts?"

p. 39, 40   "If I say the truth, why do you not believe me?

p. 41   "To what shall I liken the men of this generation?"

p. 45   "What is this, then, that is written?"

p. 46   "What do you think will happen now?"

p. 48   "Do you not see all these things?"

p. 54   "Who are you looking for?"

p. 54   "Do you think that I cannot now pray to my
             Father, and He will provide me with more than
             twelve legions of angels?"

p. 55   "Which of you by worrying can add one cubit to
             his stature?"

p.57, 58   "And which of you, having a servant plowing or
             tending sheep, will say to him when he has come
             in from the field, 'Come at once and sit down to
             eat'?"

p. 58   "Does he thank that servant because he did the
             things that were commanded him?"

p. 60   "Therefore if you have not been faithful in the
             unrighteous mammon, who will commit to your
             trust the true riches?"

p. 60   "Is not life more than food?"

p. 60   "Why do you take thought for clothing?"

p. 61   "Are you not of more value than they?"

p. 61   "Now if God so clothes the grass of the field,
             which today is, and tomorrow is thrown into the
             oven, will He not much more clothe you, O you
             of little faith?"

p. 65   "Why do you call me good?

p. 68   "Do I have such a friend in you?"

p. 69   "What will a man give in exchange for his soul?

p. 70   "Whose image and inscription does it have?"

p. 72   "...if she loses one piece, does she not light a
             candle, and sweep the house, and seek diligently
             till she find it?

p. 74, 75   "Will you lay down your life for my sake?"

p. 75   "Are there not twelve hours in the day?"

p. 77   "Why do you sleep?"

p. 77   "Could you not watch with me one hour?"

p. 78   "Simon! Do you love me more than these?

p. 79   "Do you love me?"

p. 80   "Simon, son of Jonah, do you love me?"

p. 80   "Do you love me?"

p. 82   "Why judge ye not of yourselves what is right?"

p. 84   "What is your name?"

p. 86   "How much then is a man better than a sheep?"

p. 86   "Are not five sparrows sold for two copper coins? And not one of them is forgotten before God."

p. 87   "If a son shall ask bread … will a father give him a stone?"

p. 88   "Will you also go away?

p. 88   "Have not I chosen you twelve?"

p. 90   "Do you suppose that I came to give peace on earth?

p. 91   "Are you able to drink the cup that I drink, and be baptized with the baptism that I am baptized with?"

p. 93   "Why do you persecute me?"

p. 93   "Have you come out, as against a robber, with swords and clubs to take me?

p. 95   "If they have called the master of the house Beelzebub, how much more will they call those of his household?"

p. 97   "Now my soul is troubled, and what shall I say? 'Father, save me from this hour?

p. 98   "Why do you make this commotion and weep?"

p. 100   "Why do you call attention to the splinter in your brother's eye?"

p. 103   "Which of you shall have an ass or an ox fall into a pit and will not straightway pull him out on the Sabbath day?"

p. 103   "Don't you violate your own laws?"

p. 104   "How can you escape the condemnation of hell?"

p. 104   "How can you believe, who receive honor from one another, and do not seek the honor that comes from God only?"

p. 110   "Have you not read, 'I am the God of Abraham, the God of Isaac, and the God of Jacob?"

p. 114   "Friend, how did you come in here without a wedding garment?"

p. 116   "Were there not any found who returned to give glory to God—except this foreigner?"

p. 118   "Have you not so much as read?"

p. 118   "Did you never read in the Scriptures?"

p. 120   "O faithless and perverse generation, how long shall I be with you? How long shall I bear with you?"

p. 121   "Just how is it that ye do not understand?"

p. 122   "If I have told you earthly things and you do not believe, how will you believe if I tell you heavenly things?

p. 123   "Which is easier, to say, 'Your sins are forgiven you,' or to say, 'Arise and walk'?

p. 124   "Do you not understand this parable? How then will you understand all the parables?"

p. 127   "What do you reason in your hearts?"

p. 128, 129 "How can you, being evil, speak good things? For out of the abundance of the heart the mouth speaks."

p. 130   "Why do you call me Lord…and not do what I say?"

p. 137   "What did Moses command you?"

p. 139   "Why do you strike me?"

p. 140   "What kind of conversation is this that you have with one another as you walk and are sad?"

p. 140   "Ought not the Christ to have suffered these things to enter into His glory?"

p. 143   "Do men gather grapes from thornbushes or figs from thistles?

p. 144   "Do men gather grapes from thorns or figs from thistles?"

p. 146   "And if you have not been faithful in what is another man's, who will give you what is your own?"

p. 149   "From whom do the kings of the earth take customs or taxes, from their sons or from strangers?"

p. 150   "Are the children then free?

p. 150   "What good is it to love those who love you?"

p. 151   "How do you make salt salty again?"

p. 153   "Are you angry with me because I made a man whole?"

p. 153   "Many good works I have shown you from my Father. For which of those works do you stone me?

327

p. 154   "Which of you convicts me of sin?

p. 157   "What is written in the law? What is your reading of it?"

p. 158   "So which of these three do you think was neighbor to him who fell among the thieves?"

p. 164   "Tell me, therefore, which of them will love him more?"

p. 164   "Do you see this woman?"

p. 165   "Why trouble you the woman?"

p. 168   "This night your soul will be required of you; then whose will those things be which you have provided?"

p. 172   "Because I said to you, 'I saw you under the fig tree,' do you believe? You will see greater things than these."

p. 175   "Who touched me?"

p. 177   "How is it ye have no faith?"

p. 178   "Where is your faith?"

p. 178, 179 "Why did you doubt?"

p. 180, 182 "Whence shall we buy bread that these may eat?"

p. 183   "How many loaves have you?"

p. 185   "Whoever lives and believes in Me shall never die. Do you believe this?"

p. 186, 187 "Do you believe that you will never die?"

p. 186, 187 "Did I not say to you that if you would believe you would see the glory of God?"

p. 188   "Why do you reason because you have no bread?"

p. 188   "Do you not yet perceive nor understand?"

p. 188   "Is your heart still hardened?"

p. 188   "Having eyes, do you not see?"

p. 188   "Having ears, do you not hear?"

p. 188   "Do you not remember?"

p. 188   "When I broke the five loaves for the five thousand, how many baskets full of fragments did you take up?"

p. 188   "Also, when I broke the seven for the four thousand, how many large baskets full of fragments did you take up?"

p. 188   "How is it you do not understand?"

p. 188   "When I sent you with nothing, did you lack anything?"

p. 189   "Why do you tempt me?"

p. 191   "Shall not God avenge His own elect, though He bear long with them?"

p. 191   "Shall not God avenge His own elect which cry after Him day and night?"

p. 196   "Do you know what I've done to you?

p. 197   "Friend, why have you come?"

p. 198   "Judas, are you betraying the Son of Man with a kiss?"

p. 204   "Why do you ask me? Ask them which heard me … they know what I said."

p. 205   "What have I to do with thee?"

p. 206   "What was it that you discussed among yourselves?"

p. 207   "If a shepherd has one hundred sheep and one of them is lost, does he not leave the ninety-nine and go and search until he finds that one lost sheep?"

p. 208   "What is that to you?"

p. 209   "How is it that you sought me?"

p. 209   "Did you not know that I would be about my Father's business?"

p. 211, 212 "Who do they say that I am?"

p. 214   "Sayest thou this thing of thyself or did others tell it thee of me?"

p. 217   "Why are you so sad?"

p. 218   "Do you believe on the Son of God?"

p. 219   "How many loaves do you have?"

p. 221   "Can the blind lead the blind?"

p. 221   "Shall they not both fall into a ditch?"

p. 226   "Are you a master of all Israel and don't know these things?"

p. 227   "Let me ask you a question, did the Father commission John the Baptist or not?"

p. 228   "Does this offend you?"

p. 228   "What, then, if you should see the Son of Man ascend where He was before?"

p. 229   "Why are you conspiring to kill me?"

p. 230   "Saul, why are you persecuting me?"

p. 231   "Why do you not understand my speech?

p. 232   "Is it not written in your law, 'I said, "You are Gods"'?"

p. 234-236 "What things?"

p. 240   "Have I been with you so long, and yet you have not known me, Philip?"

p. 240 "He who has seen me has seen the Father; so how can you say, 'Show us the Father'?"

p. 240 "Do you not believe that I am in the Father, and the Father in me?"

p. 241 "What did you go out into the wilderness to see? A reed shaken by the wind?

p. 241, 242 "What did you go out to see? A man clothed in soft garments?"

p. 242 "But what did you go out to see? A prophet?"

p. 242 "My God, my God, Why hast thou forsaken me?"

p. 244 "Why is it that you call me Lord and don't [simply] do what I say?"

p. 248 "Who made Me a judge or an arbitrator over you?"

p. 251 "What do you think about the Christ [Messiah]? Whose Son is He?"

p. 251 "How then does David in the Spirit call Him 'Lord'...?"

p. 251 "If David then calls Him 'Lord,' how is He his Son?"

p. 252 "How say the scribes that Christ is the son of David?"

p. 254 "Why do you transgress the commandment by your tradition?"

p. 257 "But if ye believe not his writings, how shall ye believe my words?"

p. 260 "What were you discussing with them?"

p. 262 "How then will the Scriptures be fulfilled?"

p. 262 "If the ... Scriptures cannot be broken, then how can this be?"

p. 264 "What is written in the law? What is your reading of it?"

p. 264 "Did not Moses give you the law, yet none of you keeps the law?"

p. 266 "For if they do these things in the green wood, what will be done in the dry?"

p. 268 "Can the friends of the bridegroom mourn as long as the bridegroom is with them?"

p. 268 "What are you looking for?"

p. 269 "How can Satan cast out Satan?"

p. 269 "By whom then do you sons cast them out?"

p. 270 "Would Satan cast out Satan?"

p. 272 "For which of you, intending to build a tower, does not sit down first and count the cost, whether he has enough to finish it?

p. 272 "What king, going to make war against another king, does not sit down first and consider whether he is able [to do so]?"

p. 275 "What does it profit if a man gains the whole world and loses his own soul, or is 'cast away'?"

p. 276-280 "Do you now believe?"

p. 281 "Do you think the reason that they were destroyed is because these men were sinners above all the rest?"

p. 281 "And those eighteen upon whom the tower of Siloam fell, do you think that they were sinners above all Galileans?"

p. 286, 289 "Who is my mother and my brethren?"

p. 290   "Why does this generation seek after a sign?"

p. 291   "To what shall we liken the kingdom of God? Or with what parable shall we picture it?"

p. 292   "To what shall I liken the Kingdom of Heaven?"

p. 295   "Foolish ones! Did not He who made the outside make the inside also?"

p. 296, 297 "Where is the guest chamber?"

p. 297   "Did not God make that which is inside as well as that which is outside?"

p. 300   "Fools and blind! For which is greater, the gold or the temple that sanctifies the gold?

p. 300   "Which is greater, the gift or the altar that sanctifies the gift?"

p. 303   "Who is that faithful and wise steward?"

p. 307   "What will I, if it already be kindled?"

p. 308   "Have you understood all these things?"

p. 312   "How is it that ye cannot discern this time?"

p. 314, 319 "When the Son of man cometh, shall He find faith on the earth?"

Contact Information

Don Harris
3590 Roundbottom Road
Suite F158512
Cincinnati, Ohio 45244-3026
RedLetterQuestions@ThinkRedInk.com
www.ThinkRedInk.com
888-578-7867